# THE BIG FAT JOKE BOOK

COMPILED BY GEOFF YOUNG

In researching this book, I received invaluable help from four people, whose sense of humour matched mine. They sent rafts of their own jokes my way, for which I was very grateful. In no particular order, thanks go to Ron and Di Wright, Margaret Eskrick and Pawl Victor.

A catalogue record for this book is available from the National Library of New Zealand.

ISBN 978-1-988516-51-6

An Upstart Press Book
Published in 2018 by Upstart Press Ltd
Level 4, 15 Huron Street, Takapuna 0622
Auckland, New Zealand



Designed by CVD Limited (www.cvdgraphics.nz)
Printed by McPhersons, Australia

# CONTENTS

# INTRODUCTION

This book has been collated for the sake of a good laugh. Everyone likes a joke, surely. There were the ones we giggled at as children — you know, the ones that involved farting. One I remember as an under-10-year-old went like this: 'Fatty and skinny were having a bath, Fatty did a fart and made Skinny laugh.' Hilarious? Well, it made me laugh at the time.

Our taste in jokes changes with age, of course. There was a time when a joke was not funny unless it contained copious swear words or extra-crude sex. That's probably still the case, but this book has tried — manfully, I may add — to steer away from too much profanity. A rule of thumb as a child was that if a joke made Grandma laugh — or smile at least — then it was okay. The ones you deemed a bit risqué or ones she wouldn't understand were kept out of the repertoire at a family gathering. She probably did understand just about anything we could have thrown her way, though, because she was a wise old boot.

So, to this book. It is an adults' joke book. There are no Fatty and Skinny non-jokes but plenty of political jokes, which means one Donald Trump gets a pounding, and the

Employment chapter seemed to throw up plenty of anti-lawyer yarns. One of the largest chapters is Domestic Bliss. Now this is not as sexist as cynics might assume. Women cop a lot, but give a lot back, which is as it should be. Sexism does rear its ugly head in the ubiquitous Blondes chapter. There's no getting away from it with the blondes, but these days the odd blonde gets her own back and her brunette sister gets to cop the odd jibe, plus blond blokes. So, if you don't like, or are offended by, blonde jokes, the chapter is not too long. Kids also get a good go in these pages. Smart little bastards they mostly are, but funny with it.

Plus, we have a Dark and Risqué chapter which contains the jokes that Grandma would purse her lips at, and, yes, probably would not understand. We do, though, and if you have a risqué bent, you'll have fun in that chapter. Old Geezers is not a chapter poking fun at the oldies. They tend to surprise us with inventive ways to have fun and how to deal to snivelling, grasping relatives. Kiwi jokes, inevitably, tend to be dominated by sheep. They must have been written by Australians, who also get plenty of borax poked their way. We have a few jokes poking fun at the usual suspects — the Irish, the Poles, and the rednecks of Alabama — but we figure that Aussies and Kiwis are big enough and ugly enough to take all the piss-taking that's going, so the Homegrown and Across the Border chapters are quite chunky. Rounding the book out are the Animal Kingdom, Sporting Life, Entertainment, Oldies but Goodies, and Religion chapters. In short, a bit of a laugh for every joke junkie. Enjoy.

# ACROSS THE BORDER

Quite naturally, Australia cops a lot in this section. Jibes across the ditch are a sort of rite of passage, mostly for Kiwi men. The same goes for the Aussies. Wasn't it former New Zealand Prime Minister Robert Muldoon — not renowned for his humour — who famously quipped that the annual exodus of Kiwis to Australia raised the average IQ of both countries?

**Q:** How many Frenchmen does it take to change a light bulb?
**A:** Five. One to hold the light bulb and four to turn the house.

### JUICY FRUIT

A German asks a Mexican if they have any Jews in Mexico. The Mexican says, 'Sí, we have orange jews, apple jews, and grape jews!'

**Q:** How do you know you're in the presence of a real person from Colorado?
**A:** He carries his $3000 mountain bike atop his $500 car.

### WAY WITH WORDS

Mahatma Gandhi often walked barefoot which produced an impressive set of callouses on his feet. He also ate very little, making him rather frail, and with his odd diet he often suffered from bad breath. This made him a super calloused fragile mystic hexed with halitosis.

**Q:** Why are there no ice cubes in Poland?
**A:** Because they lost the recipe.

### WET IRISHMEN

Two men from Dublin are walking to the annual Dublin Fair, when it starts to rain.

'Patrick, put your umbrella up, it's raining.'

'I can't, Mick, it's got holes in it.'

'Holes in it? Then why did you bring it with you?'

'I didn't think it would rain.'

**Q:** Why did Captain Kirk go into the ladies' room?
**A:** Because he wanted to go where no man had gone before.

**Q:** Why is North Korea not as fun as South Korea?
**A:** Because it has no Seoul.

**Q:** What do the Starship *Enterprise* and toilet paper have in common?
**A:** They both probe Uranus and wipe out Klingons.

## GO ON, MY SUN

China, Russia, and Poland venture into space. China says they'll go to Pluto because it's the furthest. Russia says they'll go to Jupiter because it's the biggest. Poland says they'll go to the Sun. Russia and China warn that they'll melt. They reply, 'We'll go at night.'

**Q:** What's the difference between Massachusetts and Connecticut?
**A:** The Kennedys don't own Connecticut.

## SURVEY SHAMBLES

A worldwide survey was conducted by the United Nations. The only question asked was: 'Would you please give your honest opinion about solutions to the food shortage in the rest of the world?' The survey was a huge failure. In Africa they didn't know what 'food' meant. In Eastern Europe they didn't know what 'honest' meant. In Western Europe they didn't know what 'shortage' meant. In China they didn't know what 'opinion' meant. In the Middle East they didn't know what 'solution' meant. In South America they didn't know what 'please' meant. And in the United States they didn't know what 'the rest of the world' meant.

## CIA INTELLIGENCE

The CIA is trying to get into Russia but they can't find someone who has Russian characteristics. They adopt a kid at birth and teach him how to drink vodka by the gallon, play the Russian guitar and speak with a perfect accent.

The child grows up and travels to Moscow one day and goes to a bar. He speaks to the barman in a wonderful accent.

'You have a wonderful accent but you're not Russian,' says the barman.

'Of course I am,' the man says, outraged, and gets out his guitar and plays it beautifully.

'You are a great guitar player but you're not Russian,' the barman says again.

Not happy, the man starts ordering vodka by the gallon and chugs it.

Surprised but not convinced, the barman says, 'I know you're not Russian because no Russians are black.'

## ACID TEST

A DuPont, Delaware, chemist walks into a pharmacy and asks the pharmacist, 'Do you have any acetylsalicylic acid?'

'You mean aspirin?' says the pharmacist.

'That's it! I can never remember that word.'

## WARM HANDS

An American tourist walks out of a Mexican train station when he notices he isn't wearing his watch. A Mexican man is resting under a nearby tree beside a donkey.

The American approaches the Mexican and asks, 'Excuse me, do you know what the time is?'

The Mexican looks at the donkey, grabs its balls, and replies, '4.30.'

The American asks, 'How do you know that?'

The Mexican replies, 'Well, you get a handful of the

donkey's balls and lift them up so you can see that clock across the street.'

**Q:** What do you call a fake noodle?
**A:** An impasta!

## DOCTOR PIZZA

Two old friends cross paths after not seeing one another for almost a decade.

Utkarsh: 'What are you doing these days?'
Sparsh: 'PHD.'
Utkarsh: 'Wow! You're a doctor!'
Sparsh: 'No, Pizza Home Delivery.'

**Q:** Why do the French eat snails?
**A:** They don't like fast food.

## SON OF A BIRCH!

Two tall trees, a birch and a beech, are growing in the woods. A small tree begins to grow between them, and the beech says to the birch, 'Is that a son of a beech or a son of a birch?' The birch says he cannot tell, but just then a woodpecker lands on the sapling.

The birch says, 'Woodpecker, you're a tree expert. Can you tell if that is a son of a beech or a son of a birch?'

The woodpecker takes a taste of the small tree and replies, 'It is neither a son of a beech nor a son of a birch. It is, however, the best piece of ash I have ever poked my pecker into.'

My friend thinks he's smart. He told me an onion is the only food that makes you cry, so I threw a coconut at his face.

My friend told me he had the body of a Greek god. I had to explain to him that Buddha is not Greek.

**Q:** How do you get a Lincoln graduate off your front porch?
**A:** Pay for the pizza.

### WORTH A WAIL!

I was sitting in a bar one day and two really large women came in, talking in an interesting accent. So I said, 'Cool accent, are you two ladies from Ireland?'

One of them snarled at me, 'It's Wales, Dumbo!'

So I corrected myself, 'My apologies, so are you two whales from Ireland?'

**Q:** What do you call a Hawaiian murder mystery?
**A:** A hula-dunnit.

### JAAPIE REASONING

Four men, one each from China, Australia, New Zealand and South Africa, are arguing about who has the best stuff.

The man from China says they have the biggest wall.

The Aussie says they have the best grass.

The Kiwi says they have the best flag.

The dude from South Africa says they have the springbok: it jumps over the wall, shits on the grass and wipes its ass with the flag.

If beauty was a drop of water, you'd be the Sahara Desert.

**Q:** What's the difference between an Australian wedding and an Australian funeral?
**A:** One less drunk at the funeral.

**Q:** What's the difference between yoghurt and Australia?
**A:** Yoghurt has some culture.

### YOU ASKED FOR IT

An Australian man and his wife are sitting in the living room.

Bruce says: 'Just so you know, Shirl, I never want to live in a vegetative state, dependent on some machine and fluids from a bottle. If that ever happens, just pull the plug.'

Shirl gets up, unplugs the TV and throws out all his beer.

**Q:** Why do so many Australian men suffer from premature ejaculation?
**A:** Because they have to rush back to the pub to tell their mates what happened!

### FOSTER'S LAGER

Two Aussies are adrift in a lifeboat. While going through the locker, one of them finds an old lamp. He rubs it and a genie suddenly appears. The genie tells them that he only grants one wish.

The lamp finder blurts out: 'Turn the entire ocean into Foster's!'

The genie claps his hands and immediately the sea turns into beer.

The genie disappears and only the gentle lapping of beer on the hull breaks the stillness as the two men consider their circumstances.

The second Aussie turns to the first and says, 'Nice going, mate! Now we're going to have to piss in the boat.'

### MILITIA MADNESS

Want to join a militia? Idaho's your state. Here are some terms to learn:

Commander: Whoever starts the unit.

Second in command: His best friend.

Auxiliary commander: His wife.

Captain: New guy.

Militia headquarters: The basement of whoever has the fax machine.

Squad: Guys in the ambulance who come out when a militia member accidentally shoots himself during training.

## FAIR DINKUM

An Englishman wants to marry an Irish girl and is told he needs to become Irish before he can do so. It is a very simple operation where they remove 5 per cent of your brain.

Anyway, the Englishman wakes up after the operation and the doctor comes up to him looking all worried and says, 'I am terribly sorry, there's been a mistake to be sure, we accidentally removed 50 per cent of your brain instead of 5 per cent!'

The Englishman sits up and simply says, 'She'll be right, mate.'

Chicago got started after a bunch of people in New York said, 'Gee, I'm enjoying the crime and the poverty, but it just isn't cold enough.'

## HOOK, LINE AND SINKER

An Aussie pirate walks into a bar with a wooden leg, a hook for a hand and an eye patch.

The barman says, 'Sheesh, how'd you lose the leg?'

The pirate says, 'Arrrrgh, a shark took it off at the knee.'

The barman says, 'That's no good, what about the hand?'

The pirate says, 'Arrrrgh, lost it in a bloody bar brawl.'

The barman says, 'Jeez, well what about the eye then?'

The pirate says, 'That's easy. A seagull crapped in it.'

The barman says, 'What?!' The pirate says, 'Arrrrgh . . . I'd only had the hook one day.'

**Q:** What's the difference between Australian sports fans and puppies?

**A:** Eventually, the puppies will grow up and stop whining so much.

## BRAGGARDS HO

Three hang-glider pilots, one from Australia, one from South Africa and the other from New Zealand, are sitting around a campfire near Ayers Rock, each bragging about the bravado for which they are famous. A night of tall tales begins . . .

Kevin the Kiwi says, 'I must be the meanest, toughest hang-glider dude there us. Why, just the other day, I landed in a field and scared a crocodile that got loose from the swamp. Et ate sux men before I wrestled ut to the ground weth my bare hends end beat uts bliddy 'ed un.'

Jerry from South Africa typically can't stand to be bettered. 'Well, you guys, I lended orfter a 200-mile flight on a tiny treck, ind a 15-foot Namibian desert snike slid out from under a rock and made a move for me. I grebbed thet borsted with my bare hinds and tore its head orf ind sucked the poison down in one gulp. Ind I'm still here today.'

Barry the Aussie remained silent, slowly poking the fire with his penis.

**Q:** What do they call 100 John Deeres circling a McDonald's in Iowa?

**A:** Prom night.

## AFGHANS TAKE BISCUIT

While waiting to finalise their Australian residential status, two Afghani men start chatting. As they part, they agree to meet in a year's time and see who has adapted better to the Australian way of life. True to their word, they meet after the year is up.

The first says to the second, 'We have integrated so well . . . yesterday, I ate a meat pie and drank a VB while watching my son play Aussie Rules.'

The second man replies, 'F--k off, towelhead.'

## FLYING SOLO

A burnt-out advertising executive decides he's had enough of the rat race and buys a property way out west. No electricity, no phones — no company. After a few weeks, he's read everything he can and is getting a bit bored. One afternoon he sees dust way in the distance heading towards him. A little while later a crusty old bushie gets out of a battered Holden ute and puts out his hand.

'Hello mate, I'm your closest neighbour, live about twenty miles up the road. Thought we'd chuck ya a bash to welcome you to the area.'

'Sounds great,' says the ad-man.

'I hear you city boys like your drugs and drink so we'll get that in for ya.'

'Sounds awesome,' says the ad-man.

'We tend to get a bit punchie and horny round here after all those drugs and drink though. Can ya handle yerself if a blue kicks off or a bit of sex is on the cards?'

'I'll go alright,' say the ad-man. 'This all sounds great, what time should I come and what should I wear?'

'Doesn't really matter,' says the bushie, 'it's only going to be you and me.'

On Boston traffic: The last person to get across Boston in under three hours was yelling, 'The British are coming! The British are coming!'

### MAINE MISERY

After surveying property along the New Hampshire and Maine border, some engineers decided the boundaries needed to be changed. So they stopped to tell a farmer that he was no longer in Maine but in New Hampshire.

'Good,' said the farmer. 'I couldn't take another one of those Maine winters.'

### WOULD YOU ADAM AND EVE IT?

**Q:** How do you know when you're staying in a Mississippi hotel?

**A:** When you call the front desk and say, 'I've got a leak in my sink', and the person at the front desk says, 'Go ahead.'

A Briton, a Frenchman and a Russian are viewing a painting of Adam and Eve frolicking in the Garden of Eden.

'Look at their reserve, their calm,' muses the Brit. 'They must be British.'

'Nonsense,' the Frenchman disagrees. 'They're naked, and so beautiful. Clearly, they are French.'

'No way! They have no clothes and no shelter,' the Russian points out. 'They have only an apple to eat, and they are being told they live in a paradise. Obviously, they are Russian.'

## BATTLER SHIRL

An old Australian battler lies dying in his bed. He calls over Shirley, his faithful wife of 60 years, and says, 'Shirl, when we started out, tried to buy a business in the depression, and went bust, you were with me.'

'Oh, yes, Bruce,' she says.

'Then the war started, I joined up, and was sent to the front line, where I lost me legs. You stayed with me.'

'Oh, yes, Bruce,' she says.

'Then, I came home, couldn't get a job, due to me disability, and bought a farm.'

'Oh, yes, Bruce,' she says.

'The farm flooded, then just when we got over that, there was a bushfire, and then the drought, which wiped us right out, and you still stayed with me.'

'Oh, yes, Bruce.'

'Now, here I am, in excruciating pain, about to die, useless, and you're still with me.'

'Yes, Bruce.'

'Shirl.'

'Yes, Bruce?'

'You're bloody bad luck.'

## DORKLANDERS

A man from Taumarunui walks into a bar and asks, 'Wanna hear a joke about people from Auckland?'

The bartender says, 'Listen, pal, I'm from Auckland, and I won't appreciate it. The man sitting next to you is 120 kilos, and he's from Auckland too. And the bouncer, that huge guy over there, is also from Auckland. So, do you still want to tell that joke?'

'No,' says the guy from Taumarunui. 'Not if I have to explain it three times.'

**Q:** If someone who speaks two languages is bilingual, and someone who speaks many languages is multilingual, then what do you call someone who speaks one language?

**A:** An American.

## CRIMINAL COWBOY

This cowboy walks into a bar and orders a beer. His hat is made of brown wrapping paper, his shirt and vest are made of waxed paper, and his chaps, pants and boots are made of tissue paper. Pretty soon, they arrest him for rustling.

Charles Dickens walks into a bar and orders a martini. The bartender asks, 'Olive or twist?'

A man walks into a bar with a chunk of asphalt under one arm. The man says, 'Beer, please, and one for the road.'

## NICE ONE, BUDHI

An Indian cattle herder named Budhi Ram was overseeing his herd in a remote mountainous pasture. Suddenly, a brand-new BMW advanced towards him out of a cloud of dust. The driver, a young man in a Brioni suit, Gucci shoes, Ray-Ban sunglasses and YSL tie, leaned out the window and asked the cowboy, 'If I tell you exactly how many cows and calves you have in your herd, will you give me a calf?'

Budhi Ram looks at the man, obviously a yuppie, then looks at his peacefully grazing herd and calmly answers, 'Sure, why not?'

The young man parks his car, whips out his MacBook Air, connects it to his iPhone, and surfs to a NASA page on the internet, where he calls up a GPS satellite to get an exact fix on his location, which he then feeds to another NASA satellite that scans the area in an ultra-high-resolution photo. The young man then opens the digital photo in iPhoto and exports it to an image-processing facility in Hamburg, Germany. Within seconds, he receives an email on his iPhone that the image has been processed and the data stored. He then accesses an MS-SQL database through an ODBC connected Excel spreadsheet with email on his iPhone and, after a few minutes, receives a response. Finally, he prints out a full-colour,150-page report on his hi-tech, miniaturised LaserJet printer, turns to Budhi Ram and says, 'You have exactly 1586 cows and calves.'

'That's right. Well, I guess you can take one of my calves,' says Budhi Ram.

He watches the young man select one of the animals

and looks on with amusement as he stuffs it into the boot of his car. Then Budhi Ram says to the young man, 'Hey, if I can tell you exactly who you are and what your business is, will you give me back my calf?'

The young man thinks about it for a second and then says, 'Okay, why not?'

'You're Rahul Gandhi,' says Budhi Ram.

'Wow! That's correct,' says the yuppie idiot, 'but how did you guess that?'

'No guessing required,' answered Budhi Ram. 'You showed up here even though nobody called you; you want to get paid for an answer I already knew, to a question I never asked; you used millions of dollars' worth of equipment trying to show me how much smarter than me you are; and you don't know a thing about how working people make a living — or about cows, for that matter. This is a herd of sheep . . . now give me back my dog.'

## MOTHER'S LOGIC

A Jewish mother is taking leave of her son, who has been called up to serve in the Czar's army against the Turks.

'Don't exert yourself too much,' she admonishes him. 'Kill a Turk and rest. Kill another Turk and rest again . . .'

'But mother,' he exclaims, 'What if the Turk kills me?'

'Kill you?' she cries out. 'Why? What have you done to him?'

**Q:** What rock group has four men that don't sing?
**A:** Mount Rushmore.

## SMILE WITH THE IRISH

Paddy spies a letter lying on his doormat. It says on the envelope 'DO NOT BEND'. Paddy spends the next two hours trying to figure out how to pick it up.

Paddy shouts frantically into the phone, 'My wife is pregnant and her contractions are only two minutes apart!'

'Is this her first child?' asks the doctor.

'No,' shouts Paddy, 'this is her husband!'

An old Irish farmer's dog goes missing and the farmer is inconsolable. His wife says 'Why don't you put an advert in the paper?' He does, but two weeks later the dog is still missing.

'What did you put in the paper?' his wife asks.

'Here, boy,' he replies.

Paddy's in jail. A guard looks in his cell and sees him hanging by his feet.

'What on earth are you doing?' he asks.

'Hanging myself,' Paddy replies.

'It should be around your neck,' says the guard.

'I know,' says Paddy, 'but I couldn't breathe.'

Paddy rings his new girlfriend's doorbell, holding a big bunch of flowers. She opens the door, sees the flowers, and drags him in. She lies back on the couch, pulls her skirt up, rips her knickers off and says, 'This is for the flowers!'

'Don't be silly,' says Paddy, 'you must have a vase somewhere!'

## WET FLIGHT

Shortly after take-off on an outbound, evening Aer Lingus flight from Dublin to Boston, the lead flight attendant nervously made the following painful announcement in her lovely Irish brogue:

'Ladies and gentlemen, I'm so very sorry, but it appears that there has been a terrible mix-up by our catering service. I don't know how this has happened, but we have 103 passengers on board, and unfortunately, we received only 40 dinner meals. I truly apologise for this mistake and inconvenience.'

When the muttering of the passengers had died down, she continued:

'Anyone who is kind enough to give up their meal so that someone else can eat, will receive free and unlimited drinks for the duration of our 10-hour flight.'

Her next announcement came about two hours later:

'If anyone is hungry, we still have 40 dinners available.'

## IRISH CRAIC

Friendship is when people know all about you . . . but like you anyway.

It doesn't matter how big your house is, how much money you have, or that you wear expensive clothes. Our graves will be the same size. Stay humble.

Do you know that great feeling when you get into bed, fall straight to sleep and wake up feeling refreshed and ready to take on the day? No, me neither.

## UNDERSTANDING COP

An elderly Irishman bought a sports car to recapture his youth and drove on the main road at 120 mph. Then he saw a police car behind him, blue lights flashing. 'I'm too old for this nonsense,' he thought, so he pulled over.

The police officer said, 'Sir, my shift ends in 10 minutes. If you can give me a good reason why you were speeding, I'll let you go.'

The old man said, 'Years ago my wife ran off with a policeman. I thought you were bringing her back.'

'That'll do,' said the policeman. 'On yer way.'

The brain is the most amazing organ. It works 24 hours a day, 365 days a year from birth until you fall in love.

Every woman's dream is that her ideal man takes her in his arms, throws her on the bed . . . and cleans the whole house while she sleeps.

I don't like to think before I speak . . . I like to be just as surprised as everyone else about what I say.

**Q:** What did our parents do when they were bored with no internet?
**A:** I asked my 18 brothers and sisters, and they didn't know either.

**Q:** How many Australian men does it take to change a light bulb?
**A:** None. It's a woman's job.

### SENSITIVE KIND

Three Aussie guys, Shane, Ricky and Jeff, were working on a high-rise building project in Wagga Wagga. Unfortunately, Shane falls off the scaffolding and is killed instantly.

As the ambulance takes the body away, Ricky says, 'Someone should go and tell his wife.'

Jeff says, 'Okay, I'm pretty good at that sensitive stuff, I'll do it.'

Two hours later, he comes back carrying a case of Foster's.

Ricky says, 'Where did you get that, Jeff?'

'Shane's wife gave it to me.'

'That's unbelievable,' Ricky replies, 'you told the lady her husband was dead and she gave you the beer?'

'Well, not exactly,' says Jeff. 'When she answered the door, I said to her, "You must be Shane's widow." She said, "No, I'm not a widow." And I said, 'I'll bet you a case of Foster's you are.'

### A GENTLE SHOVE

Monty Kelly, a rich man who lived near Darwin, decided that he wanted to throw a party. So he invited his buddies, including Darel, the only Aborigine in the neighbourhood. The party was held around the pool in the backyard of Monty's mansion. Everyone was having a good time, dancing, eating prawns and oysters, and drinking, flirting and telling lies.

At the height of the party, the host said, 'I have a 16-foot man-eating crocodile in my pool and I'll give a million dollars to anyone who has the balls to jump in.'

The words were barely out of Monty's mouth when there was a loud splash and everyone turned around and saw Darel in the pool fighting the croc, jabbing the croc in the eyes with his thumbs, throwing punches, doing all kinds of stuff like head butts and choke holds, biting the croc on the tail and flipping the croc through the air like some kind of judo instructor.

The water was churning and splashing everywhere. Both Darel and the croc were screaming and raising hell. Finally, Darel strangled the croc and let it float to the top like a dead goldfish. He slowly climbed out of the pool. Everybody was staring at him in disbelief.

Then Monty said, 'Well, Darel, I reckon I owe you a million dollars.'

'Nah, you all right boss, I don't want it,' said Darel.

'Man, I have to give you something.' said Monty. 'You won the bet. How about a new car?'

'No thanks. I don't want it,' answered Darel.

'Come on,' said Monty. 'I insist on giving you something. That was amazing. How about a new Rolex watch and some stock options?'

Again, Darel said, 'No.'

Confused, Monty asked, 'Well, Darel, then what do you want?

Darel said, 'I just want the bastard who pushed me in.'

### KEEP TRYING, BRUCE

Bruce went to the police station and asked to speak to the burglar who had broken into his house the previous night.

'You'll get your chance in court,' the desk sergeant told him.

'I have to know how he got into the house without waking my wife,' pleaded Bruce. 'I've been trying to do that for years.'

### ROOS FLOOR RANDY

Texan farmer Randy goes to Australia for a vacation. There he meets Glen, an Aussie farmer, and gets talking. The Aussie shows off his big wheat field and the Texan says, 'Oh yeah. We have wheat fields that are at least twice as large.'

Then they walk around the ranch a little, and Glen shows off his herd of cattle. Randy immediately says, 'We have longhorns that are at least twice as large as your cows.'

The conversation has almost died when the Texan sees a herd of kangaroos hopping through the field and he asks, 'And what are those?'

'Glen,' the Aussie replies with an incredulous look, 'don't you have any grasshoppers in Texas?'

### HELLO SAILOR!

An old Canadian sailor and an American gunbunny were sitting in the Duke of Buckingham pub arguing about who'd had the tougher career.

'I did 30 years in the 29th Field Artillery,' the American declared proudly, 'and fought in three of my country's wars. Fresh out of boot camp I hit the beach at Okinawa, clawed my way up the blood-soaked sand, and eventually took out an entire enemy machine-gun nest with a single grenade. As a sergeant, I fought in Korea alongside General MacArthur. We pushed back the enemy inch by bloody inch all the way up to the Chinese border, always under a barrage of artillery and small-arms fire. Finally, as a gunny sergeant, I did three consecutive combat tours in Vietnam. We humped through the mud and razor grass for 14 hours a day, plagued by rain and mosquitoes, ducking under sniper fire all day and mortar fire all night. In a fire-fight, we'd fire until our arms ached and our guns were empty, then we'd charge the enemy with bayonets!'

'Ah,' said the sailor with a dismissive wave of his hand, 'lucky gunbunny, all shore duty, huh?'

### TALE WAGGER

An Englishman, an Irishman and a Scotsman were confessing their secret vices to each other.

'I'm a terrible gambler,' said the Englishman.

'I'm a terrible drinker,' said the Scotsman.

'My vice is much less serious,' said the Irishman, 'I just like to tell tales about my friends.'

**Q:** What is every Californian's favourite part about the winter?
**A:** Watching all of the bad weather on TV.

## ACROSS THE BORDER

Sign seen in the window of a shop in Enniskillen, County Fermanagh, Northern Ireland: 'The bargain basement is on the first floor.'

## LIGHT BULBS AS WELL?

Andrew called in to see his Scottish friend Angus to find he was stripping the wallpaper from the walls. Rather obviously, he remarked 'You're decorating, I see.'

To which Angus replied, 'No. I'm moving house.'

## ACTING THE GOAT

A busload of retired Kiwis was touring Switzerland. On the third day, they visited a farm known for its excellent-quality goat cheese. The young farmer's wife gave them a tour, a cheese-making demonstration, and finally some samples. As the retirees were tasting the cheeses, she pointed to a pasture full of goats.

'This is a special pasture where we let our older goats graze happily after they can no longer give milk. In New Zealand, what do you do with your old goats?'

An old lady piped up, 'Honey, they take us on bus tours.'

## DIRTY TRICK

In order to help jump-start the economy, the Immigration Department has announced that this year they will stop focusing on overstayers and begin the deportation of retired people. It's predicted that this will not only help lower health-care costs, but it turns out that retirees are much easier to catch. Plus, they rarely can remember how to get back home.

**Q:** What European capital has the most ghosts?
**A:** Boo-dapest!

### FAIR REPLY

An Arkansas state trooper pulls over a pickup truck on I-40. He says to the driver, "Got any ID?"

The driver asks, "'Bout what?'

Barbara Walters, of the news magazine show *20/20*, did a story on gender roles in Kabul, Afghanistan, several years before the Afghan conflict. She noted that women customarily walked five paces behind their husbands. She recently returned to Kabul and observed that women still walk behind their husbands. Despite the all-too-brief overthrow of the oppressive Taliban regime, the women seemed happy to maintain the old custom.

Ms Walters approached one of the Afghan women and asked, 'Why do you now seem happy with an old custom that you once tried so desperately to change?'

The woman looked Ms Walters straight in the eye, and without hesitation said, 'Land mines.'

Moral of the story (no matter what language you speak or where you go): Behind every man, there's a smart woman.

It's so hot in Arizona, cows are giving evaporated milk and the trees are whistling for dogs.

## BRIGHT LIEUTENANT

While in Kuwait, shortly before deployment to Iraq, a major general told our unit that we should expect to cross 'into Iraq in less than 24 hours'. He then opened the floor to questions.

A lieutenant stood up and asked, 'Is that 24 hours our time or 24 hours their time?'

While on manoeuvres in the Mojave Desert, our convoy got lost, forcing our lieutenant to radio for help.

'Are you near any landmarks that might help us locate you?' the base operator asked him.

'Yes,' said the lieutenant. 'We are directly under the moon.'

## FAT TO THE FIRE

While fishing off Myrtle Beach, South Carolina, a Yankee tourist capsized his boat. Petrified, he yelled to an old guy standing on the shore, 'Are there any gators around here?!'

'Naw,' the man hollered back, 'they ain't been around for years.'

Feeling safe, the tourist started swimming towards shore. Halfway there, he asked the guy, 'How'd you get rid of the gators?'

'We didn't do anything,' the old guy said. 'The sharks got 'em.'

A mummy covered in chocolate and nuts has been discovered in Egypt. Archaeologists believe it may be Pharaoh Rocher . . .

### PIZZA DE RÉSISTANCE

A military lab has developed a pizza that boasts a shelf life of three years without being frozen. A magazine has asked its readers to name this durable dish. Here's what they came up with:

The Lasting Supper
In-dough-structible
Pizza de Résistance
Auld Lang Slice
Eternal Piece

### LONG NIGHT

An Alaskan was on trial in Anchorage. The prosecutor leaned menacingly towards him and asked, 'Where were you on the night of October to April?'

**Q:** How can you tell if an Oklahoman is married?
**A:** There's dried chewing tobacco on both sides of the pickup truck.

### KA-BOOM

A tough old badlands rancher in South Dakota once told his grandson that the secret to long life was to sprinkle a little gunpowder on his oatmeal every morning. The grandson did this religiously and he lived to be 93. When he died, he left 14 children, 28 grandchildren, 35 great-grandchildren . . . and a 15-foot hole in the wall of the crematorium.

## ON CHOPPY WATER

Sven in Wisconsin notices his neighbour has a sign in his yard: 'Boat for Sale.'

'Ole,' he says, 'you don't own a boat. All you got is your old tractor and your combine.'

'Yup,' says Ole, 'and they're boat for sale.'

**Q:** What occupies the last six pages of the Lada user's manual?

**A:** The bus and train timetables.

## SLAPSTICK ON TRAIN

An Englishman, a Frenchman, a ravishing blonde and an old woman are sharing a compartment on a train as it winds its way through the Alps. Every now and then the train passes through a tunnel, during which time the compartment is plunged into complete darkness. On one such occasion, a ringing slap is heard and as the train passes back into daylight, the Frenchman is rubbing his sore, red cheek.

The old lady thinks, 'I bet that dirty Frenchman fondled the blonde and she struck the pervert.'

The blonde thinks, 'I bet that filthy Frenchman was looking to grope me in the dark, mistook the old lady for me and she slapped him.'

The Frenchman thinks, 'I bet that perfidious Englishman touched up the blonde in the dark and she slapped me by mistake.'

The Englishman thinks, 'I can't wait for another tunnel so I can slap that French twat again.'

**Q:** What does sex in a canoe and American beer have in common?
**A:** They're both f---ing close to water.

## YALE HO

On his first trip to Boston, a man from North Carolina met a girl at a bar and asked her, 'Do you go to Harvard?'

The girl responded, 'Yale.'

'OKAY. DO YOU GO TO HARVARD?!'

**Q:** What is the West Virginia state flower?
**A:** The satellite dish.

## SWEET HOME ALABAMA

When a visitor to a town in Alabama spotted a dog attacking a boy, he grabbed the animal and throttled it with his bare hands. An impressed reporter saw the incident and told him the next day's headline would scream: 'Valiant Local Man Saves Child by Killing Vicious Animal'.

'I'm not from this town,' said the hero.

'Then,' the reporter said, 'it will say "Alabama Man Saves Child by Killing Dog".'

'Actually,' said the man, 'I'm from New Hampshire.'

'In that case,' the reporter grumbled, 'the headline will be "Yankee Kills Family Pet".'

**Q:** What's a seven-course meal in North Dakota?
**A:** A hamburger and a six-pack.

## FLATTERY

Travelling outside Taos, New Mexico, a man comes upon a Native American lying in the middle of the road with his ear pressed against the blacktop.

'What are you doing?' asks the man.

The tribesman replies, 'Woman, late 30s, three kids, one barking dog in late model, four-door station wagon, travelling at 65 mph.'

'Amazing! You can tell all of that just by listening to the ground?'

'No,' says the Native American. 'They ran over me five minutes ago.'

I moved to New York City for my health. I'm paranoid, and it was the only place where my fears were justified.

**Q:** Why do Germans love Americans?
**A:** Because Americans are the most hated people in the world now.

## BETWEEN ROCK AND HARD PLACE

A man wakes up at the Albury Hospital on the Victoria/NSW border bandaged from head to toe. The doctor comes in and says, 'Ah, I see you've regained consciousness. Now you probably won't remember, but you were in a huge pile-up on the Hume Highway. You're going to be okay, you'll walk again and everything, but your penis was severed in the accident and we couldn't find it.'

The man groans, but the doctor goes on, 'You have

$9000 in insurance compensation coming and we now have the technology to build a new penis. They work well but they don't come cheap. It's roughly $1000 an inch.'

The man perks up.

'So,' the doctor says, 'you must decide how many inches you want. I understand that you have been married for more than 30 years and this is something you should discuss with your wife. If you had a five-incher before and get a nine-incher now, she might be a bit put out. If you had a nine-incher before and you decide to only invest in a five-incher now, she might be disappointed. It's important that she plays a role in helping you make a decision.'

The man agrees to talk it over with his wife.

The doctor comes back the next day. 'So, have you spoken with your wife?'

'Yes, I have,' says the man.

'And has she helped you make a decision?'

'Yes,' says the man.

'What is your decision?' asks the doctor.

'We're getting granite benchtops.'

**Q:** What's the difference between a smart Russian and a unicorn?

**A:** Nothing, they're both fictional characters.

### STALIN'S ENEMIES OF THE STATE

When Stalin was in office, he once noted that there were mice in his study and complained to President Kalinin about this.

The President thought for a moment and suggested, 'Why don't you put up a sign reading "Collective Farm"? Half the mice will die of hunger and the other half will run away.'

Paddy says to Mick, 'Christmas is on Friday this year.' Mick says, 'Let's hope it's not the 13th then.'

## DODGY BATCH

Two Indian junkies accidentally snorted curry powder instead of cocaine. Both are in hospital . . . one's in a korma; the other's got a dodgy tikka.

## LAND MINE BONUS

An Englishman has started his own business in Afghanistan. He's making land mines that look like prayer mats. It's doing well. Prophets are going through the roof.

Japanese scientists have created a camera with a shutter speed so fast, they can now photograph a woman with her mouth shut.

'The United States is a nation of laws: badly written and randomly enforced.' — *Frank Zappa*

'The 100 per cent American is 99 per cent idiot.' — *George Bernard Shaw*

'The trouble with her is that she lacks the power of conversation but not the power of speech.' — *George Bernard Shaw*

'I would like to live in Manchester, England. The transition between Manchester and death would be unnoticeable.' — *Mark Twain*

## KELLY'S A RIGHT TIT

Kelly limps into his favourite bar.

'My God! What happened to you?' the barman asked as he hobbled in on a crutch, with one arm in a cast.

'I got in a tiff with O'Riley,' whispered Kelly to the barman.

'O'Riley? He's just a wee fellow,' the barman said, surprised. 'He must have had something in his hand.'

'That he did,' Kelly said, 'a shovel it was.'

'Dear Lord, didn't you have anything in *your* hand?'

'Aye, that I did — Mrs O'Riley's right tit — and a beautiful thing it is, but not much use in fight.'

## ESKIMO NELL

An Eskimo is travelling through Auckland when his car breaks down. A Kiwi farmer driving by decides to stop and help. After checking under the hood, he looks up and says to the Eskimo, 'Looks like you've blown a seal, mate.'

The Eskimo shouts back, 'So what, you f--k sheep!'

## YOU'RE IN THE QUEUE!

A Russian fellow back in the bad old days of communism has saved and saved and finally can buy an automobile. He goes to the state store to order his car and is informed that it will be delivered in 10 years. The man then asks: 'Will it be here in the morning or the afternoon?'

'Why are you concerned? It's quite some time from now.'

'Because the plumber is coming in the morning.'

## WIFE WITH THE LUCK

Two naive blokes were driving home across the desert and were in need of some fuel. They pass a sign that says: 'Free sex with fill-up.'

'Hey man,' says one of them, 'I've heard of that. Let's try it.' So they stop.

'Can I help you?'

'Yeah, fill 'er up.'

A few minutes later: 'That'll be $18.50 please.'

'Hey, wait a minute, your sign says free sex with fill-up.'

'Oh, why yes it does, but it is conditional. I am thinking of a number between one and 20, what is it?'

First guy, 'Five.'

Second guy, 'Eight.'

'No, I'm sorry gentlemen, it was two. Well, better luck next time.'

The two naive blokes leave and are a bit perturbed.

'Aw man, we were ripped off!'

'Nah, I don't think so. Last week my wife went in there twice and won both times!'

## RUSSIA WITH LOVE

One day an old Jewish Pole, living in Warsaw, has his last light bulb burn out. To get a new one, he'll have to stand in line for two hours at the store, and they'll probably be out by the time he gets there, so he goes up to his attic and starts rummaging around for an old oil lamp he vaguely remembers seeing. He finds an old brass lamp in the bottom of a trunk that has seen better days. He starts to polish it and, poof!, a genie appears in a cloud of smoke.

'Ho ho, mortal,' says the genie, stretching and yawning, 'for releasing me I will grant you three wishes!'

The old man thinks for a moment, and says, 'I want Genghis Khan resurrected. I want him to reunite his Mongol hordes, march to the Polish border, and then decide he doesn't want the place and march back home.'

'No sooner said than done!' thunders the genie. 'Your second wish?'

'Okay. I want Genghis Khan resurrected. I want him to reunite his Mongol hordes, march to the Polish border, and then decide he doesn't want the place and march back home.'

'Hmmm. Well, all right. Your third wish?'

'I want Genghis Khan resurrected. I want him to reunite his–'

'Okay okay okay. Right. What's this business about Genghis Khan marching to Poland and turning around again?'

The old man smiles. 'He has to pass through Russia six times.'

## MIKHAIL THE CHAUFFEUR

Comrade Gorbachev is being driven from his dacha to Moscow and is in a hurry. He is getting irritated with the slowness of his driver. 'Can't you go any faster?' he says angrily.

'I have to obey the speed limits,' says the driver.

Finally, Gorbachev orders the driver into the back and takes the wheel. Sure enough, a patrol car soon pulls them over. The senior officer orders the junior to write up the ticket. But the junior officer comes back and says he can't give them a ticket, the person in the car is too important.

'Well, who is it?' the senior officer asks.

'I didn't recognise him,' says the junior officer, 'but Comrade Gorbachev is his chauffeur.'

## TEXAN GETS MESSAGE

A Texan in New York City needed to call a nearby community from a pay phone.

'Deposit $1.85 please,' instructed the operator.

Pulling himself up to his full height and dropping into his thickest Texas drawl, he objected, 'Ma'am, I'm from Texas, and in Texas we can place a call to Hell and back for $1.85!'

'I understand, sir,' retorted the operator, 'but in Texas, that's a local call.'

## BLAME GAME

A Jew and a Chinese man are travelling on a train together. After a while, the Jew stands up and gives the Chinese man a tremendous slap.

'What are you doing?' says the stricken Chinese.

'That's for Pearl Harbor,' says the Jew.

'But I am Chinese! The Japanese were responsible for that,' says the Chinese.

'Japanese, Chinese — all the same.'

They resume their seats for a while. Then the Chinese gets up and mightily kicks the Jew.

'Hey! what's going on?'

'That's for the *Titanic*!' says the Chinese.

'But the *Titanic* was hit by an Iceberg!'

'Iceberg, Weissberg — all the same.'

## GOD'S MONEY MYSTERY

A nice young worker from Australia Post was sorting through her regular envelopes, when she discovered a letter addressed as follows: GOD, c/o Heaven. Upon opening the envelope, a letter enclosed told of how a little old lady who had never asked for anything in her life was desperately in need of $100 and was wondering if God could send her the money. Well, the young lady was deeply touched and collected $90 from her fellow workmates and sent it off to the old lady.

A few weeks later, another letter arrived addressed to God, so the young lady opened it and it read: 'Thank you for the money, God, I deeply appreciate it. However, I only received $90. It must have been those bastards at the Post Office.'

## IT'S A DEAL

One Russian and one Polish workman were digging the foundations for a new road. After several hours of hard toil, the Polish guy hits his shovel on something hard in the ground. Both men work hurriedly to dig the object out and discover that it's a treasure chest. On opening it, they find jewels, coins and gold beyond their wildest dreams. Both are wild with happiness and dance around madly.

When they have calmed down, the Russian takes the Polish workman's hand and earnestly says, 'Sir, we will share this just like Russian and Polish comrades should,' and the Polish guy says, 'Oh no, it should 50/50!'

## SWEET, SOFT PUMPKIN

Recently, a female sheriff's deputy arrested a young man who was fornicating with a pumpkin in the middle of a field at night. The next day, at the courthouse, he was charged with lewd and lascivious behaviour, public indecency and public intoxication. He explained how he was passing the pumpkin patch on his way home from a drinking session when he decided to stop.

'You know how a pumpkin is soft and squishy inside, and there was no one around for miles, or at least I thought there was no one around,' he stated, before going on to say that he pulled over to the side of the road, picked out a pumpkin that he felt was appropriate to his purpose, cut a hole in it and proceeded to satisfy his pressing need. 'Guess I was really into it, y'know?' he commented with evident embarrassment. In the process of doing the deed, he failed to notice the approaching sheriff's car and was unaware of his audience until the deputy approached him.

'It was an unusual situation, that's for sure,' said the deputy. 'I walked up to him and he's just humping away at this pumpkin. I said excuse me, sir, but do you realise that you're having sex with a pumpkin? He froze and was clearly very surprised that I was there, and then he looked me straight in the face and said, "A pumpkin? Shit, is it midnight already?"'

## EXPENSIVE THOUGHTS

A young Scottish lad and lass were sitting on a low stone wall, holding hands, smiling and gazing out over the loch. For several minutes they sat silently. Then finally the girl looked at the boy and said, 'A penny for your thoughts, Angus.'

'Well, um, I was thinkin' . . . perhaps it's aboot time for a wee kiss.'

The girl blushed, leaned over and kissed him lightly on the cheek and then he blushed. The two turned once again to gaze out over the loch.

A few more minutes passed and the girl spoke again. 'Another penny for your thoughts, Angus.'

'Well, uh, I was thinkin' noo, perhaps it's aboot time for a wee cuddle.'

The girl blushed, leaned over and cuddled him for a few seconds. And he blushed. And the two turned once again to gaze out over the loch.

After a while, she again said, 'Another penny for your thoughts, Angus.'

'Well, ah, I was thinkin' perhaps it's aboot time you let me put my hand on your leg.'

The girl blushed, took his hand and put it on her knee and he blushed. Once again, the two turned to gaze out over the loch before the girl spoke softly.

'Another penny for your thoughts, Angus.'

The young man glanced down with a furrowed brow. 'Well, noo,' he said, 'my thoughts are a wee bit more serious this time.'

'Really?' said the lass in a whisper, filled with anticipation.

'Aye,' said the lad, nodding. The girl looked away in shyness, began to blush, and bit her lip in anticipation of the ultimate request. And he said, 'Dae ye nae think it's aboot time ye paid me the first three pennies?'

## SAY IT AS IT IS, MICHAEL

'It is absolutely bizarre that the people who can't tell us what the f---ing weather is next Tuesday can predict with absolute precision what the f---ing global temperatures will be in 100 years' time. It's horseshit.'

— 'enlightened' Luddite quote from Michael O'Leary, boss of Irish airline Ryanair, a 'Quote of the Week' from the *Mail on Sunday*

## PRESS DOOZEYS

News headlines from various American newspapers:

'Forecasters call for weather on Monday' (subhead: 'They're hesitant to predict snowstorm here')

'Amphibious pitcher makes debut' (subhead: 'Venditte becomes first pitcher in 20 years to pitch with both arms in MLB game')

'Cows lose their jobs as milk prices drop'

'Miracle cure kills fifth patient'

'Man accused of killing lawyer receives a new attorney'

'State population to double by 2040; babies to blame'

'Missippi's literacy program shows improvement'

'Breathing oxygen linked to staying alive'

'Police arrest everyone on February 22nd'

'Thursday is cancelled'

'Bridge closure date: Thursday or October' (subhead: 'State's detour plans draw criticism')

## ACROSS THE BORDER

'Most earthquake damage is caused by shaking'

'Federal agents raid gun shop, find weapons' (subhead: 'Store owner arrested previously')

'Safety meeting ends in accident'

'Murderer says detective ruined his reputation'

'Utah poison control centre reminds everyone not to take poison'

'Bugs flying around with wings are flying bugs'

'Students cook & serve grandparents'

'Alton attorney accidentally sues himself'

'Hospitals resort to hiring doctors' (subhead: 'Physician shortage prompting move, administrators say')

'Farmer using cannon to protect watermelons'

'Voters to vote on whether to vote'

'Museums full of history'

'Goat accused of robbery' (from a Nigerian newspaper)

# ANIMAL KINGDOM

Animals can't talk. We all know that. But the animals in this chapter chatter away like there's no tomorrow. It sometimes seems strange to read of an animal talking like a human in a typical human situation. But, hey, how can you make a joke about animals without them turning into us? So, get set for plenty of laughs as you wolf your way through this chapter . . .

## RUGBY, ANIMAL STYLE

The animals were bored. Finally, the lion had an idea. 'I know a really exciting game that the humans play called rugby. I've seen it on TV.' He proceeded to describe it to the rest of the animals and they all got excited about it, so they decided to play.

They went out to the field and chose teams and were ready to begin. The lion's team received the kick-off. They were able to get two rucks and then decided to kick.

The mule punted and the rhino was back deep for the kick. He caught the ball, lowered his head and charged. First, he crushed a roadrunner, then two rabbits. He gored a wildebeest, knocked over two cows, and broke through to daylight and scored a try. Unfortunately, they lacked a placekicker, and the score remained 5–0.

Late in the first half the lion's team scored a try and the mule kicked the extra points. The lion's team led at halftime 7–5.

In the changing room, the lion gave a pep talk. 'Look, you guys. We can win this game. We've got the lead and they only have one real threat. We've got to keep the ball away from the rhino, he's a killer. Mule, when you kick off, be sure to keep it away from the rhino.'

The second half began. Just as the mule was about to kick off, the rhino's team changed formation and the ball went directly to the rhino. Once again, the rhino lowered his head and was off running. First, he stomped two gazelles. He skewered a zebra and bulldozed an elephant out of the way. It looked like he was home free. Suddenly, at the 22-metre line, he dropped down dead. There were no other animals anywhere near him. The lion went over to see what had happened. Right next to the dead rhino he saw a small centipede.

'Did you do this?' he asked the centipede.

'Yeah, I did,' the centipede replied.

The lion retorted, 'Where were you during the first half?'

'I was putting on my boots.'

## VERY BATTY

Two bats are hanging upside down on a branch. One asks the other, 'Do you recall your worst day last year?'

The other responds, 'Yes, the day I had diarrhoea!'

**Q:** What do you call a rabbit that has fleas?
**A:** Bugs bunny.

## BEAR-FACED LIES

A priest, a minister, and a rabbi want to see who's best at his job. So they each go into the woods, find a bear, and attempt to convert it. Later they get together.

The priest begins: 'When I found the bear, I read to him from the Catechism and sprinkled him with holy water. Next week is his first communion.'

'I found a bear by the stream,' says the minister, 'and preached God's holy word. The bear was so mesmerised that he let me baptise him.'

They both look down at the rabbi, who is bleeding heavily from an arm wound. 'Looking back,' he says, 'maybe I shouldn't have started with the circumcision.'

**Q:** How do you get 500 old cows in a barn?
**A:** Put up a bingo sign.

**Q:** What has more lives than a cat?
**A:** A frog because it croaks every night.

## SERVES HIM RIGHT!

A man is fishing and he catches a crocodile.

The crocodile pleads with him, 'Please let me go! I'll grant you any wish you desire.'

The man says, 'Okay, I wish my penis could touch the ground.'

The crocodile then bites his legs off.

**Q:** Why did the fish blush?
**A:** Because it saw the ocean's bottom.

## BACKWARD CHRISTIAN SOLDIERS

Two devout Christian guys are walking through a game park and they come across a lion that has not eaten for days. The lion starts chasing the two men.

They run as fast as they can and then one guy starts getting tired and decides to say a prayer: 'Please turn this lion into a Christian, Lord.' He looks to see if the lion is still chasing and he sees the lion on its knees.

Happy to have his prayer answered, he turns around and heads towards the lion. As he comes closer to the lion, he hears it saying a prayer: 'Thank you Lord for the food I am about to receive.'

## FISHY TALE

A boy is selling fish on a corner. To get his customers' attention, he is yelling, 'Dam fish for sale! Get your dam fish here!'

A pastor hears this and asks, 'Why are you calling them dam fish?'

The boy responds, 'Because I caught these fish at the dam.'

The pastor buys a couple of fish, takes them home to his wife, and asks her to cook the dam fish. The wife responds, surprised, 'I didn't know it was acceptable for a preacher to speak that way.' He explains to her why they are dam fish.

Later at the dinner table, he asks his son to pass the dam fish.

'That's the spirit, Dad!' responds his son. 'Now pass the f---ing potatoes!'

**Q:** What animal should you never play cards with?
**A:** A cheetah.

## ANIMAL CRACKERS

An elephant and a camel are talking. The elephant asks, 'Why do you have boobs on your back?'

The camel replies, 'Ha! That's a funny question coming from an animal with a willy hanging from his face.'

## ELEPHANTITIS

**Q:** What did the elephant say to a naked man?
**A:** Hey, that's cute but can you breathe through it?

**Q:** What's grey, stands in a river when it rains and doesn't get wet?
**A:** An elephant with an umbrella!

**Q:** Why does an elephant wear sneakers?
**A:** So that he can sneak up on mice!

**Q:** What do you call an elephant that doesn't matter?
**A:** An irrelephant.

**Q:** What's big and grey and wears a mask?
**A:** The elephantom of the opera!

**Q:** What's grey and moves at 100 km/h?
**A:** A jet-propelled elephant!

**Q:** Why does the elephant bring toilet paper to the party?
**A:** Because he is a party pooper.

I suppose when you've seen one lion catch an elephant, you've seen a maul.

**Q:** Why did the elephants get kicked out of the pool?
**A:** Because their trunks kept on falling down.

**Q:** What do you get when you cross an elephant with a dairy cow?
**A:** Peanut butter.

**Q:** What do you call an elephant at the North Pole?
**A:** Lost!

## FROG'S BIG MOUTH

A 92-year-old man is walking through a park and sees a frog. He picks up the frog and it says, 'If you kiss me, I will turn into a beautiful princess and be yours for a week.'

The old man puts the frog in his pocket. The frog screams, 'Hey, if you kiss me, I will turn into a beautiful princess and make love to you for a whole month.'

The old man looks at the frog and says, 'At my age, I'd rather have a talking frog.'

**Q:** What type of sandals do frogs wear?
**A:** Open-toad!

## A TALL STORY

A man and his pet giraffe walk into a bar and start drinking. As the night goes on, they get drunk, and the giraffe finally passes out. The man decides to go home.

As he's leaving, the man is approached by the barman who says, 'Hey, you're not gonna leave that lyin' here, are ya?'

'Hmph,' says the man. 'That's not a lion — it's a giraffe.'

## MAGILLA GORILLA

A man walks out on his front porch one day and sees a gorilla in the tree on his front lawn. He calls animal control and about an hour later a man shows up with a ladder, a pit bull, and a shotgun.

The animal control employee tells the man, 'I'm here to get the gorilla out of your tree. I'm going to use this ladder to climb up the tree and shake the branch the gorilla is on to knock him to the ground. The pit bull is trained to go after anything that falls from the tree and bites their balls which calms the animal down, so I can put him in the truck.'

The man says, 'Okay, I see what the ladder and the pit bull are for but what is the shotgun for?'

The animal control employee says, 'Oh, that's for you. In case I fall out of the tree instead of the gorilla.'

**Q:** Why couldn't the leopard play hide-and-seek?
**A:** Because he was always spotted.

Light travels faster than sound. This is why some people appear bright until you hear them speak.

## MONKEY BUSINESS

A boy with a monkey on his shoulder was walking down the road when he passed a policeman who said, 'Now, now young lad, I think you had better take that monkey to the zoo.'

The next day, the boy was walking down the road with the monkey on his shoulder again, when he passed the same policeman. The policeman said, 'Hey there, I thought I told you to take that monkey to the zoo.'

The boy answered, 'I did! Today I'm taking him to the pictures.'

## CLAP-HAPPY

It was a baby mosquito's first day to fly out from home. When the baby came back home later that day, the father mosquito asked, 'How was your journey?'

The baby mosquito replied, 'It went great. Everyone was clapping for me!'

**Q:** How come oysters never donate to charity?
**A:** Because they are shellfish.

## PANDA ANTICS

A panda walks into a bar, sits down, and orders a sandwich. He eats, pulls out a gun, and shoots the waiter dead.

As the panda stands to go, the barman shouts, 'Hey! Where are you going? You just shot my waiter and you didn't pay for the food!'

The panda yells back, 'Hey, man, I'm a panda. Look it up!'

The bartender opens his dictionary to 'panda': 'A tree-climbing mammal of Asian origin, characterised by distinct black and white colouring. Eats, shoots, and leaves.'

## PARROT FASHION

Late one night a burglar broke into a house and while he was sneaking around he heard a voice say, 'Jesús is watching you.'

He looked around and saw nothing. He kept on creeping and again heard, 'Jesús is watching you.'

In a dark corner, he saw a cage with a parrot inside.

The burglar asked the parrot, 'Was it you who said Jesús is watching me?'

The parrot replied, 'Yes.'

Relieved, the burglar asked, 'What is your name?'

The parrot said, 'Clarence.'

The burglar said, 'That's a stupid name for a parrot. What idiot named you Clarence?'

The parrot answered, 'The same idiot that named the rottweiler Jesús.'

## ARCTIC ANTICS

A family of polar bears have just come out of hibernation. The Arctic weather is still bitterly cold, with the snow and ice stretching as far as the eye can see. The baby polar bear struggles in the deep snow and ice. He asks his mother, 'Am I a real polar bear, Mum?'

His mother replies, 'What sort of nonsense is that? Of course you're a real polar bear. Your daddy's a polar bear and I'm a polar bear. We made you and of course you're a polar bear.'

They trudge on and the baby polar bear catches up to his father and asks, 'Daddy, am I a real polar bear?'

His father smiles and says, 'Of course you are, son. Your mother is a polar bear and I'm a polar bear. We made you, so you are a polar bear.'

The baby polar bear is still not satisfied, so he sidles up to his big sister. 'Am I a real polar bear, sis?' he asks.

His sister answers, 'What a dumb question that is. Of course you're a real polar bear. Mum's a real polar bear,

Dad's a real polar bear, I'm a real polar bear. So that makes you a real polar bear. Why are you asking this dopey question anyway?'

The baby polar bear says, 'Because I'm bloody freezing!'

## BRAINY POODLE

A wealthy old woman decides to go on a photo safari in Africa, taking her poodle along for company. One day the poodle starts chasing butterflies and before long discovers that he's lost. Wandering about, he notices a hungry-looking leopard heading rapidly in his direction. The poodle thinks, 'Uh, oh!'

Noticing some bones on the ground close by, he immediately settles down to chew on the bones with his back to the approaching cat. Just as the leopard is about to leap, the poodle exclaims loudly, 'Boy, that was one delicious leopard! I wonder if there are any more around here?'

Hearing this, the leopard halts his attack in mid-strike, a look of terror comes over his face and he slinks away into the trees. 'Whew!' says the leopard. 'That was close! That poodle nearly had me.'

Meanwhile, a monkey who had been watching the whole scene from a nearby tree figures he can put this knowledge to good use and trade it for protection from the leopard. So off he goes, but the poodle sees him heading after the leopard with great speed, and figures that something must be up.

The monkey soon catches up with the leopard, spills the

beans and strikes a deal for himself with the leopard. The leopard is furious at being made a fool of and says, 'Here, monkey, hop on my back so you can watch me chew that poodle to bits!'

Now the poodle sees the leopard coming with the monkey on his back and thinks, 'What am I going to do now?' But instead of running, the dog sits down with his back to his attackers, pretending he hasn't seen them yet, and waits until they get just close enough to hear.

'Where's that damn monkey?' the poodle says. 'I sent him off an hour ago to bring me another leopard!'

## DODGY RIDE

You are on a horse, galloping at a constant speed. On your right side is a sharp drop-off, and on your left side is an elephant travelling at the same speed as you. Directly in front of you is another galloping horse but your horse is unable to overtake it. Behind you is a lion running at the same speed as you and the horse in front of you.

What must you do to safely get out of this highly dangerous situation?

Get your drunk ass off the merry-go-round!

## ROSE BETWEEN LILY AND DAISY

There are five cows on a farm, one mumma cow and four baby calves. The first baby walks up to the mum and asks, 'Mumma, why is my name Rose?'

The mummy cow replies, 'Well, honey, a rose petal fell on your head when you were born.'

The next calf comes up and asks, 'Mumma, why is my name Lily?'

The mother replies, 'Because, honey, a lily petal fell on your head when you were born.'

The third baby comes up and asks, 'Mumma, why is my name Daisy?'

The mumma cow again replies, 'Well, when you were born a daisy petal fell on your head.'

The final baby walks over and says, 'Duh huh guh nuh!'

The mumma cow says, 'Shut up, Tree Trunk.'

**Q:** Why do the French eat snails?
**A:** Because they don't like fast food.

**Q:** What's the difference between a guitar and a fish?
**A:** You can tune a guitar, but you can't tuna fish.

## MOTHER BEAR IS TOP

It's a sunny morning in the Big Forest and the bear family is just waking up. Baby Bear goes downstairs and sits in his small chair at the table. He looks into his small bowl. It's empty! 'Who's been eating my porridge?' he squeaks.

Father Bear arrives at the table and sits in his big chair. He looks into his big bowl. It's also empty! 'Who's been eating my porridge?' he roars.

Mother Bear sticks her head out the kitchen door and yells, 'For Pete's sake, how many times do we have to go through this? It was Mother Bear who got up first. It was Mother Bear who woke everybody else in the house up. It was Mother

Bear who unloaded the dishwasher from last night and put everything away. It was Mother Bear who went out into the cold early morning air to fetch the newspaper. It was Mother Bear who set the table. It was Mother Bear who put the cat out, cleaned the litter box and filled the cat's water and food dish. And now that you've decided to come downstairs and grace me with your presence, listen good because I'm only going to say this once: I haven't made the f---ing porridge yet!'

**Q:** What do cats eat for breakfast?
**A:** Mice Krispies.

**Teacher:** 'Name a bird with wings but can't fly.'
**Student:** 'A dead bird, sir.'

## LOVE A DUCK!

One day a duck walks into a store and asks the manager if he sells grapes. The manager says, 'No, we don't sell grapes.'

The duck goes home and comes back the next day and asks the same question. The manager says the same thing again, 'No, we do not sell grapes.'

The duck goes home, comes back the next day, and asks the manager if they sell grapes. This time the manager says, 'No, we don't sell grapes! If you ask one more time, I will nail your beak to the floor!'

The duck goes home. It comes back the next day and asks the manager if he has any nails. The manager says, 'No, I don't have any nails.'

The duck says, 'Okay, good. Do you sell grapes?'

## PICKY FROG

A chicken walks into a library, goes up to a librarian and says, 'Book book book.' The librarian decides that the chicken wants a book so he gives the chicken a book and the chicken walks away.

About 10 minutes later the chicken comes back with the book, looking a bit agitated, saying, 'Book book book.' The librarian decides the chicken wants another book so he takes the old book back and gives the chicken another book.

The chicken walks out the door. Ten minutes later the chicken comes back again, very agitated, saying, 'Book book book!' so quickly it almost sounds like one word. The chicken puts the book on the librarian's desk and looks up — waiting for another book. This time the librarian gives the chicken another book and decides that something weird is happening.

He follows the chicken out the door and into the park, all the way to the pond. In the pond is a frog sitting on a lily pad. The chicken gives the book to the frog, who then says, 'Reddit, reddit.'

## SEVEN-ALL UP

**Q:** If you were forced to go through one of the following doors, which door do you go through with 100 per cent certainty you'd stay alive: a door with a man with a gun behind it, a door with a tiger who hasn't eaten in seven years behind it, or a door with an electric chair behind it?

**A:** The one with the tiger behind it, because if it hasn't eaten in seven years it's dead.

**Q:** How do fish get high?
**A:** Seaweed.

### POETRY TIME

Roses are red.
Your blood is too.
You look like a monkey
And belong in a zoo.
Do not worry,
I'll be there too.
Not in the cage,
But laughing at you.

### KINKY!

I saw a young teenage kid on the subway today. He had a Mohawk hairstyle dyed yellow, green, and red.

He caught me staring at him and in a nasty voice asked, 'What the f--k are you looking at?'

I replied, 'Sorry, but when I was about your age I had sex with a parrot. I thought maybe you were my son.'

**Q:** What's the difference between a BMW and a porcupine?
**A:** A BMW has pricks on the inside!

## VARIATION ON A THEME

Bob: 'Why did the chicken cross the road?'
Joe: 'To get to the idiot's house.'
Bob: 'Knock knock.'
Joe: 'Who's there?'
Bob: 'The chicken.'

## DOGGONE CLEVER

A dog walks into a butcher's shop and the butcher asks, 'What do you want?' The dog points to steak in a glass case. 'How many kilograms?' The dog barks twice. 'Anything else?' The dog points to some pork chops and barks four times. So the butcher wraps up a two-kilogram steak and four pork chops, and places the bag in the dog's mouth. He then takes money from a purse tied around the dog's neck and sees him out.

A customer, who has been watching in amazement, follows the dog to a house several blocks away, where it rings the doorbell to be let in. As the owner appears at the door, the customer says, 'What a remarkable dog!'

'Remarkable?' snorts the owner. 'This is the second time this week he's forgotten his keys.'

## BOMBS AWAY

A man boards a plane and is seated next to an air marshal and his 'sniffing dog'. Soon, the plane takes off and the marshal says, 'Sniffer, search.'

The dog walks along the aisle and stops next to a woman. He then returns to his seat and puts a paw on the marshal's arm. 'Good boy,' says the marshal.

'What happened?' asks the man.

'That woman is in possession of marijuana. We'll arrest her when we land.'

Once again, Sniffer searches the aisles. He stops beside a man, then returns to his seat, and places two paws on the marshal's arm. 'That man is carrying cocaine,' the marshal explains.

The dog walks up the aisle again, then races back, jumps into his seat, and shits all over it.

'What's going on?!' demands the man.

The marshal nervously replies, 'He just found a bomb!'

## BLIND CHEEK

Two guys were out walking their dogs on a hot day when they pass by a pub. The first guy says, 'Let's go in there for a pint.'

The second guy, says, 'They won't let us in with our dogs.'

First guy: 'Sure they will, just follow my lead.'

He goes up to the pub, and sure enough the doorman says, 'I can't let you in here with that dog.'

He replies, 'Oh, I'm blind and this is my seeing-eye dog.'

The doorman says, 'Okay then, come on in.'

The second guy sees this and does the same thing. He goes up to the pub, and the doorman says, 'You can't come in here with a dog.'

He replies, 'I'm blind and this is my seeing-eye dog.'

The doorman responds, 'You have a chihuahua for a seeing-eye dog?'

The second guy stops for a second, and exclaims, 'They gave me a chihuahua?'

## CUSTOMISED CHOOK

Several years ago, we headed to Opunake to visit some relatives. I had a new car and was having fun driving fast on the twisty coastal road from New Plymouth. As we zoomed along, I noticed a three-legged chicken keeping pace with me. I slowed to get a better look at the speedster when it turned and went down a dirt road. I stopped, turned around and followed it.

After a short ride, we came upon a house with an older couple sitting on the porch and dozens of three-legged chickens in the yard. I asked them, 'Are these your chickens? They're the fastest I've ever seen.'

The old man said, 'Yep.'

So I asked him where they came from, and he replied, 'When the kids were younger, they always fought over the chicken legs, so we decided to breed a three-legged chicken.'

I nodded and said, 'Well, they are fast, but what do they taste like?'

'Not rightly sure,' he admitted. 'We never could catch one.'

## POODLE TROUBLES

A poodle and a collie are walking down the street when the poodle suddenly unloads on his friend. 'My life is a mess,' he says. 'My owner is mean, my girlfriend's having an affair with a German shepherd, and I'm as nervous as a cat.'

'Why don't you go and see a psychiatrist,' suggests the collie.

'I can't,' says the poodle. 'I'm not allowed on the couch.'

## LOOKS LIKE A WEE NUN

A penguin walks into a bar, goes to the counter, and asks the barman, 'Have you seen my brother?'

The barman says, 'I don't know. What does he look like?'

## CRAPPY STORY!

My collection of vintage kitchen utensils includes one whose intended purpose was always a mystery. It looks like a cross between a metal slotted spoon and a spatula, so I use it as both. When not in use, it is prominently displayed in a decorative ceramic utensil caddy in my kitchen.

The mystery of the spoon/spatula was recently solved when I found one in its original packaging at a garage sale.

It's a pooper-scooper.

**Q:** What do you call a cat that ate a mallard?
**A:** A duck filled fatty puss!

## HEALTHY DIET

**Q:** What do we learn from animals like buffaloes, elephants and cows?
**A:** That not everyone can lose weight by eating greens and salads and walking as well.

**Q:** Why are frogs always so happy?
**A:** They eat whatever bugs them.

**Q:** Why can't you hear a pterodactyl pee?
**A:** Because the 'p' is silent.

## PIGGING OUT

A farmer is out walking with a prospective buyer when they see a beautiful pig in the yard, except it has a wooden leg.

The buyer asks, 'Why the wooden leg?'

The farmer replies, 'That pig is so smart, I let it drive the kids to school.'

'Great, but why the wooden leg?'

'The pig is so smart it has a degree in horticulture and philosophy.'

'Amazing! But why the bloody wooden leg?'

'Well, when you have a pig that smart you don't eat it all at once!'

## HORSE SENSE

A man walks into a bar and the barman says, 'If you can make that horse over there laugh, you can get free drinks for the rest of the night.'

The man walks over, says something to the horse, it laughs, and he walks back over to the bar to collect his free drinks.

The next night, the man goes back to the bar and the barman asks the man if he can make the horse cry.

The man walks over, does something to the horse, and it starts to cry.

The barman asks, 'How did you make it cry?'

The man replies, 'Well, to make the horse laugh last night I told it I had a bigger dick and to make it cry tonight I showed it.'

**Q:** Why did the blind man give up skydiving?
**A:** Because it was scaring the hell out of his dog!

## GOD NO HELP

A man needed a horse, so he went to a temple and got one. Before he left, the priest told him that it was a special horse. In order to make the horse go, you say 'Thank God' and for it to stop you say 'Amen'.

So the man left, and a few minutes later he dozed off in his saddle. Hours later, he woke up and his horse was racing him towards the edge of a cliff. Just in time, he shouted 'Amen!' and the horse stopped a few inches from the edge.

'Whew,' said the man, 'thank God!'

## HOW NOW BROWN COW

There was a farmer who had a brown cow and a white cow and he wanted to get them bred, so he borrowed his neighbour's bull and turned it loose in the pasture. He told his son to watch and come in and tell him when the bull was finished. 'Yeah Daddy, yeah Daddy,' said the little boy.

After a while the boy came into the living room where his father was talking with some friends. 'Say, Pop,' said the boy.

'Yes,' replied his father.

'The bull just f---ed the brown cow.'

There was a sudden lull in the conversation. The father said, 'Excuse me', and took his son outside.

'Son, you mustn't use language like that in front of company. You should say, "The bull *surprised* the brown cow." Now go and watch and tell me when the bull *surprises* the white cow.'

The father went back inside the house. After a while, the boy came in and said, 'Hey, Daddy.'

'Yes, son. Did the bull surprise the white cow?'

'He sure did, Pop! He f---ed the brown cow again!'

## WISE CHOICE OF WORDS

Attorney: 'At the scene of the accident, did you tell the constable you had never felt better in your life?'

Farmer: That's right.'

Attorney: 'Well, then, how is it that you are now claiming you were seriously injured when my client's auto hit your wagon?'

Farmer: 'When the sheriff arrived, he went over to my horse, who had a broken leg, and shot him. Then he went over to Rover, my dog, who was all banged up, and shot him. When he asked me how I felt, I just thought under the circumstances, it was a wise choice of words to say I've never felt better in my life.'

## LOAD OF OLD BOLLOCKS

A city boy went duck hunting in the country one day. While hunting, he shot a duck which fell on the property of a farmer. The boy crawled over the fence to claim his kill.

But the farmer, seeing what had happened, rushed out with his shotgun and yelled, 'See here! That duck belongs to me.'

The city boy replies, 'But I shot the duck, therefore it belongs to me.'

The farmer says, 'It fell on my property so it belongs to me.'

They continue to argue, each claiming ownership of the duck. After a while, the farmer says, 'We should settle this the old-fashioned country way.'

The city boy asks, 'What is the "old-fashioned country way"?'

The farmer explains, 'First, I kick you in the groin. Then, you kick me in the groin and we continue in this fashion until one of us gives up. The one who wins gets the duck.'

The city boy, willing to do anything to get his duck and leave, agrees to the contest. The farmer draws back his leg and kicks the city boy in the groin with all his might. The city boy, in horrible pain, falls to the ground moaning and groaning.

After about 10 minutes, the city boy stands up shakily and croaks, 'It's my turn now.'

The farmer says, 'Oh, you can have the duck,' and leaves.

### PARROT HEAVEN

This man had a parrot that knew only one sentence, which was 'Let's make love'. The parrot said it all the time, embarrassing the owner no end.

Finally, he went to his parish priest and told him of his parrot problem. The priest replied, 'I have a parrot who also only knows one sentence. He always says "Let us pray". Bring your parrot over Sunday after Mass, and I'm sure your parrot will be praying by the end of the day.'

So, as directed, the owner brought the parrot over to the

presbytery after Mass. The parrot, spying the priest's parrot, opened his mouth and blurted out, 'Let's make love.'

The priest's parrot closed his eyes, looked up at Heaven and said, 'My prayers have been answered.'

## ACCIDENT PRONE

Johnny and Dave own a meat business. They are driving down a dirt road in their meat truck and hit something big. Bang!

'What the hell was that?!' said Johnny.

Dave said, 'I have no idea.'

Johnny said, 'Go have a look.'

Dave comes back and said, 'We've hit a cow.'

Johnny asked if it was any good.

Dave said, 'Its head is crushed.'

Johnny said, 'Well, cut its head off, skin it, gut it and put it in the back with the rest.'

So they drive down the road and hit a sheep.

Johnny asked if it was any good. Dave said yes.

Johnny said, 'Skin it, gut it and chuck it in the back with the rest.'

They drove down the road a little bit more, then another bang!

'What the f--k was that?!' said Johnny. 'Go have a look.'

Dave came back and said, 'We've hit a pig.'

Johnny said, 'Is it any good? Yeah? Skin it, gut it and chuck it in the back with the rest.

Dave comes back and says, 'What do you want me to do with his motorbike.'

### POLITE LION

This Christian was thrown into the ring with a lion. Terrified, he fell on his knees and started praying. At the same time, the lion dropped down on its knees and started praying too.

The Christian, overjoyed, exclaimed, 'Thank God! Another Christian!'

To which the lion replied, 'I don't know about you, but I'm saying grace.'

# BLONDES

Yes, the blondes are back. For the bulk of the world's population, the insults fly thick and fast. We wondered whether blonde jokes were allowed, or even relevant in our more chastened world. But yes, the backers said go ahead, chuck them in! So, here they are. A few of them even take a poke at brunettes and bloke blonds, but the majority are aimed squarely at the dim-witted female blondes. Some are funny and, admittedly, others are perhaps a bit lame, but they are all in the eye of the beholder.

### THIRD GRADER

There were three third graders walking down the street — a redhead, a brunette and a blonde. Which one had the best figure?

The blonde, she was 18.

### SEE YA LATER ALLIGATOR

A young blonde was on vacation in the depths of Louisiana. She wanted a pair of real alligator shoes in the worst way, but she didn't want to pay the high prices the local vendors were asking. After becoming very frustrated with the 'no haggle' attitude of one of the shopkeepers, the blonde shouted, 'Maybe I'll just go out and catch my own alligator so I can get a pair of shoes at a reasonable price!'

The shopkeeper said, 'By all means, be my guest. Maybe you'll luck out and catch yourself a big one!'

Determined, the blonde turned and headed for the swamps, set on catching herself an alligator. Later in the day, the shopkeeper is driving home when he spots the young woman standing waist deep in the water, shotgun in hand.

Just then, he sees a huge three-metre alligator swimming quickly towards her. She takes aim, kills the creature and with a great deal of effort hauls it onto the swamp bank.

Lying nearby were several more of the dead creatures. The shopkeeper watches in amazement. Just then the blonde flips the alligator on its back, and frustrated, shouts out, 'Darn, this one isn't wearing any shoes either!'

**Q:** Why do blondes wear their hair up?
**A:** To catch everything that goes over their heads.

## BLIND TO DANGER

A blind man enters a bar and find his way to a bar stool. After ordering a drink, and sitting there for a while, the blind guy yells to the bartender, 'Hey, you wanna hear a blonde joke?'

The bar immediately becomes absolutely quiet. In a husky, deep voice, the woman next to him says, 'Before you tell that joke, you should know something. The bartender is blond, the bouncer is blond and I'm a six-foot tall, 90-kilogram blonde with a black belt in karate. What's more, the fella sitting next to me is blond and he's a weightlifter. The woman to your right is a blonde, and she's a pro wrestler. Think about it seriously, mister. You still wanna tell that blonde joke?'

The blind guy says, 'Nah, not if I'm gonna have to explain it five times.'

## SOME FRIEND

A blonde, a redhead, and a brunette were all lost in the desert. They found a lamp and rubbed it. A genie popped out and granted them each one wish.

The redhead wished to be back home. Poof! She was back home.

The brunette wished to be at home with her family. Poof! She was back home with her family.

The blonde said, 'Awwww, I wish my friends were here.'

**Q:** What's the difference between a blonde and a supermarket trolley?

**A:** The supermarket trolley has a mind of its own.

## BLONDE CRINGE

There was a blonde who just got sick and tired of all the blonde jokes. One evening, she went home and memorised all the US state capitals.

Back in the office the next day, some guy started telling a dumb blonde joke. She interrupted him with a shrill announcement, 'I've had it up to here with these blonde jokes. I want you to know that this blonde went home last night and did something probably none of you could do. I memorised all the state capitals.'

One of the guys said, 'I don't believe you. What's the capital of Delaware?'

'D,' she answered.

## IN THE SWIM

There was a blonde, a redhead and a brunette. They were all trapped on an island and the nearest shore was 50 kilometres away.

The redhead swam, trying to make it to the other shore. She swam 15 kilometres, then drowned.

The brunette swam 24 kilometres before drowning.

The blonde swam 25 kilometres, got tired, and swam back.

**Q:** Why can't a blonde dial 911?
**A:** She can't find the eleven.

## BLONDE COWBOY

A sheriff in a small town in Wyoming walks out in the street and sees a blond-haired cowboy coming towards him with nothing on but his cowboy hat, his gun and his boots. He arrests him for indecent exposure. As he is locking him up, he asks, 'Why in the world are you walking around like this?'

The cowboy says, 'Well, it's like this sheriff. I was in this bar down the road and this pretty little redhead asks me to go out to her motor home with her. So I did.

'We go inside and she pulls off her top and asks me to pull off my shirt. So I did.

'Then she pulls off her skirt and asks me to pull off my pants. So I did.

'Then she pulls off her panties and asks me to pull off my shorts. So I did.

'Then she gets on the bed and looks at me kind of sexy and says, "Now go to town cowboy."

'So here I am.'

## THE GRIDIRON GAME

A guy took his blonde girlfriend to her first football game. They had great seats right behind their team's bench. After the game, he asked her how she liked the experience.

'Oh, I really liked it,' she replied, 'especially the tight pants and all the big muscles, but I just couldn't understand why they were killing each other over 25 cents.'

Nonplussed, her date asked, 'What do you mean?'

'Well, they flipped a coin, one team got it, and then for the rest of the game, all they kept screaming was, "Get the quarterback! Get the quarterback!" I'm like, hello? It's only 25 cents!'

## TV TIMES

A robber comes into the store and steals a TV.

A blonde runs after him and says, 'Wait, you forgot the remote!'

**Q:** What do a blonde and a beer bottle have in common?
**A:** They're both empty from the neck up.

### COLGATE?

A blonde drops off her dress to the dry cleaners.

The lady says, 'Come again.'

The blonde says, 'No, it's toothpaste this time.'

**Q:** What do you call a blonde with two brain cells?
**A:** Pregnant.

### UNMASKED

A young brunette goes into the doctor's office and says that her body hurts wherever she touches it.

'Impossible,' says the doctor. 'Show me.'

She takes her finger and pushes her elbow and screams in agony. She pushes her knee and screams, pushes her ankle and screams and so it goes on, everywhere she touches makes her scream.

The doctor says, 'You're not really a brunette, are you?'

She says, 'No, I'm really a blonde.'

'I thought so,' he says. 'Your finger is broken.'

**Q:** How do blonde brain cells die?
**A:** Alone.

## EASILY MISTAKEN

A blonde walks into an electronics store and tells the salesman, 'I want that TV' and points to the display.

He looks at her and tells her, 'I'm sorry, I'm not allowed to sell that to blondes.' So the blonde, all ticked off, walks out of the store.

An hour later, she walks back into the same store with a black wig on. She walks up to the salesman and says, 'I want to buy that TV' and points to the display.

He looks at her and says, 'I'm sorry, but I already told you we can't sell that to blondes.'

So she walks out of the store mad again without a TV. A few weeks later she gets a makeover, new hair colour and everything, and she walks back into that electronics store.

She walks up to the salesman and says, 'I want to buy that TV' and points to the display.

The salesman shakes his head and tells her, 'I told you twice already, I can't sell that to blondes.'

The blonde looks at him and says, 'How do you know that I'm a blonde?'

He looks at her and states, 'Because, that's a microwave.'

**Q:** Why did the blonde die in a helicopter crash?
**A:** She got cold and turned off the fan.

## JUST A FERRARI

A blonde, wanting to earn some money, decided to hire herself out as a handyman-type and started canvassing a wealthy neighbourhood. She went to the front door of the first house and asked the owner if he had any jobs for her to do.

'Well, you can paint my porch. How much will you charge?'

The blonde said, 'How about 50 dollars?'

The man agreed and told her that the paint and ladders that she might need were in the garage.

The man's wife, inside the house, heard the conversation and said to her husband, 'Does she realise that the porch goes all the way around the house?'

The man replied, 'She should. She was standing on the porch.'

A short time later, the blonde came to the door to collect her money. 'You're finished already?' he asked.

'Yes,' the blonde answered, 'and I had paint left over, so I gave it two coats.'

Impressed, the man reached into his pocket for the $50.

'And by the way,' the blonde added, 'that's not a Porch, it's a Ferrari.'

**Q:** Why are blonde jokes so short?
**A:** So brunettes can remember them.

## KIDNAP CAPER

A blonde was down on her luck. In order to raise some money, she decided to kidnap a kid and hold him for ransom. So she went to the playground, grabbed a kid, took him behind a tree, and told him, 'I've kidnapped you.'

She then wrote a note saying, 'I've kidnapped your kid.

Tomorrow morning, put $10,000 in a paper bag and put it under the pecan tree next to the slide on the north side of the playground. Signed, Blonde.'

The blonde then taped the note to the kid's shirt and sent him home to show it to his parents.

The next morning the blonde checked, and sure enough, a paper bag was sitting beneath the pecan tree.

The blonde opened the bag and found the $10,000 with a note that said, 'How could you do this to a fellow blonde?'

## HEAVENLY BODY

Upon arrival, a concerned St Peter met a blonde at the Pearly Gates. 'I'm sorry,' St Peter said, 'but Heaven is suffering from an overload of goodly souls and we have been forced to introduce an entrance exam for new arrivals to ease the burden of heavenly arrivals.'

'That's cool,' said the blonde, 'What does the entrance exam consist of?'

'Just three questions,' said St Peter.

'Which are?' asked the blonde.

'The first,' said St Peter, 'is, Which two days of the week start with the letter "T"? The second is, How many seconds are there in a year? The third is, What was the name of the swagman in the song "Waltzing Matilda"? Now,' said St Peter, 'go away and think about those three questions and when I call upon you, I shall expect you to have those answers for me.'

So the blonde went away and gave those three questions some considerable thought.

The following morning, St Peter called upon the blonde and asked if she had considered the questions, to which she replied, 'I have.'

'Well then,' said St Peter, 'Which two days of the week start with the letter "T"?'

The blonde said, 'Today and Tomorrow.'

St Peter pondered this answer for some time and decided that indeed the answer could be applied to the question.

'Well, then, could I have your answer to the second of the three questions?' St Peter went on. 'How many seconds are there in a year?'

The blonde replied, 'Twelve!'

'Only twelve?' exclaimed St Peter. 'How did you arrive at that figure?'

'Easy,' said the blonde, 'there's the second of January, the second of February, right through to the second of December, giving a total of 12 seconds.'

St Peter looked at the blonde and said, 'I need some time to consider your answer before I can give you a decision.' And he walked away shaking his head.

A short time later, St Peter returned to the blonde. 'I'll allow the answer to stand, but you need to get the third and final question absolutely correct to be allowed into Heaven. Now, can you tell me the answer to the name of the swagman in the song "Waltzing Matilda"?'

The blonde replied eagerly, 'Of the three questions, I found this the easiest to answer.'

'Really!' exclaimed St Peter. 'And what is the answer?'

'It's Andy.'

'Andy?'

'Yes, Andy,' said the blonde.

This totally floored St Peter, and he paced this way and that, deliberating the answer. Finally, he couldn't stand the suspense any longer, and turning to the blonde, asked, 'How in God's name did you arrive at that answer?'

'Easy,' said the blonde. 'Andy sat, Andy watched, Andy waited till his billy boiled.'

And so the blonde entered Heaven . . .

**Q:** What do you call a blonde with half a brain?
**A:** Gifted!

## STOP THAT CAR

There's a blonde and a brunette in a car. The brunette is driving while the blonde is in the passenger seat. They're going down a steep hill when the brunette realises that the brakes don't work. The brunette tells the blonde that the brakes don't work and they will drive off the side of the cliff at the bottom of the hill if they can't stop.

The blonde replies, 'Don't worry! There's a stop sign ahead.'

**Q:** How do you sink a submarine full of blondes?
**A:** Knock on the door.

## YOU'RE HIRED

Three blondes were all applying for the last available position on the Northern Territory Highway Patrol. The detective conducting the interview looked at the three of them and said, 'So y'all wanna be cops, huh?' The blondes all nodded.

The detective got up, opened a file drawer, and pulled out a folder. Sitting back down, he opened it, pulled out a picture, and said, 'To be a detective, you have to be able to detect. You must be able to notice things such as distinguishing features and oddities like scars and so forth.'

So he stuck the photo in the face of the first blonde and withdrew it after about two seconds. 'Now,' he said, 'did you notice any distinguishing features about this man?'

The blonde immediately said, 'Yes, I did. He has only one eye!'

The detective shook his head and said, 'Of course he has only one eye in this picture! It's a side profile of his face. You're dismissed.'

The first blonde hung her head and walked out of the office.

The detective then turned to the second blonde, stuck the photo in her face for two seconds, pulled it back, and said, 'What about you? Notice anything unusual or outstanding about this man?'

'Yes. He only has one ear.' The detective put his head in his hands and exclaimed, 'Didn't you hear what I just told the previous applicant? This is a side picture profile of the man's face.'

The second blonde sheepishly walked out of the office.

The detective turned his attention to the third and last blonde and said, 'This is probably a waste of time, but . . .' He flashed the photo for a couple of seconds and withdrew it, saying, 'All right, did you notice any distinguishing or unusual features about this man?'

The blonde said, 'I sure did. This man wears contact lenses.'

The detective frowned, took another look at the picture, and began looking at some of the papers in the folder.

He looked up at the blonde with a puzzled expression and said, 'You're absolutely right. His bio says he wears contacts. How in the world could you tell that by looking at his picture?'

The blonde rolled her eyes and said, 'Well, helloooooooooo! With only one eye and one ear, he certainly can't wear glasses.'

**Q:** Why couldn't the blonde add 10 + 5 on a calculator?
**A:** She couldn't find the '10' button.

Did you hear about the blonde that got excited? She finished a jigsaw puzzle in six months, when the box said, 'two to four years'.

**Q:** How do you get a blonde's eyes to twinkle?
**A:** Shine a torch in her ear.

## MORE THAN A TRILLION?

A blonde is watching the news with her husband when the newscaster says, 'Six Brazilian men die in a skydiving accident.'

The blonde starts crying, sobbing, 'That's horrible!'

Confused, her husband replies, 'Yes, dear, it is sad, but they were skydiving, and there is always that risk involved.'

After a few minutes, the blonde, still sobbing, says, 'How many is a Brazilian?'

## DOGGONE BLONDE

Tired of constant blonde jokes, a blonde dyes her hair brown. She then goes for a drive in the country and sees a farmer herding his sheep across the road.

'Hey, farmer, if I guess how many sheep are here, can I keep one?'

The shepherd is puzzled but agrees.

She blurts out, '352!'

He is stunned but keeps his word and allows her to pick a sheep.

'I'll take this one,' she says proudly. 'It's the cutest!'

'Hey lady,' says the farmer, 'if I guess your real hair colour, can I have my dog back?'

## RUMBLED

A blonde, a brunette and a redhead are running from the police. They run into an old barn and hide in potato sacks. The officer chasing them walks into the barn looking for them. He kicks the first sack with the redhead inside and the redhead says, 'Woof woof!'

The cop, also a blond, thinks it's a dog, so he walks to the next one. He kicks the second bag with the brunette, and she says, 'Meow meow!'

The cop believes it's a cat and moves on. He kicks the third bag with the blonde, and the blonde yells, 'Potato potato!'

## DISTRACTED DEALERS

Two bored casino dealers are waiting at the craps table. A very attractive blonde woman from Hamilton arrives and bets $20,000 on a single roll of the dice.

She says, 'I hope you don't mind, but I feel much luckier when I play topless.'

With that, she strips to the waist, rolls the dice, and yells, 'Come on, Waikato girl needs new clothes!'

As the dice bounce and come to a stop, she jumps up and down and squeals, 'Yes! Yes! I won! I won!'

She hugs each of the dealers, picks up her winnings, and her clothes, and quickly departs. The dealers stare at each other dumbfounded.

Finally, one of them asks, 'What did she roll?'

The other answers, 'I don't know, I thought *you* were watching.'

**Q:** What do you call a blonde with a brain?
**A:** A golden retriever.

## SPARE PARTS

Three blondes are on a road trip. As they are driving through the desert, their car breaks down. They have no phone to call anyone, so they decide to walk to the nearest city, several miles away. They each decide to take one thing to make the journey better.

The first blonde takes the radio and says, 'If we get bored, we can put the radio on and listen to music.'

The second blonde decides to take a wheel, explaining, 'In case one of us gets really tired, we can go inside the wheel and be rolled.'

The third blonde takes the car door, saying, 'In case it gets too hot, we can roll down the window!'

## UNLUCKY!

Brunette: 'Where were you born?'
Blonde: 'Australia.'
Brunette: 'Which part?'
Blonde: 'My whole body.'

## FIRE, FIRE

A blonde's neighbour's house was on fire so she called 111. The blonde told the operator, 'My neighbour's house is on fire!'

The operator asked, 'Where are you?'

The blonde answered, 'At my house.'

The operator replied, 'No, I'm asking how do we get there?'

The blonde said, 'In a fire truck, duh!'

**Q:** What did the blonde say when she found out she was pregnant?
**A:** I wonder if it's mine.

### SKIP TO THE LOO!

A blonde is overweight, so her doctor puts her on a diet. 'I want you to eat regularly for two days, then skip a day and repeat for two weeks and you'll lose at least half a kilogram,' he directs her.

When the blonde returns, she's lost nearly a whole kilogram. The doctor exclaims, 'That's amazing! Did you follow my diet?'

The blonde nods. 'I thought I was going to drop dead every third day from all the skipping!'

### HAVE YOU GOT GREEN BALLS?

A blonde golfer goes into the pro shop and looks around frowning. Finally, the pro asks her what she wants.

'I can't find any green golf balls,' the blonde golfer complains.

The pro looks all over the shop, and through all the catalogues, and finally calls the manufacturers and determines that sure enough, there are no green golf balls.

As the blonde golfer walks out the door in disgust, the pro asks her, 'Before you go, could you tell me why you want green golf balls?'

'Well, obviously, because they would be so much easier to find in the sand traps!'

## CLOSE CALL

A blonde, a brunette and a redhead all work at the same office for a female boss who always goes home early.

'Hey girls,' says the brunette, 'let's go home early tomorrow. She'll never know.'

The next day, they all leave right after the boss does. The brunette gets some extra gardening done, the redhead goes to a bar, and the blonde goes home to find her husband having sex with the female boss. She quietly sneaks out of the house and returns at her normal time.

'That was fun,' says the brunette the next day. 'We should do it again sometime.'

'No way,' says the blonde. 'I almost got caught!'

A brunette and blonde are walking in the park when the brunette says, 'Aw, look at the dead birdie.'

The blonde looks up and says, 'Where?'

## BRIDGE TOO FAR

A blonde and a brunette are watching a TV show. The brunette bets the blonde $10 that the man in the episode would jump off a bridge. The man jumps off the bridge and the blonde pays the brunette $10.

The brunette feels guilty because she had already seen the episode, so she confesses to the blonde.

The blonde says, 'I've seen it too, but I didn't think he would jump again.'

## TWIN PACK JOY

A couple is trying to have a baby. Finally, the blonde tells her husband, 'Honey, I have great news! We're pregnant, and we're having twins.'

The husband is overjoyed and says to his wife, 'Honey that's wonderful, but how do you know so soon that we're having twins?'

She nods her head and says, 'Well, I bought the twin-pack pregnancy test and they both came out positive!'

## HOT AND COLD TRUTH

A blonde sees a thermos in a store. She asks an assistant, 'What's that and what's it for?'

The man answers, 'It's a thermos that keeps hot things hot and cold things cold.'

The blonde says, 'I'll take it.'

When she gets to work, her blonde boss asks, 'What's that?'

The blonde worker says, 'It's a thermos. It keeps cold things cold and hot things hot.'

'Whatcha got in it?'

'A cup of coffee and a Popsicle.'

## FAIR ENOUGH!

A blonde goes on a hot date and ends up making out with the guy in his car. The guy asks if she would like to go in the back seat.

'No!' yells the blonde.

Things get even hotter, and the guy asks again.

'For the last time, no!' says the blonde.

Frustrated, the guy asks, 'Well, why the hell not?'

The blonde says, 'Because I wanna stay up here with you!'

## BENEVOLENT COP

A blond police officer pulls over a blonde driver and says, 'You failed to stop at the red light. Let me see your driver's licence.'

The blonde asks, 'What does that look like?'

The blond cop answers, 'It's rectangular and has your picture on it.'

The blonde looks around inside her purse and mistakes her mirror for the licence. When she hands it to the blond officer, he looks at it and replies, 'Oh, I didn't know you were also an officer. You can go!'

## SNOW IDEA!

A blonde woman was stuck in her car in a snowstorm in Queenstown when she remembered her dad's advice: 'If you ever get stuck in a snowstorm, wait until a snowplough drives by and then follow it.'

Eventually, she saw a snowplough so she followed it. After 30 minutes or so, the snowplough driver stopped, got out, and walked up to the woman's car asking, 'Lady, why are you following me?'

She explained what her father had told her and the driver said, 'Well, I'm done with The Warehouse parking lot now. Do you want to follow me to the New World?'

## QUICK FLIGHT

A blonde calls Air New Zealand and asks, 'Can you tell me how long it'll take to fly from Wellington to Christchurch?'

The airline man replies, 'Just a minute.'

'Thank you,' the blonde says, and hangs up.

# DOMESTIC BLISS

This chapter throws up plenty of sarcasm, bitchiness and downright nastiness from both sexes. Jokes based around the home take plenty of forms: women getting 'sarky' answers when seeking approval for their appearance; men getting the same when they make dickheads of themselves on numerous occasions. Whichever side you back, you'll get plenty of laughs here.

## BLAZING SADDLES

During lunch at work, I ate three plates of beans (which I know I shouldn't). When I got home, my husband seemed excited to see me and said delightedly, 'Darling, I have a surprise for dinner tonight.'

He then blindfolded me and led me to my chair at the dinner table. I took a seat and just as he was about to remove my blindfold, the telephone rang. He made me promise not to touch the blindfold until he returned and went to answer the call.

The beans I had consumed were still affecting me and the pressure was becoming unbearable, so while my husband was out of the room I seized the opportunity, shifted my weight to one leg and let one go.

It was not only loud, but it smelled like a fertiliser truck running over a skunk in front of a garbage dump! I took my napkin from my lap and fanned the air around me vigorously. Then, shifting to the other leg, I ripped off three more. The stink was worse than cooked cabbage.

Keeping my ears carefully tuned to the conversation in the other room, I went on releasing atomic bombs like this for another few minutes. The pleasure was indescribable.

Eventually, the telephone farewells signalled the end of my freedom, so I quickly fanned the air a few more times with my napkin, placed it on my lap and folded my hands back on it feeling very relieved and pleased with myself.

My face must have been the picture of innocence when my husband returned, apologising for taking so long.

He asked me if I had peeked through the blindfold and I assured him I had not. At this point, he removed the blindfold, and 12 dinner guests seated around the table, with their hands to their noses, chorused, 'Happy Birthday!'

'I tended to place my wife under a pedestal.' — *Woody Allen*

## THIRSTY BUG

A boy asks his father, 'Dad, are bugs good to eat?'

His father relies, 'That's disgusting. Don't talk about things like that over dinner.'

After dinner, the father asks, Now, son, what did you want to ask me?'

'Oh, nothing,' the boy says. 'There was a bug in your soup, but now it's gone.'

'Love: a temporary insanity, curable by marriage.'—
*Ambrose Bierce*

## GOOD LUCK, CHUCK

Four men are in the hospital waiting room because their wives are having babies. A nurse approaches the first guy and says, 'Congratulations! You're the father of twins.'

'That's odd,' answers the man. 'I work for the Minnesota Twins!'

A nurse then tells the second man, 'Congratulations! You're the father of triplets!'

'That's weird,' answers the second man. 'I work for the 3M company!'

A nurse goes up to the third man saying, 'Congratulations! You're the father of quadruplets.'

'That's strange,' he answers. 'I work for the Four Seasons Hotel!'

The last man begins groaning and banging his head against the wall.

'What's wrong?' the others ask.

'I work for 7 Up!'

'That's okay, honey. I used to believe in things too.'—
*Homer Simpson*

## DEERY ME!

A man kills a deer and takes it home to cook for dinner. He and his wife decide they won't tell the kids what kind of meat it is, but will give them a clue and let them guess.

The dad said, 'Well, it's what Mummy calls me sometimes.'

The little girl screamed to her brother, 'Don't eat it. It's an arsehole!'

'Every time I look at you I get a fierce desire to be lonesome.' — *Oscar Levant*

## DREAM WEAVER

A woman was taking an afternoon nap. When she woke up, she told her husband, 'I just dreamed that you gave me a pearl necklace. What do you think it means?'

'You'll know tonight,' he said.

That evening, the man came home with a small package and gave it to his wife. Delighted, she opened it to find a book entitled 'The Meaning of Dreams'.

## LETTING IT RIP

A woman goes to her boyfriend's parents' house for dinner. This is her first time meeting the family and she is very nervous. They all sit down and begin eating a fine meal. The woman is beginning to feel a little discomfort, thanks to her nervousness and the broccoli casserole. The gas pains are almost making her eyes water. Left with no other choice, she decides to relieve herself a bit and lets out a dainty little fart. It wasn't loud, but everyone at the table heard the poot.

Before she even had a chance to be embarrassed, her boyfriend's father looked over at the dog that had been snoozing at the woman's feet, and said in a rather stern voice, 'Ginger!'

'That was great' the woman thought, and a big smile spread across her face. A couple of minutes later, she was beginning to feel the pain again. This time, she didn't hesitate. She let a much louder and longer fart rip.

The father again looked at the dog and yelled, 'Dammit, Ginger!' Once again, the woman smiled and thought, 'Yes!'

A few minutes later, the woman had to let another one rip. This time she didn't even think about it. She let rip a fart that rivalled a train whistle blowing.

Again, the father looked at the dog with disgust and yelled, 'Dammit, Ginger, get away from her before she shits on you!'

After years of research, scientists have discovered what makes women happy.

Nothing.

### HUMOUR ME!

A wife asked her husband, 'What do you like most in me — my pretty face or my sexy body?'

He looked her over from head to toe and replied, 'I like your sense of humour!'

Man: I know how to please a woman.
Woman: Then please leave me alone.

## OOOH, NASTY!

A child asked his father, 'How were people born?'

So his father said, 'Adam and Eve made babies, then their babies became adults and made babies, and so on.'

The child then went to his mother, asked her the same question and she told him, 'We were monkeys, then we evolved to become like we are now.'

The child ran back to his father and said, 'You lied to me!'

His father replied, 'No, your mum was talking about her side of the family.'

## PASTA ME SMELLING SALTS

A wealthy man was having an affair with an Italian woman for a few years. One night, during one of their rendezvous, she told him she was pregnant. Not wanting to ruin his reputation or his marriage, he paid her a large sum of money if she would go to Italy to have the child. If she stayed in Italy, he would also provide child support until the child turned 18.

She agreed but wondered how he would know when the baby was born. To keep it discreet, he told her to mail him a postcard, and write 'Spaghetti' on the back. He would then arrange for child support.

One day, about nine months later, he came home to his confused wife. 'Honey,' she said, 'you received a very strange postcard today.'

'Oh, just give it to me and I'll explain it later,' he said.

The wife handed the card over and watched as her

husband read it, turned white, and fainted. On the card was written: 'Spaghetti, Spaghetti, Spaghetti. Two with meatballs, one without.'

### TAKES SHINE OFF

A Polish man married a Canadian girl after he had been in Canada a year or so, and although his English was far from perfect, the couple got on very well. One day, though, he rushed into a lawyer's office and asked if he could arrange a divorce for him, 'Very quick!' The lawyer explained that the speed of getting a divorce would depend on the circumstances, and asked these questions:

Lawyer: 'Have you any grounds?'
Pole: 'An acre and half, and a nice three-bedroom house.'
Lawyer: 'No, I mean what is the foundation of the case?'
Pole: 'It is made of concrete, bricks and mortar.'
Lawyer: 'Does either of you have a real grudge?'
Pole: 'No, we have a carport and don't need a grudge.'
Lawyer: 'I mean, what are your relations like?'
Pole: 'All my relations live in Poland.'
Lawyer: 'Is there any infidelity in your marriage?'
Pole: 'Yes, we have hi-fidelity stereo set and DVD player with 6.1 sound.'
Lawyer: 'No, I mean does your wife beat you up?'
Pole: 'No, I'm always up before her.'
Lawyer: 'Why do you want this divorce?'
Pole: 'She going to kill me!'
Lawyer: 'What makes you think that?'

Pole: 'I got proof.'
Lawyer: 'What kind of proof?'
Pole: 'She going to poison me. She buy bottle at drug store and I read label. It say Polish Remover.'

## GEM OF AN IDEA

A woman decided to have her portrait painted. She told the artist, 'Paint me with diamond earrings, a diamond necklace, emerald bracelets and a ruby pendant.'

'But you are not wearing any of those things.'

'I know,' she said. 'It's in case I should die before my husband. I'm sure he will remarry right away, and I want his new wife to go nuts looking for the jewellery.'

## THRILL SEEKER

'The thrill is gone from my marriage,' Brian told his best friend Mike.

'Why not add some intrigue to your life, and have an affair?' his friend suggested.

'But what if my wife finds out?'

'Heck, we are in the twenty-first century, Brian. Go ahead and tell her about it!'

So Brian went home and said, 'Dear, I think an affair will bring us closer together.'

'Forget it,' said his wife. 'I've tried that many times — it never worked.'

## DASHING DAVE

The wedding was over, and the reception was in full swing. Dave, an usher, was having a great time with other members of the wedding party. His wife, Betty, was not.

'Don't be too mad at Dave,' a friend told her. 'He did a terrific job. I'd be glad to have him usher at my wedding.'

'Yeah,' Betty replied, 'I wish he had been an usher at mine.'

## WOULD YOU ADAM AND EVE IT?

Adam and Eve had an ideal marriage. He didn't have to hear about all the men she could have married, and she didn't have to hear about the way his mother cooked.

## A FESTIVE RUSE

A man in Auckland calls his son in Wellington the day before Christmas Eve and says, 'I hate to ruin your day but I have to tell you that your mother and I are divorcing; 45 years of misery is enough.'

'Dad, what are you talking about?' the son screams.

'We can't stand the sight of each other any longer,' the father says. 'We're sick of each other and I'm sick of talking about this, so you call your sister in Christchurch and tell her.'

Frantically, the son calls his sister, who explodes on the phone. 'Like hell they're getting divorced!' she shouts, 'I'll take care of this!'

She calls her parents in Auckland immediately and screams at her father 'You are NOT getting divorced.

Don't do a single thing until I get there. I'm calling my brother back, and we'll both be there tomorrow. Until then, don't do a thing, DO YOU HEAR ME?' and hangs up.

The old man hangs up his phone and turns to his wife. 'Sorted! They're coming for Christmas — and they're paying their own way.'

## GOLFER'S DILEMMA

A guy stands over his tee shot for what seems an eternity: looking up, looking down, measuring the distance, figuring the wind direction and speed.

Finally, his exasperated playing partner says, 'What's taking so long? Hit the damn ball!'

The guy answers, 'My wife is up there watching me from the clubhouse. I want to make this a perfect shot.'

'Forget it, man,' says his partner. 'You'll never hit her from here.'

## OVER-EXPOSED

A man is getting into the shower just as his wife is finishing her shower, when the doorbell rings. The wife quickly wraps herself in a towel and runs downstairs. When she opens the door, there stands Bob, the next-door neighbour.

Before she says a word, Bob says, 'I'll give you $800 to drop that towel.'

After thinking for a moment, the woman drops her towel and stands naked in front of Bob. After a few seconds, Bob hands her $800 and leaves. The woman wraps the towel around herself again and goes back upstairs.

When she gets to the bathroom, her husband asks, 'Who was that?'

'It was Bob from next door,' she replies.

'Great,' the husband says, 'did he say anything about the $800 he owes me?'

Moral of the story: If you share critical information pertaining to credit and risk with your shareholders in time, you may be in a position to prevent avoidable exposure.

## VIVA LAS VEGAS

A man comes home to find his wife of 10 years packing her bags. 'Where are you going?' demands the surprised husband.

'To Las Vegas! I found out that there are men that will pay me $500 cash to do what I do for you for free!'

The man pondered that thought for a moment, and then began packing his bags.

'What do you think you are doing?' she screamed.

'I'm going to Las Vegas with you . . . I want to see how you're going to live on $1000 a year!'

## MAKE UP YOUR MIND!

A wife got so mad at her husband she packed his bags and told him to get out. As he walked to the door, she yelled, 'I hope you die a long, slow, painful death.'

He turned around and said, 'So, you want me to stay?'

## NICE SURPRISE?

Stan is seconds away from receiving a vasectomy when his brother Tom and sister-in-law Sophie barge in holding their newborn baby. 'Stop! You can't do this!' exclaims the brother.

'And why not?' asks Stan.

'Don't you want to have a beautiful baby someday? Like Sophie and I have here?'

Stan says nothing. The brother grows impatient, 'C'mon Stan, I want a nephew. Stan, make me an uncle.'

Stan can't take it any more. He gives Sophie an apologetic look and asks his brother, 'You're sure you want a nephew?'

'Yes,' Tom replies. 'It would be an honour.'

'Well, congratulations, you're holding him.'

## A TOSSER

A man came home from work, sat down in his favourite chair, turned on the TV, and said to his wife, 'Quick, bring me a beer before it starts.'

She looked a little puzzled, but brought him a beer. When he finished it, he said, 'Quick, bring me another beer. It's gonna start.'

This time she got a little angry, but brought him a beer. When it was gone, he said, 'Quick, another beer before it starts.'

She blows her top. 'That's it, you bastard! You waltz in here, flop your fat ass down, don't even say hello to me and then expect me to run around like your slave. Don't you realise that I cook and clean and wash and iron all day long?'

The husband sighed. 'Oh shit, it started!'

## A SAD MAN!

A husband says to his wife, 'I bet you can't tell me something that will make me both happy and sad at the same time.'

The wife thinks about it for a few moments and replies, 'Your dick is bigger than your brother's.'

## SERIAL CHEATER

Boy: 'Hey, I like you and I was wondering if you would be my girlfriend.'
Girl: 'I have a boyfriend.'
Boy: 'I have a math test tomorrow.'
Girl: 'What does that have to do with anything?'
Boy: 'I thought we were listing things we could cheat on.'

**Q:** Why didn't the man report his stolen credit card?
**A:** The thief was spending less than his wife.

## BOZO BERNIE

Bernie was invited to his friend's home for dinner. Morris, the host, prefaced every request to his wife with endearing terms, calling her Honey, My Love, Darling, Sweetheart, or Pumpkin.

Bernie looked at Morris and remarked, 'That's really nice, that after all these years you've been married, you keep calling your wife those pet names.'

Morris hung his head and whispered, 'To tell you the truth, I forgot her name three years ago!'

## TOO HI-TECH

Dear Tech Support,

Last year I upgraded from Boyfriend 5.0 to Husband 1.0 and noticed a distinct slowdown in overall system performance — particularly in the flower and jewellery applications, which operated flawlessly under Boyfriend 5.0.

In addition, Husband 1.0 uninstalled many other valuable programs, such as Romance 9.5 and Personal Attention 6.5 and then installed undesirable programs such as NRL 5.0, EPL 3.0, and Golf Clubs 4.1. Conversation 8.0 no longer runs, and Housecleaning 2.6 simply crashes the system. I've tried running Nagging 5.3 to fix these problems, but to no avail.

What can I do?

Signed, Desperate

Dear Desperate,

First keep in mind, Boyfriend 5.0 is an Entertainment Package, while Husband 1.0 is an Operating System.

Please enter the command 'http: I Thought You Loved Me.html' and try to download Tears 6.2 and don't forget to install the Guilt 3.0 update. If that application works as designed, Husband 1.0 should then automatically run the applications Jewellery 2.0 and Flowers 3.5.

But remember, overuse of the above application can cause Husband 1.0 to default to Grumpy Silence 2.5, Happy Hour 7.0 or Beer 6.1. Beer 6.1 is a very bad program that will download the Snoring Loudly Beta.

Whatever you do, DO NOT install Mother-in-law

1.0 (it runs a virus in the background that will eventually seize control of all your system resources). Also, do not attempt to reinstall the Boyfriend 5.0 program. These are unsupported applications and will crash Husband 1.0.

In summary, Husband 1.0 is a great program, but it does have limited memory and cannot learn new applications quickly. You might consider buying additional software to improve memory and performance. We recommend Food 3.0 and Hot Lingerie 7.7.

Good Luck,
Tech Support

## DOING PORRIDGE

A woman wakes during the night to find that her husband is not in their bed. She puts on her robe and goes downstairs to look for him. She finds him sitting at the kitchen table with a cup of coffee in front of him. He appears deep in thought, just staring at the wall.

She watches as he wipes a tear from his eye and takes a sip of coffee. 'What's the matter, dear?' she whispers as she steps into the room. 'Why are you down here at this time of night?'

The husband looks up. 'Do you remember 20 years ago when we were dating, and you were only 15?' he asks solemnly.

The wife is touched, thinking her husband is so caring and sensitive. 'Yes, I do,' she replies.

The husband pauses. The words are not coming easily. 'Do you remember when your father caught us in the back seat of my car?'

'Yes, I remember,' says the wife, lowering herself into a chair beside him.

The husband continues, 'Do you remember when he shoved a shotgun in my face and said, 'Either you marry my daughter, or I will send you to jail for 20 years!'

'I remember that too,' she replies softly.

He wipes another tear from his cheek and says, 'I would have got out today!'

### POCKET ROCKET

A man walks into a bar and orders a shot, then he looks into his shirt pocket and orders another one. After he finishes, he looks into his pocket again and orders another shot.

The bartender is curious and asks the man why he looks into his pocket before ordering each shot.

The man replies, 'I have a picture of my wife in my pocket, and when she starts to look good, I go home.'

### CLOUDY DAY

Me: 'Would you like to be the sun in my life?'
Her: 'Awww . . . Yes!'
Me: 'Good, then stay 92.96 million miles away from me.'

### LAUGHING MATTER

A man tells his wife, 'Honey, your mother fell down the stairs 15 minutes ago.'

The wife yells at him, 'Why are you just telling me now?'

He said, 'Because I couldn't stop laughing.'

## BLISSFUL DEATH

A husband and wife have four boys. The odd part of it is that the older three have red hair, light skin and are tall, while the youngest son has black hair, dark eyes and is short.

The father falls ill and is lying on his deathbed when he turns to his wife and says, 'Honey, before I die, be completely honest with me. Is our youngest son my child?'

The wife replies, 'I swear on everything that's holy that he is your son.'

With that, the husband passes away. The wife then mutters, 'Thank God he didn't ask about the other three.'

Scientists have discovered a food that diminishes a woman's sex drive by 90 per cent.

It's called a wedding cake.

I wonder what my parents did to fight boredom before the internet.

I asked my 17 brothers and sisters and they didn't know either.

## GIFT FOR LIFE

A man got his mother-in-law a cemetery plot for Christmas. It came with a coffin, tombstone, the works. Next Christmas comes around and the husband gets her nothing.

When the mother-in-law asks, 'Why didn't you get me a gift?' the husband says, 'You haven't used the one I got you last year!'

### TASTY PRESENT

Three brothers wanted to give their blind mother a birthday gift. The first got her a big beautiful house. The second got her a brand-new luxury vehicle with a driver. The third got her a talking parrot to keep her company. When they all got together, they wanted to know which gift she liked most.

She said they were all great but she thanked her third son because she liked the chicken dinner best!

A man admitted he lied on his income tax return: he listed himself as the head of the household.

### BAD LUCK!

You know you're getting old when your wife says, 'Honey, let's run upstairs and make love,' and you answer, 'I can't do both.'

### ELEVATED OPINION

An Amish husband, wife and son travel to the city on vacation. They visit a shopping mall and while the mother is shopping, the father and son are standing in awe in front of an elevator, having no idea what it was.

As they watch, an elderly lady walks into the strange silver doors and the doors close. The father and son watch as the numbers go up, and then back down. When the doors open, a beautiful young woman walks out.

The father leans over and whispers to the son, 'Son, quick, go get your mother!'

## WHAT A BOSS

Worker: 'Sir, can I have a day off next week to visit my mother-in-law?'

Boss: 'Certainly not!'

Worker: 'Thank you so much sir! I knew you would be understanding.'

## TWENTY LEROYS

A woman had 20 children: 10 girls, 10 boys, all of their names were Leroy — boys spelt Leroy and girls spelt Leroigh. She met a man one day and told him how many children she had and what their names were.

'Why did you name all of your children Leroy/Leroigh?' the man asked.

The woman laughed. 'So that it's easy to call them all together. For example, Leroy/Leroigh, time for bed, time for supper.'

The man asked, 'How do you call them if you only need one of the children?'

The woman cackled. 'By their last names, of course!'

## ART LOVERS

At an art gallery, a woman and her 10-year-old son were having a tough time choosing between one of my paintings and another artist's work. They finally went with mine.

'I guess you decided you prefer an autumn scene to a floral,' I said.

'No,' said the boy. 'Your painting's wider, so it'll cover three holes in our wall.'

My wife says she's leaving me because she thinks I'm too obsessed with astronomy. What planet is she on!

### PARTY POOPER

A man has six children and is very proud of his achievement. He is so proud of himself that he starts calling his wife 'mother of six' in spite of her objections.

One night they go to a party. The man decides that it's time to go home and wants to find out if his wife is ready to leave as well. He shouts at the top of his voice, 'Shall we go home "mother of six"?'

His wife, irritated by her husband's lack of discretion, shouts right back, 'Anytime you're ready, father of four.'

### TAKE THAT SUCKER

Typical macho man married typical good-looking lady and after the wedding he laid down the following rules:

'I'll be home when I want, if I want and at what time I want and I don't expect any hassle from you. I expect a great dinner to be on the table unless I tell you that I won't be home for dinner.

'I'll go hunting, fishing, boozing and card-playing when I want with my old buddies and don't you give me a hard time about it. Those are my rules. Any comments?'

His new bride said, 'No, that's fine with me. Just understand that there will be sex here at seven every night, whether you're here or not.'

**Q:** 'Why do you always go to the balcony when your wife starts singing?'

**A:** 'So that no one will think I'm beating her.'

## CRUELTY DOUBLED

Husband and wife had a bitter quarrel on the day of their fortieth wedding anniversary.

The husband yells, 'When you die, I'm getting you a headstone that reads: "Here Lies My Wife — Cold As Ever."'

'Yeah?' she replies. 'When you die, I'm getting you a headstone that reads: "Here Lies My Husband — Stiff At Last.'

## RIGHT WORDS, RIGHT TIME

A man wakes up at home with a huge hangover. He forces himself to open his eyes and the first thing he sees is a couple of aspirins and a glass of water on the side table. He sits down and sees his clothing in front of him, all clean and pressed. He looks around the room and sees it is in perfect order. So's the rest of the house. He takes the aspirins and notices a note on the table: 'Honey, breakfast is in the oven, I left early to go shopping. Love you.'

He goes to the kitchen. Sure enough, a hot breakfast and the morning paper await him.

His son is also at the table, eating. The man asks, 'Son, what happened last night?'

His son says, 'Well, you came home after 3 a.m., drunk and delirious. You broke some furniture, puked in the hallway, and gave yourself a black eye when you walked into the door.'

Confused, the man asks, 'So, why is everything in order and so clean, with breakfast on the table waiting for me?'

His son replies, 'Oh, that? Mum dragged you to the bedroom, and when she tried to take your pants off you shouted, "Lady, get your hands off me! I'm married!"'

## LESSER OF TWO EVILS

There were two evil brothers. They were rich and used their money to keep their ways from the public eye. They even attended the same church and looked to be perfect Christians. Then their pastor retired and a new one was hired. Not only could he see right through the brothers' deceptions, but he also spoke well and true, and the church started to swell in numbers. A fundraising campaign was started to build a new assembly hall.

All of a sudden, one of the brothers died. The remaining brother sought out the new pastor the day before the funeral and handed him a cheque for the amount needed to finish paying for the new building. 'I have only one condition,' he said. 'At his funeral, you must say my brother was a saint.' The pastor gave his word and deposited the cheque.

The next day at the funeral, the pastor did not hold back. 'He was an evil man,' he said. 'He cheated on his wife and abused his family. But compared to his brother, he was a saint.'

A woman standing nude in front of a mirror says to her husband, 'I look horrible, I feel fat and ugly. Pay me a compliment.'

He replies, 'Your eyesight is perfect.'

A man was granted two wishes by God. He asked for the best drink and the best woman ever.

Next moment, he got mineral water and Mother Teresa.

## DEAR OLD DAD

Manny was almost 29 years old. Most of his friends were already married and Manny just bounced from one relationship to the next. Finally, a friend asked him, 'What's the matter, are you looking for the perfect woman? Are you *that* particular. Can't you find anyone who suits you?'

'No,' Manny replied. 'I meet a lot of nice girls, but as soon as I bring them home to meet my parents, my mother doesn't like them. So I keep on looking!'

'Listen,' his friend suggested, 'why don't you find a girl who's just like your dear ole mother?'

Many weeks passed before Manny and his friend got together again.

'Manny, did you find the perfect girl yet. One that's just like your mother?'

Manny shrugged his shoulders. 'Yes, I found one just like Mum. My mother loved her, and they became great friends.'

'Excellent. So are you and this girl engaged, yet?'

'I'm afraid not. My father can't stand her!'

There are three kinds of men in this world:

Some remain single and make wonders happen.

Some have girlfriends and see wonders happen.

The rest get married and wonder what happened!

## FART TROUBLE

A little old lady goes to the doctor and says, 'Doctor I have this problem with gas, but it really doesn't bother me too much. My farts never smell and are always silent. As a matter of fact, I've farted at least 20 times since I've been here in your office. You didn't know I was farting because they don't smell and are silent.'

The doctor says, 'I see, take these pills and come back to see me next week.'

The next week the lady comes back. 'Doctor,' she says, 'I don't know what the heck you gave me, but now my farts — although still silent — stink terribly.'

The doctor says, 'Good. Now that we've cleared up your sinuses, let's work on your hearing.'

A prospective husband in a book store: 'Do you have a book called "Husband — the Master of the House?"'

Saleswoman: 'Sir, fiction and comics are on the first floor!'

## POISON IVY

After her conviction of murder in the second degree, the district attorney, during her sentencing hearing, said, 'Mrs Grey, after you put the arsenic in the stew and served it to your husband, didn't you feel even a little remorse for what you were doing?'

'I did,' she answered calmly.

'And when was that?' inquired the DA.

'When he asked for seconds!' she replied.

A bookseller conducting a market survey asked a woman, 'Which book has helped you most in your life?'

The woman replied, 'My husband's cheque book!'

Pharmacist to customer: 'Sir, please understand, to buy anti-depression pills you need a proper prescription. Simply showing a marriage certificate and your wife's picture is not enough!'

Wives are magicians: they can change anything into an argument.

Dear Mother-in-law,

Don't teach me how to handle my children.

I am living with one of yours and he needs a lot of improvement!

When a married man says, 'I'll think about it', what he really means is that he doesn't know his wife's opinion yet.

A woman says to her doctor, 'My husband has a habit of talking in his sleep! What should I give him to cure it?'

The doctor replies, 'Give him an opportunity to speak when he's awake!'

## CRUEL!

'The letter "W" is the most dangerous in the alphabet. Because all worries start with "w" — who, why, what, when, which, whom, where, war, wine, whisky, and wealth.'

'You're forgetting one.'

'Really? Which one?'

'Wife!'

## THOUGHTFUL MAN

My husband is in infantry, and he said the most wonderful things to convince me to marry him:

The closets could all be mine since he wears the same thing every day.

I could have as many babies as I want because giving birth is free.

He would never get on my nerves, because he would always be gone.

I had to clean out my spice rack and found everything was too old and had to be thrown out.

What a waste of thyme.

## POINTED MESSAGE

The following is a tablet at the front door of an unknown house, which I'm sure many of us would like to copy. It reads:

NO UNSOLICITED CALLERS

We are too broke to buy anything

Our utilities work fine with our current providers

We have already found God

We know who we are voting for
So unless you are bringing free beer
BUGGER OFF

Since the snow came, all the wife has done is look through the window.

If it gets any worse, I'll have to let her in.

## MULLIGAN TARGET

So there's this guy who golfs with his buddies every weekend, and his wife keeps bugging him to take her along and teach her to play. He finally relents, and the following Sunday finds them on the first tee. She's never played, so he tells her to go down to the ladies' tees, watch him drive, and then try to do like he did.

She goes down to the ladies' tee, the guy hooks his drive, and the ball hits his wife, killing her.

The police come to investigate, and the coroner says, 'It's the damnedest thing I ever saw. There's an imprint on her temple, and you can read "Titlist 1".

'That was my ball,' the guy said.

'What I don't understand,' the coroner continued, 'is the one on her hip that says "Titleist 3".'

'Oh,' the guy replied, 'that was my mulligan.'

'I'll always cherish the original misconception I had of you.'
— *unknown*

### SERVES HIM RIGHT!

After a night of drink, drugs and wild sex, Jim woke up to find himself next to a really ugly woman.

That's when he realised he had made it home safely.

My mate just hired an Eastern European cleaner — took her 15 hours to hoover the house. Turns out she was a Slovak.

The old system of having a baby was much better than the new system, the old system being characterised by the fact that the man didn't have to watch.

'Familiarity breeds contempt — and children.'
— *Mark Twain*

### NICE LINE

A little boy went up to his father and asked, 'Dad, where did my intelligence come from?'

The father replied, 'Well, son, you must have got it from your mother, 'cause I still have mine.'

### OLD-FASHIONED CHAUVINIST

A doctor examining a woman who had been rushed to the emergency room took the husband aside and said, 'I don't like the looks of your wife at all.'

'Me neither, doc,' said the husband. 'But she's a great cook and really good with the kids.'

## A WOMAN SCORNED . . .

While shopping for holiday clothes, my husband and I passed a display of bathing suits. It had been at least 10 years and 10 kilograms since I had even considered buying a bathing suit, so I sought my husband's advice.

'What do you think?' I asked. 'Should I get a bikini or an all-in-one?'

'Better get a bikini,' he replied. 'You'd never get it all in one.'

He's still in intensive care.

In light of the new morality, *Playboy* is starting an edition strictly for married people. It has the same centrefold every month.

## SMART-ARSE GEORGE

There are three golfers, Bob, Max and Ted, who are looking for a fourth. Bob mentions that his friend George is a pretty good golfer, so they decide to invite him for the following Saturday.

'Sure, I'd love to play,' says George, 'but I may be about 10 minutes late, so wait for me.'

Saturday rolls around. Bob, Max and Ted arrive promptly at 9.00 a.m., and find George already waiting for them. He plays right-handed and beats them all. Quite pleased with their new fourth, they ask him if he'd like to play again the following Saturday.

'Yeah, sounds great,' says George, 'but I may be about 10 minutes late, so wait for me.'

The following Saturday, again, all four golfers show up on time, but this time George plays left-handed, and beats them all. As they're getting ready to leave, George says, 'See you next Saturday, but I may be about 10 minutes late, so wait for me.'

Every week, George is right on time, and plays great with whichever hand he decides to use. And every week, he departs with the same message.

After a couple of months, Ted gets pretty tired of this routine, so he says, 'Wait a minute, George. Every week you say you may be about 10 minutes late, but you're right on time. And you beat us either left-handed or right-handed. What's the story?'

'Well,' George says, 'I'm kind of superstitious. When I get up in the morning, I look at my wife. If she's sleeping on her left side, I play left-handed. And if she's sleeping on her right side, I play right-handed.'

'So what do you do if she's sleeping on her back?' Bob asks.

'Then I'm about 10 minutes late,' George answers.

# EMPLOYMENT

Lawyers get a terrible hammering in this chapter. Other 'hated' professions — bank managers, car salesmen, journalists, real estate agents, film moguls who think they're God's gift to women, and loan sharks — pale into relative obscurity next to the lawyers. Having said that, plenty of jokes on myriad professions fill these pages, and if your crust appears, let's hope you can see some similarity. If not, just have a good laugh.

## BOSS GETS WICKED WAY

The boss said to his secretary, 'I want to have sex with you, but I will make it very fast. I'll throw $1000 on the floor and by the time you bend down to pick it up, I'll be done.'

She thought for a moment, then called her boyfriend and told him the story. Her boyfriend said, 'Do it but ask him for $2000. Then pick up the money so fast, he won't even have enough time to undress.' She agrees.

After half an hour passes, the boyfriend calls the girlfriend and asks, 'So what happened?'

She responds, 'The bastard used coins, so I'm still picking it up!'

## BUM RAP

A doctor reaches into his smock to get a pen to write a prescription and pulls out a rectal thermometer. 'Oh, damn it,' he proclaims, 'Some arsehole has my pen!'

## CABBIE'S GOOD HAGGLE!

So two men from Dargaville were travelling to Australia. Before they left home, one of their dads gives them both a bit of advice: 'You watch them Aussie cab drivers. They'll rob you blind. Don't you go paying them what they ask. You haggle.'

At the Sydney airport, the Dargaville boys catch a cab to their hotel. When they reach their destination, the cabbie says, 'That'll be 20 dollars, lads.'

'Oh no you don't! My dad warned me about you. You'll only be getting 15 dollars from me,' says one of the men.

'And you'll only be getting fifteen from me too,' adds the other.

## COMPUTER LITERATE

Mother: 'Sweetie, make a Christmas wish.'
Girl: I wish that Santa will send some clothes to those naked girls in Dad's computer.'

## DEBT COLLECTING

A man went to his lawyer and told him, 'My neighbour owes me $500 and he won't pay up. What should I do?'

'Do you have any proof he owes you the money?' asked the lawyer.

'Nope,' replied the man.

'Okay then, write him a letter asking him for the $5000 he owes you,' said the lawyer.

'But it's only $500,' replied the man.

'Precisely. That's what he will reply and then you'll have your proof!'

**Q:** How is Christmas like your job?
**A:** You do all the work and the fat guy in the suit gets all the credit.

**Q:** Why is Santa Claus so jolly?
**A:** Because he knows where all the naughty girls live.

## MAN NAMED LUCKY

There was this guy at a bar, just looking at his drink. He stays like that for half an hour. Then a big trouble-making truck driver steps up next to him, takes the drink from the guy, and downs it.

The poor man starts crying. The truck driver says, 'Come on, man, I was just joking. Here, I'll buy you another drink. I just can't stand to see a man cry.'

'No, it's not that,' the man replies, wiping his tears. 'This day is the worst day of my life. First, I oversleep and I go in late to my office. My outraged boss fires me. When I leave the building to go to my car, it has been stolen. The police say they can do nothing. I get a cab to go home, and when I get out, I remember I left my wallet. The cab driver just drives away. I go inside my house where I find my wife in bed with the gardener. I leave my home, come to this bar, and just when I was thinking about putting an end to my life, you show up and drink my poison.'

## CURDLED MILKMAN

A couple are rushing to the hospital because the wife is going into labour. As they walk in, a doctor says to them that he has invented a machine that splits the pain between the mother and father. They agree to it and are led into a room where they get hooked up to the machine. The doctor starts it off at 20 per cent split towards the father.

The wife says, 'Oh, that's actually better.' The husband says he can't feel anything.

Then the doctor turns it to 50 per cent and the wife says that it doesn't hurt nearly as much. The husband says he still can't feel anything.

Encouraged, the doctor turns it up to 100 per cent. The husband still can't feel anything and the wife is really happy because there is now no pain for her. The baby is born. The couple go home and find the milkman groaning in pain on the doorstep.

## SPECIAL REQUEST

A little kid sends a letter to Santa that says: 'Dear Santa, I want a brother for Christmas.'

Santa writes back: 'Dear Timmy, send me your mummy.'

**Q:** What do you call the space between Kim Kardashian's breasts and butt cheeks?
**A:** Silicon Valley.

A sandwich walks into a bar. The barman says: 'Sorry, we don't serve food in here.'

Did you hear about the butcher who backed up into the meat grinder? He got a little behind in his work.

### PRETTY PUKE!

A guy is going on an ocean cruise and he tells his doctor that he's worried about getting seasick. The doctor suggests, 'Eat two kilograms of stewed tomatoes before you leave the dock.'

The guy replies, 'Will that keep me from getting sick, doc?'

The doctor says, 'No, but it'll look really pretty in the water.'

**Q:** Why did the can crusher quit his job?
**A:** Because it was soda pressing.

### IDEAS ABOVE HIS STATION

Reaching the end of a job interview, the human resources officer asks a young engineer fresh out of university, 'And what starting salary are you looking for?'

The budding engineer replies, 'In the region of $125,000 a year, depending on the benefits package.'

The interviewer inquires, 'Well, what would you say to a package of five weeks' holiday, 14 paid holidays, full medical and dental, company matching retirement fund to 50 per cent of salary, and a company car leased every two years — say, a red Ferrari?'

The engineer sits up straight and says, 'Wow! Are you kidding?'

The interviewer replies, 'Yeah, but you started it.'

## COMING A CROPPER

A lawyer runs a stop sign in Auckland and gets pulled over by a cop. Being a big-shot lawyer, he thinks he's smarter than the cop.

The policeman asks for licence and registration. The lawyer asks, 'What for?'

The cop responds, 'You didn't come to a complete stop at the stop sign.'

The lawyer says, 'I slowed down and no one was coming.'

'You still didn't come to a complete stop. Licence and registration please,' says the cop impatiently.

The lawyer says, 'If you can show me the legal difference between slow down and stop, I'll give you my licence and registration and you can give me the ticket. If not, you let me go and don't give me the ticket.'

The cop says, 'That sounds fair, please exit your vehicle.'

The lawyer steps out and the cop takes out his truncheon and starts beating the lawyer with it. The cop says, 'Do you want me to stop or just slow down?'

## PULLING THE WOOL

Two factory workers are talking. The woman says, 'I can make the boss give me the day off.'

Her male colleague replies, 'And how would you do that?'

The woman says, 'Just wait and see.' She then hangs upside down from the ceiling.

The boss comes in and says, 'What are you doing?'

The woman replies, 'I'm a light bulb.'

The boss then says, 'You've been working so much that you've gone crazy. I think you need to take the day off.'

The man starts to follow her and the boss says, 'Where are you going?'

The man says, 'I'm going home, too. I can't work in the dark!'

## BITER BITTEN

A doctor and a lawyer are talking at a party. Their conversation is constantly interrupted by people describing their ailments and asking the doctor for free medical advice. After an hour of this, the exasperated doctor asks the lawyer, 'What do you do to stop people from asking you for legal advice when you're out of the office?'

'I give it to them,' replies the lawyer, 'and then I send them a bill.'

The doctor is shocked, but agrees to give it a try. The next day, still feeling slightly guilty, the doctor prepares the bills and sends them off.

When he goes to his mailbox, he finds a bill from the lawyer.

A lawyer is standing in a long line at the box office. Suddenly, he feels a pair of hands kneading his shoulders, back, and neck. The lawyer turns around. 'What the hell do you think you're doing?'

'I'm a chiropractor, and I'm just keeping in practice while I'm waiting in line.'

'Well, I'm a lawyer, but you don't see me screwing the guy in front of me, do you?'

## HEART OF GOLD

An office of the IHC realised that the organisation had never received a donation from Hamilton's most successful lawyer. The person in charge of contributions called him to persuade him to contribute.

'Our research shows that out of a yearly income of at least $500,000, you did not give a penny to charity. Wouldn't you like to give back to the community in some way?'

The lawyer mulled this over for a moment and replied, 'First, did your research also show that my mother is dying after a long illness, and has medical bills that are several times her annual income?'

Embarrassed, the IHC rep mumbled, 'Um, no.'

The lawyer interrupts, 'Or that my brother, a disabled veteran, is blind and confined to a wheelchair?'

The stricken IHC rep began to stammer out an apology, but was interrupted again.

'Or that my sister's husband died in a traffic accident,' the lawyer's voice rising in indignation, 'leaving her penniless with three children?!'

The humiliated IHC man, completely beaten, said simply, 'I had no idea.'

On a roll, the lawyer cut him off once again, 'So if I don't give any money to them, why should I give any to you?'

## BRIGHT ONE

As a group of soldiers stood in formation at an army base, the sergeant major said, 'All right! All you idiots fall out.'

As the rest of the squad wandered away, one soldier remained at attention.

The sergeant major walked over until he was eye to eye with him, and then raised a single eyebrow.

The soldier smiled and said, 'Sure was a lot of 'em, huh, sir?'

## WHOOPS!

A young man goes into a chemist's to buy condoms. The pharmacist tells him that the condoms come in packs of three, nine or 12, and asks which ones the young man wants.

'Well,' he says, 'I've been seeing this girl for a while and she's really hot. I want the condoms because I think tonight's the night. We're having dinner with her parents and then we're going out. Once she's had me, she'll want me all the time, so you'd better give me the 12-pack!'

The young man makes his purchase and leaves. Later that evening, he sits down to dinner with his girlfriend and her parents. He asks if he may say grace and they agree.

He begins the prayer but continues praying for several minutes.

The girl leans over and says, 'You never told me that you were such a religious person.'

He leans over to her and says, 'You never told me that your father is a pharmacist.'

## GEORGE'S CRACKING LAST DAY

It was George the postie's last day on the job after 35 years of carrying the mail through all kinds of weather to the same neighbourhood. When he arrived at the first house on his route, he was greeted by the whole family there, who roundly and soundly congratulated him and sent him on his way with a big bottle of Glenfiddich whisky. At the second house they presented him with a box of cigars. The folks at the third house handed him a selection of terrific fishing lures.

At the fourth house he was met at the door by a strikingly beautiful woman in a revealing negligee. She took him by the hand, gently led him through the door, which she closed behind him, and led him up the stairs to the bedroom where she blew his mind with the most passionate love he had ever experienced.

When he had had enough they went downstairs, where she fixed him a giant breakfast of eggs, potatoes, ham, sausage, blueberry waffles and freshly squeezed orange juice. When he was truly satisfied she poured him a cup of steaming coffee. As she was pouring, George noticed a dollar bill sticking out from under the cup's bottom edge.

'All this was just too wonderful for words,' he said. 'But what's the dollar for?'

'Well,' she said, 'last night I told my husband that today would be your last day and that we should do something special for you. I asked him what to give you. He said, "F--k him. Give him a dollar." The breakfast was my idea.'

## COUNT THE DAYS

Doctor: 'I'm sorry but you suffer from a terminal illness and I only give you 10 to live.'
Patient: 'What do you mean, 10? Ten what? Months? Weeks?'
Doctor: '9, 8, 7 . . .'

## GETTING TENSE

An old teacher asked her student, 'If I say, "I am beautiful", which tense is that?'

The student replied, 'It is obviously past.'

## GET YOUR LIES FACTUAL!

Gilding the lily is a job seeker's birthright. Here are a few doozies, where the applicant claimed . . .

- to be a former CEO of the company to which he was applying
- to be fluent in two languages — one of which was pig Latin
- to be a Nobel Prize winner
- to have worked in a jail when he was really in there serving time
- he was fired 'on accident'.

**Q:** Why did the scarecrow win an award?
**A:** Because he was outstanding in his field.

**Calling the cops**

What a beat cop deals with every day:

- A cop responded to a report of a vehicle stopping at mailboxes. It was the mailman.
- A woman said her son was attacked by a cat, and the cat would not allow her to take her son to the hospital.
- A resident said someone had entered his home at night and taken five pounds of bacon. Upon further investigation, police discovered his wife had got up for a late-night snack.
- A man reported that a squirrel was running in circles on Davis Drive, and he wasn't sure if it was sick or had been hit by a car. An officer responded, and as he drove along the street, he ran over the squirrel.

**IMAGINE THE FUN!**

The military has a long, proud tradition of pranking recruits — much like the time-worn pranks apprentices are subjected to in Godzone. Here are some favourites:

- Instructed a private in the mess hall to look for left-handed spatulas.
- Sent a recruit to a medical-supplies office in search of fallopian tubes.
- Had a new guy conduct a 'boom test' on a howitzer by yelling 'Boom!' down the tube in order to 'calibrate' it.

- Ordered a private to bring back a five-gallon can of dehydrated water (in fact, the sergeant just wanted an empty water can).

## OLDER THAN GOOGLE

Before Google, there were librarians. Here are some queries posed to the poor, suffering staff of public libraries:

- A woman wanted 'inspirational material on grass and lawns'.
- 'Who built the English Channel?'
- 'Is there a full moon every night in Acapulco?'
- 'Music suitable for a doll wedding to take place between a Shirley Temple doll and a teddy bear.
- 'Can the New York Public Library recommend a good forger?'

## COPPED IT

I was walking down the street and I punched a white guy and then I was arrested for assault.

The day after I got out, I punched a black guy and I was arrested for impersonating a police officer.

## ORDER OF ONE'S EMPIRE!

A farmer in the Rangitikei near Marton noticed his neighbour standing for hours in his paddock staring into space. Intrigued by this, he asked him what he was doing.

His neighbour replied he was hoping for an OBE as he had read in the paper that OBEs were awarded for people outstanding in their field.

## GREEN ROBBER

'Your Honour,' began the defence attorney, 'my client has been characterised as an incorrigible bank robber, without a single socially redeeming feature. I intend to disprove that.'

'And how will you accomplish this?' the judge inquired.

'By proving beyond a shadow of a doubt,' replied the lawyer, 'that the note my client handed the teller was on recycled paper.'

## SATAN'S GOT A POINT

An engineer dies and reports to the Pearly Gates. St Peter checks his dossier and says, 'Ah, I see you're an engineer — you're in the wrong place.'

So the engineer reports to the gates of Hell and is let in. Pretty soon, the engineer gets dissatisfied with the level of comfort in Hell and starts designing and building improvements. After a while, they've got air conditioning, flush toilets and escalators, and the engineer is becoming a pretty popular guy.

One day God calls Satan up on the telephone and asks with a sneer, 'So, how's it going down there in Hell?'

Satan replies, 'Hey, things are going great. We've got air conditioning, flush toilets and escalators, and there's no telling what this engineer is going to come up with next.'

God replies, 'What? You've got an engineer? That's a mistake — he should never have gone down there. Send him back up here.'

Satan says, 'No way! I like having an engineer on the staff, and I'm keeping him.'

God says, 'Send him back up here or I'll sue.'

Satan laughs uproariously and answers, 'Yeah, right. And just where are YOU going to get a lawyer?'

## HONESTY DOESN'T PAY

A guy goes in for a job interview and sits down with the boss. The boss asks him, 'What do you think is your worst quality?'

The man says, 'I'm probably too honest.'

The boss says, 'That's not a bad thing. I think being honest is a good quality.'

The man replies, 'I don't care about what *you* think!'

My memory has got so bad it has actually caused me to lose my job. I'm still employed. I just can't remember where.

I asked the corporate wellness officer, 'Can you teach me yoga?'

He said, 'How flexible are you?'

I said, 'I can't make Tuesdays.'

Team work is important — it helps to put the blame on someone else.

There's a new trend in our office — everyone is putting names on their food. I saw it today, while I was eating a sandwich named Kevin.

## QUESTIONS COST

A man phones his lawyer and asks, 'How much would it cost me to have you answer three questions?'

'That would be $300,' the lawyer replies.

The man says, 'That's an awful lot of money for three questions, isn't it?'

'I guess so,' says the lawyer. 'What's your third question?'

## BETWIXT AND BETWEEN

A woman answers her phone.

'Is this Mrs Haycroft?'

'Yes.'

'Mrs Haycroft, this is Doctor Willits calling from the medical lab. Your doctor sent us your husband's samples yesterday. In the same shipment we received a similar sample from a different Mr Haycroft. Unfortunately, there was a mix-up, and we're not sure which result belongs to your husband. I'm sorry to say that either way, the news is not good.'

'Not good?' asks Mrs Haycroft.

'I'm afraid not. One of the tests came back with Alzheimer's and the other with AIDS. As I said, we're unsure which result is the correct one for your husband.'

'Oh no, that's horrible!' said Mrs Haycroft. 'I assume you'll redo the test?'

'We'd like to, but they're very expensive, and the insurance people tell us they will not pay for them again.'

'That's ridiculous! What can I possibly do now?'

'The insurance company recommends that you drive

your husband to the other side of town and leave him there. If he finds his way home, don't sleep with him.'

### ON YER BIKE!

Two engineering students were out mountain biking. One of them asked the other, 'Where'd you get that cool bike, anyway?'

His engineering friend said, 'It was weird. I was exercising in the quad the other day and this gorgeous girl coasted by on her bike. She stopped, watched me for a few minutes, jumped off the bike, took all her clothes off, and told me I could have whatever I wanted.'

The first engineering student thought a second, then nodded approvingly and said, 'Good choice. I doubt if the clothes would have fitted.'

### DOGGONE HOUNDS

A team of animal behaviourists want to see if dogs take on the personalities of their owners. They put some bones in a room and bring in a dog owned by an architect. The dog sniffs around the bones a while, starts pushing them around, and an hour later he's built the Taj Mahal.

They bring in a chemist's dog and after inspecting the bones, she starts arranging them in a pattern. An hour later she's diagrammed the chemical composition of an amino acid.

Then they bring in a musician's dog. He grinds the bones into a powder, snorts it, has sex with all the other dogs, then asks, 'When do I get paid?'

### IT'S THE PRINCIPAL

As autumn approaches and summer vacation is over, a mother wakes up her son and says it's the first day of school, so get up and get ready.

He says, 'Mum, I don't want to go back. Please don't make me. I hate school!'

She says, 'Don't be silly. It can't be that bad. I bet you can't even think of two reasons not to go.'

He says, 'Really, I mean it! All the kids hate me. And the teachers all think I'm stupid.'

She says, 'Well, those aren't really good reasons. Maybe you can try harder.'

He says, 'No, I don't want to go. Give me two good reasons I should.'

She replies, 'Well, first of all, you're almost 60 years old. And second, you're the principal.'

### BABY TALK

A lady walked into a dentist's office and said, 'I don't know which is worse, having a root canal or having a baby.'

The dentist replied, 'Well, make up your mind so I know how to tilt the chair.'

### LIMO NOT PARKED UP

After 45 years at the company and ready to retire, the boss walked into the office on his last day of work. He didn't notice his zipper was down and his fly area wide open.

His long-time assistant walked up to him and said, 'This morning when you left your house, did you close your garage door?'

The boss said he knew he'd closed the garage door and walked into his office puzzled by the question.

Later, as he checked himself in the office mirror before his final lunch in the company cafeteria, he noticed his fly was open, so he zipped it up. Then he understood his assistant's question about his 'garage door'.

He headed out, paused by her desk, smiled, and asked, 'When my garage door was open, did you see my stretch limo parked in there?'

'No,' she said, 'I didn't. All I saw was a rusty little Holden with two flat tires.'

## DICK OF A QUESTION!

Students taking the entrance exam for the Otago University medical school were perplexed by this question: 'Rearrange the letters P-N-E-S-I to spell the part of the human body that is most useful when erect.'

Those who spelled SPINE became doctors. The rest are in Parliament.

## EARLESS!

A construction worker accidentally cuts off one of his ears with an electric saw. He calls out to a guy walking on the street below, 'Hey, do you see my ear down there?'

The guy on the street picks up an ear and yells back, 'Is this it?'

'No,' replies the construction worker. 'Mine had a pencil behind it!'

'It's a plastic surgeon you need, not a doctor.' —*John Cleese*

## GREAT CHEEK!

My friend, an air force officer, was riding his scooter when he passed an airman who didn't salute. My friend stopped, turned around, and glared at the airman.

'Thanks for coming back for me,' the airman said, jumping on the back of the scooter. 'Airmen's mess, sir.'

'I find it rather easy to portray a businessman. Being bland, rather cruel and incompetent comes naturally to me.' —*John Cleese*

## ANTHEM FOR WANKERS

I had to go see my doctor because I'm having an unusual problem. I say to him, 'I've got a problem — every time I finish masturbating I sing the Australian national anthem.'

The doctor said, 'Don't worry, a lot of wankers sing that.'

'The meek shall inherit the earth, but not the mineral rights.' —*J. Paul Getty*

## DINOSAUR UNITED

[Note: This is an exact transcript of National Public Radio (NPR) interview between a female broadcaster and US Army General Reinwald who was about to sponsor a Boy Scout troop visiting his military installation.]

Woman Radio Host: 'So, General Reinwald, what things are you going to teach these young boys when they visit your base?'

General Reinwald: 'We're going to teach them climbing, canoeing, archery, and shooting.'

Woman Radio Host: 'Shooting! That's a bit irresponsible, isn't it?'

General Reinwald: 'I don't see why, they'll be properly supervised on the rifle range.'

Woman Radio Host: 'Don't you admit that this is a terribly dangerous activity to be teaching children?'

General Reinwald: 'I don't see how, we will be teaching them proper rifle discipline before they even touch a firearm.'

Woman Radio Host: 'But you're equipping them to become violent killers.'

General Reinwald: 'Well, you're equipped to be a prostitute, but you're not one, are you?'

[The radio went silent and the interview ended.]

**Q:** What's the difference between a lawyer and a leech?

**A:** After you die, a leech stops sucking your blood.

## PARROT FLUMMOXED

A magician worked on a cruise ship in the Caribbean. The audience would be different each week, so the magician did the same tricks each week. However, there was a problem. The captain's parrot saw the shows each week and began to understand how the magician did every trick.

Once he understood, he started shouting out the secrets in the middle of the show:

'Look, it's not the same hat.'

'Look, he's hiding the flowers under the table.'

'Hey, why are all the cards the ace of spades?'

The magician was furious but couldn't do anything — it was, after all, the captain's parrot. One day, the ship had an accident and sank.

The magician found himself with the parrot, adrift on a piece of wood, in the middle of the ocean. They stared at each other with hatred, but did not utter a word. This went on for a day, then another, and another.

Finally, after a week, the parrot said, 'Okay, I give up. Where the heck is the boat?'

Oh, you hate your job? Why didn't you say so? There's a support group for that.

It's called EVERYBODY, and they meet at the bar.

'Honesty is the best policy — when there is money in it.' — *Mark Twain*

## NASTY FOUR-LETTER WORD

A man is recovering from surgery when the surgical nurse appears and asks him how he is feeling.

'I'm okay. But I didn't like the four-letter word the doctor used in surgery,' he answered.

'What did he say,' asked the nurse.

'OOPS.'

**Q:** What do you have when you have a lawyer buried up to his neck in sand?
**A:** Not enough sand.

## SOCKS ON FOR 'SEX'!

One man was explaining to another why he fired his secretary: 'Two weeks ago,' he said, 'was my forty-fifth birthday and I wasn't feeling too hot that morning. I went into the kitchen for breakfast knowing that my wife would be pleasant and say "happy birthday" and probably have a present for me. She didn't even say "good morning" let alone "happy birthday". I said to myself, "Well, that's wives for you. The children will remember." But the children came into breakfast and didn't say a word. And when I started to the office, I was feeling pretty low and despondent.

'As I walked into my office, Janet said, "Good morning, boss. Happy birthday," and I felt a little bit better that someone had remembered. I worked until noon. About noon, Janet knocked on my door and said, "You know it's such a beautiful day and it is your birthday, so let's go to lunch, just you and me." I said, "By George, that is the greatest thing I have heard all day. Let's go."

'We went to lunch. We didn't go where we normally go. We went out into the country to a private place. We had two martinis and enjoyed lunch tremendously. On the way back to the office, she said, "You know, it's such a beautiful day, we don't need to go back to the office, do we?" I said, "No, I guess not." She said, "Let's go by my apartment, and I'll fix you another martini."

'So we went to her apartment. We enjoyed another martini and smoked a cigarette and she said, "Boss, if you don't mind, I think I'll go into the bedroom and slip into something more comfortable" and I allowed her as I didn't mind at all.

'She went into the bedroom and in about six minutes she came out carrying a big birthday cake followed by my wife and children. All were singing "Happy Birthday" and there I sat with nothing on but my socks.'

## PIGS IN MUD!

A farmer decides that his three sows should be bred, and contacts his buddy down the road, who owns three male pigs. They agree on a stud fee and the farmer puts the sows in his pickup and takes them down the road to the males.

He leaves them all day, and when he picks them up that night, asks the man how he can tell if it 'took' or not. The breeder replies that if, the next morning, the sows were grazing on grass, they were pregnant, but if they were rolling in the mud as usual, they probably weren't.

Comes the morn, the sows are rolling in the mud as usual, so the farmer puts them in the truck and takes them back for a second full day of frolic. This continues for a week, since each morning the sows are rolling in the mud.

About the sixth day, the farmer wakes up and tells his wife, 'I don't have the heart to look again. This is getting ridiculous, *and* expensive. You check today.'

With that, the wife peeks out the bedroom window and starts to laugh.

'What is it?' asks the farmer excitedly. 'Are they grazing at last?'

'Nope,' says the wife. 'Two of them are jumping up and down in the back of your truck, and the other one is honking the horn!'

### TRICKY LAWYER

Middle of the night, middle of nowhere, two cars both slightly cross over the white line in the centre of the road. They collide and a fair amount of damage is done, although neither driver is hurt. It's impossible to place blame for the accident on either however.

They both get out. One is a doctor, one is a lawyer. The lawyer calls the police on his cell phone; they'll be there in 20 minutes.

It's cold and damp, and both men are shaken up. The lawyer offers the doctor a drink of brandy from his hip flask, the doctor accepts, drinks and hands it back to the lawyer, who puts it away.

'Aren't you going to have a drink?' the doctor says.

'After the police get here,' replies the lawyer.

### ANAESTHETIC IS NO JOKE

A plumber, an electrician, a dentist and a computer programmer are fast friends: buddies for life, eternal bachelors . . . until the programmer announces he is getting married.

Never ones to pass up a golden opportunity, the three compadres find out the name and location of the hotel where the programmer will be honeymooning and bribe the desk clerk to let them in to rig a few 'welcome' surprises.

A week after returning from the honeymoon, the programmer meets his buddies in a bar for drinks, and half-heartedly chuckles with them over the gags.

Pointing to the plumber, he says, 'Yeah, the drippy tap you couldn't turn off was a neat trick.'

And to the electrician: 'And a flickering table lamp with no off switch was cute, too.'

Then, shaking a fist at the dentist, 'But, you! YOU! Novocaine in the Vaseline was one cheap shot!'

## IN QUITE A PICKLE

Bill worked in a pickle factory. He had been employed there for a number of years when he came home one day to confess to his wife that he had a terrible compulsion. He had an urge to stick his penis in the pickle slicer. His wife suggested that he should see a therapist to talk about it, but Bill indicated that he'd be too embarrassed. He vowed to overcome the compulsion on his own.

One day a few weeks later Bill came home absolutely ashen. His wife could see at once that something was seriously wrong. 'What's wrong, Bill?' she asked.

'Do you remember that I told you how I had this tremendous urge to put my penis in the pickle slicer?'

'Oh, Bill, you didn't.'

'Yes, I did.'

'My God, Bill, what happened?'

'I got fired.'

'No, Bill. I mean, what happened with the pickle slicer?'
'Oh, she got fired too.'

## LOGIC RULES. OKAY?

A new sales assistant was hired at a department store in Palmerston North. On his first day, the sales manager took him around to show him the ropes. They were passing by the gardening section, when they heard a customer asking for grass seed. The sales manager stepped in.

Sales manager: 'Excuse me, but will you be needing a hose to water your lawn?'

Customer: 'I guess so. I'll take one.'

Sales manager: 'And how about some fertiliser and weed-killer?'

Customer: 'Um, okay.'

Sales manager: 'Here's a couple of bags. You'll also need a lawn mower to cut the grass when it starts growing too long.'

Customer: 'I'll take one of those too.'

After the customer had left, the sales manager turned to the assistant. 'You see?' he said. 'That's the way to make a good sale. Always sell more than what the customer originally came in for.'

Impressed, the assistant headed off for the pharmaceutical section, where he was to work. Soon, a man strolled in.

Man: 'I'd like to buy a pack of Tampax, please.'

Assistant: 'Sure, and would you like to buy a lawn mower too?'

Man: 'Why would I want to do that?'
Assistant: 'Well, your weekend's shot to hell anyway, so you might as well mow the lawn.'

### JACK'S A DULL BOY

In a company there are two employees, Jack and Jill, doing the same job. Both have been model employees and have been much valued by the firm. However, due to financial setbacks, the company is forced to let one of them go. But which one?

The boss decides on a plan. He will watch Jack closely for one day, monitoring his performance. The next day, he will similarly scrutinise Jill. Then he will announce which one he is going to keep and which one will have to be fired.

The first day, Jack comes in early. He works hard all morning, not even taking a coffee break. He skips lunch. He works hard all afternoon, doesn't spend any time on the phone, and leaves late.

Noticing this, the boss begins to think, 'If they're both such diligent workers, the choice is going to be even harder.'

The next day, Jill comes in late, complaining of a headache. She takes some aspirin and hangs out at the water fountain talking to her friends. She takes an extra-long coffee break. She leaves early for lunch and comes back late. She's unproductive in the afternoon, spending much of her time calling her friends and telling them how miserable she feels. She takes some more aspirin and leaves early.

The boss takes note of this. His mind is made up.

So, the next day, the boss calls Jill into his office. He tells her, 'Jill, I am afraid I either have to lay you or Jack off.'

Jill replies, 'Well, you're going to have to jack off because *I've* got a headache.'

## A TOXIC PIPELINE

Three engineering students were gathered together discussing the possible designers of the human body.

One said, 'It was a mechanical engineer. Just look at all the joints.'

Another said, 'No, it was an electrical engineer. The nervous system has many thousands of electrical connections.'

The last said, 'Actually it was a civil engineer. Who else would run a toxic waste pipeline through a recreational area?'

## TWO FOR THE PRICE OF ONE

A woman was at the pharmacy and asked, 'Can I get Viagra here?'

The old pharmacist replied, 'Yes.'

She asked, 'Can I get it over the counter?'

He responded, 'If you give me two of them, you can.'

WARNING: Patients will be charged extra for annoying the doctor with any self-diagnosis gotten off the internet.
— notice in an Oregon doctor's practice

# ENTERTAINMENT

This chapter covers a multitude of sins. Acting and actors feature a bit and the great 'service industry' also gets a mention. There are a couple of naughtier items, but nothing your little old grandma would blush at.

## BEACH BUDDIES

A man is lying on the beach, wearing nothing but a cap over his crotch. A woman passing by remarks, 'If you were any sort of a gentleman, you would lift your hat to a lady.'

He replies, 'If you were any sort of a sexy lady, the hat would lift by itself.'

Waiter: These are the best eggs we've had for years!
Customer: Well, bring me some you haven't had around for that long!

## FALLEN ON HARD TIMES

A cowboy lay sprawled across three entire seats in the posh Amarillo theatre's lower section. When the usher came by and noticed this he whispered to the cowboy, 'Sorry, sir, but you're only allowed one seat.'

The cowboy groaned but didn't budge. The usher became

more impatient. 'Sir, if you don't get up from there, I'm going to have to call the manager.' The cowboy just groaned.

The usher marched briskly back up the aisle. In a moment he returned with the manager. Together the two of them tried repeatedly to move the cowboy, but with no success.

Finally, they summoned the police. The cop surveyed the situation briefly, then asked, 'All right buddy, what's your name?'

'Sam,' the cowboy moaned.

'Where ya from, Sam?'

With pain in his voice, Sam replied, 'The balcony.'

### FORMAL ATTIRE

An American, a Vietnamese, a Mexican, a Brazilian, a Canadian, a German, a Turk and a Russian walk into a fancy restaurant.

When they got to the front desk, they were kicked out because they didn't have a Thai.

### HONESTY

Two men visit a prostitute. The first man goes into the bedroom and comes out 10 minutes later and says, 'Heck, my wife is better than that.'

The second man goes in. He comes out 10 minutes later and says, 'You know? Your wife IS better.'

## WHAT A WALLY

Insult: Hey, you're not much of a looker, but I'll date you.
Response: Thanks. You must be very open-minded. Was that how your brain slipped out?

## LEGS II

A man goes to a bar and sees a fat girl dancing on a table. He walks over to her and says, 'Wow, nice legs!'

She is flattered and replies, 'You really think so?'

The man says, 'Oh, definitely! Most tables would have collapsed by now.'

## IN THE POO

A Kiwi, a German guy and an American dude climb a mountain because they each want to be granted a wish from the genie on the top. When they make it to the top, they find the lamp and all rub it.

The genie appears and says, 'For your wish to be granted, you must yell it out while you are jumping off the mountain.'

So the German jumps off and yells, 'I wish to be a fighter plane!'

'So be it,' the genie says, and the German becomes a plane.

The American jumps off and yells, 'I wish to be an eagle!'

'So be it,' the genie says, and the American becomes an eagle and flies away.

The Kiwi runs to the edge, accidentally trips on a rock, and yells, 'I wish to b– oh SHIT!'

### SWEET NUMBER

Three guys travel to Saudi Arabia and get lost in Riyadh. They walk into a tent that they think was the one they rented, but actually belongs to a prince with three hot wives.

The prince comes home and thinks his wives are cheating on him. As a punishment, he tells the men that their penises will have to be cut off in some way relating to their occupation.

He asks the first guy what his job was. 'I'm an employee at the shooting range,' he replies.

'Then we'll shoot your dick off!' the prince says.

'I'm a fireman,' the second guy says. 'Then we'll burn your cock off!' says the prince.

The third guy smiles and says, 'I'm a lollipop salesman.'

Some guy called me a tool. So, I got hammered and nailed his girlfriend. Guess he was right.

### WHISKEY PROMISE

Two Irish friends are drinking together at one of their homes. One takes out a bottle of Irish whiskey and asks the other, 'Will you pour this bottle out on my grave if I die first?'

His friend replies, 'Do you mind if I pass it through my kidneys first?'

## TALKING GIRLY

Yesterday, scientists in the United States revealed that beer contains small traces of female hormones.

To demonstrate their theory, they fed 100 men 12 pints of beer and observed that 100 per cent of them started talking nonsense and couldn't drive.

## RIGHT OUT OF ORDER

A man walks into a bar and sits down. He asks the bartender, 'Got any cigarettes?'

The bartender replies, 'Sure, the cigarette machine is over there.'

So, the man walks over to the machine and as he is about to order some cigarettes, the machine suddenly says, 'Oi, you bloody idiot.'

Surprised, the man says, 'That's not very nice.'

He returns to his bar stool without any cigarettes and asks the bartender for some peanuts. The bartender passes the man a bowl of peanuts and the man hears one of the peanuts say, 'Ooh, I like your hair.'

The man says to the bartender, 'Hey, what's going on here? Your cigarette machine is insulting me and this peanut is coming on to me. Why's this?'

The bartender replies, 'Oh, that's because the cigarette machine is out of order and the peanuts are complimentary.'

### CANNIBAL DEMOCRACY

There were two cannibals who captured a man. They decided it would be fair if they started eating him from opposite ends.

After a few minutes, the one who started at the head asked the other one, 'How's it going down there?'

And the other one replies, 'I'm having a ball!'

### BARMAN'S RUSE

An old guy walked into a bar and the barman asked for ID.

'You've got to be kidding,' he said. 'I'm almost 70 years old.'

The bartender apologised, but said he had to see the proof.

The guy showed his ID, then paid and told the bartender to keep the change.

'The tip's for questioning my age,' he said.

The bartender put the change in the tip cup. 'Thanks,' he said. 'Works every time.'

### CARTONS OF CULTURE

Two cartons of yoghurt walk into a bar. The barman, who is a tub of cottage cheese, says to them, 'We don't serve your kind in here.'

One of the yoghurt cartons says to him, 'Why not? We're cultured individuals.'

### MUSICAL TALES

Most of our music store customers have a story about their old vinyl collection. Once, a man asked how much a record cost. My co-worker quoted him the price, then added, 'But there's a surcharge if we have to listen to how your mother made you throw out all your old vinyl records.'

### DUH!

A Twitter exchange between an angry customer and an apologetic Domino's Pizza:

Customer: Yoooo. I ordered a pizza and it came with no toppings on it or anything. It's just bread.

Domino's: We're sorry to hear about this!

Customer (minutes later): Never mind, I opened the pizza upside down.

Did you hear about the restaurant on the moon? Great food, no atmosphere.

### UNDERSTANDING JUDGE

A defendant isn't happy with how things are going in court, so he gives the judge a hard time.

Judge: 'Where do you work?'

Defendant: 'Here and there.'

Judge: 'What do you do for a living?'

Defendant: 'This and that.'

Judge: 'Take him away.'

Defendant: 'Wait! When will I get out?'

Judge: 'Sooner or later.'

### ALARMED!

I came home from work this evening and said to my wife, 'Are we having salad for dinner?'

'Yes, we are, how did you know?' she asked.

I replied, 'Because I can't hear the smoke alarm.'

### STAR STRUCK

An actress who suffered from an inferiority complex was complaining to her psychiatrist. 'I'm a nothing!' she cried. 'I can't sing. I can't remember my lines. I can't dance. I can't even act. I really don't belong in show business.'

'Why don't you quit?' the doctor asked.

'I can't,' moaned the actress. 'I'm a Star!'

**Q:** What do you call an ABBA toilet?
**A:** What a loo?

### MY OATH!

A very self-centred actor was hauled into a court as a witness. When asked to state his occupation, he announced quite confidently, 'I am the world's greatest actor.'

'Why did you tell them that?' a friend inquired afterward.

'Had to,' was the answer. 'I was under oath.'

## TIME TUNNEL

'Time separates the best of friends,' said one woman to another.

'How true,' replied the other. 'Twenty years ago, we were both fifteen — now you're 35 and I'm 29!'

## CELEBRITY COFFEE

A new celebrity restaurant chain is opening up nationwide. It's a partnership between Kareem Abdul-Jabbar, Ryan Coffee and Sugar Ray Leonard. They're going to call it 'Coffee with Kareem and Sugar'.

## MILKYBAR KID

Sad news at the Nestlé factory today when a member of staff was seriously injured when a pallet of chocolate fell more than 20 metres and crushed him underneath. He tried in vain to attract attention but every time he shouted, 'The Milkybars are on me!' everyone just cheered.

## SHEER MADNESS

Walking into the lingerie store, the hard-of-hearing customer says to the clerk, 'I'd like to buy a pair of stockings for my wife.'

The clerk says, 'Sheer?'

And the man replies, 'No. She's in another store.'

## TRUTH RULES

A woman was in a gambling casino for the first time. At the roulette table she says, 'I have no idea what number to play.'

A young, good-looking man nearby suggests she play her age. Smiling at the man, she puts her money on number 25. The wheel is spun, and 30 comes up.

The smile vanishes from the woman's face and she faints.

## SOMETHING FOR THE WEEKEND

A white-haired old man walked into a jewellery store on a Friday, with a beautiful young lady at his side. 'I'm looking for a special ring for my girlfriend,' he said.

The jeweller looked through the stock and took out an outstanding ring priced at $5000.

'I don't think you understand — I want something very unique,' the man said.

At that, the now very excited jeweller went and fetched the special stock from the safe. 'Here's one stunning ring at $40,000.' The girl's eyes sparkled, and the man said that he would take it. 'How are you paying?' asked the jeweller.

'I'll pay by cheque — but, of course, the bank will want to make sure that everything is in order, so I'll write a cheque and you can phone the bank tomorrow, and then I'll fetch the ring on Monday.'

Monday morning, the very disappointed jeweller phoned the man. 'You lied, there's no money in that account.'

'I know, sorry, but can you imagine what a FANTASTIC weekend I had?'

## LOBE LOAD

A man is at work one day when he notices that his co-worker is wearing an earring. This man knows his co-worker to be normally a conservative fellow, and is curious about his sudden change in fashion sense. The man walks up to him and says, 'I didn't know you were into earrings.'

'Don't make a big deal, it's only an earring,' he replies sheepishly.

His friend falls silent for a few minutes, but then his curiosity prods him to say, 'So, how long have you been wearing one?'

'Ever since my wife found it in my truck.'

## SMART-ARSE POLLY

On reaching his plane seat a man is surprised to see a parrot strapped in next to him. He asks the stewardess for a coffee whereupon the parrot squawks, 'And get me a whisky!'

The stewardess, flustered, brings back a whisky for the parrot and forgets the coffee. When this omission is pointed out to her the parrot drains its glass and bawls, 'And get me another whisky.'

Quite upset, the hostie comes back shaking with another whisky but still no coffee. Unaccustomed to such treatment, the man tries the parrot's approach: 'I've asked you twice for a coffee. Go and get it now!'

The next moment, both he and the parrot have been wrenched up and thrown out of the emergency exit by two burly stewards.

Plunging downwards the parrot turns to him and says, 'For someone who can't fly, you complain too much!'

## PROF'S A SPOIL-SPORT

A PhD student, a postgraduate and their professor are walking through Albert Park near Auckland University and they find an antique oil lamp. They rub it and a genie comes out in a puff of smoke. The genie says, 'I usually only grant three wishes, so I'll give each of you just one.'

'Me first! Me first!' says the PhD student. 'I want to be in Fiji, driving a speedboat with a gorgeous woman.' Poof! He's gone.

'Me next! Me next!' says the postgrad. 'I want to be in Hawaii, relaxing on the beach with a professional hula dancer on one side and a beer on the other.' Poof! He's gone.

'You're next,' the genie says to the professor. The professor says, 'I want those guys back in the lab after lunch.'

## SCOTCH MISSED

After a hard day at work I decided to ride my bicycle to Christchurch city centre to wind down a bit. I came into town and decided I'd go to a liquor store to get a bottle of Scotch. I came out of the store and since my bike had a basket in front, I put the bottle in there.

It occurred to me that if I fell over with the bike, the bottle of Scotch would break. So, I decided to drink the Scotch and then head home. So, I did.

Good thing, too, as I fell over 10 times on the way home.

## BEER PROBLEM

A man walks into a bar and says, 'Give me a beer before the problems start.' He drinks the beer and then orders another, saying, 'Give me a beer before the problems start.'

The bartender looks confused but gives him another beer.

This goes on for a while, and after the fifth beer the bartender is totally confused and asks the man, 'When are you going to pay for these beers?'

The man answers, 'Now the problems start!'

## SERIOUSLY UNFUNNY

Three comedians are relaxing in the dressing room of a nightclub after a late gig. They've heard one another's material so much that they've reached the point where they don't need to say the jokes any more to amuse each other, they just need to refer to each joke by a number.

'Number 37!' cracks the first comic, and the others break up.

'Number 53!' says the second person, and they howl.

Finally, the third comic says '44!' He gets nothing from the other comics.

'What?' he asks, 'Isn't "44" funny?'

'Sure, it's usually hilarious,' they answer. 'But the way you tell it . . .'

Photographer: 'Now say cheese.'
Dim girl: 'Actually, I'm dieting, so can I say oats or something that's a little healthier?'

## EVERYBODY HAPPY IN PORN?

Porn movies are positive movies: no murder, no war, no fight, no conspiracy, no cheating, no racism, no religious fanatics, no language problem, no crying or teasing, good cooperation, good coordination, natural acting, everybody enjoys the climax, lots of love, always a very happy ending for all characters! And the best part? No matter which point you start watching, you will understand the story.

## LETTER SCRAMBLE

What happens when you rearrange the letters?

DORMITORY — DIRTY ROOM
PRESBYTERIAN — BEST IN PRAYER
ASTRONOMER — MOON STARER
DESPERATION — A ROPE ENDS IT
THE EYES — THEY SEE
GEORGE BUSH — HE BUGS GORE
THE MORSE CODE — WHERE COME DOTS
SLOT MACHINES — CASH LOST IN ME
ANIMOSITY — IS NO AMITY
ELECTION RESULTS — LIES LET'S RECOUNT
SNOOZE ALARM — ALAS! NO MORE ZS
A DECIMAL POINT — I'M A DOT IN PLACE
THE EARTHQUAKES — THAT QUEER SHAKE
ELEVEN PLUS TWO — TWELVE PLUS ONE

And, the mother of them all:

MOTHER-IN-LAW — WOMAN HITLER

### BIN MISTAKEN

'That is him,' I said to my wife in the shopping centre. 'That's Kenny Baker, the actor who played R2-D2 in *Star Wars*.'

'Are you sure?' she asked. 'It doesn't look like him, go on over and ask.'

A couple of minutes later, I walked back over to her. 'Well, what did he say?'

'Nothing.' I said. 'It's a rubbish bin.'

### SPLASH SLASH!

I went on the Splash Mountain roller coaster and the woman next to me wouldn't stop screaming her fool head off.

Seriously, it was like she'd never seen a penis before.

### CUSHY NUMBER

The easiest job on the planet has to be the DJ at a classical music station. It's a sweet gig: 'Here's Beethoven's 9th Symphony in D Minor. I'll be back in an hour and a half.'

### GORE NONSENSE

While driving on the main highway through Gore, a man strummed a guitar he held in his lap. A policeman pulled him over, got out of the police car, and walked over to the driver.

'Do you know you're a menace to the safety of hundreds of people?' the cop asked.

'No,' the driver said. 'How does it go? Hum a few bars and I'll fake it.'

## GOTTA URN IT!

I asked the people in my audience, 'What is the ideal weight for a stand-up comedian?'

Three and a half pounds, including the urn, seemed to be the consensus answer.

## HE BLEW IT

An actor had been out of work for 15 years because he always forgot his lines. Then one day he got a call from a director who wanted him for a significant part in a play. All he had to say was, 'Hark! I hear the cannon roar!'

After much worry, the actor decided to take the role. Opening night arrived, and while he waited in the wings, he muttered to himself, 'Hark! I hear the cannon roar! Hark! I hear the cannon roar!'

The time for the entrance finally came and as the actor made his appearance, he heard a loud BARRROOOOM!

He turned around and said, 'What the hell was that?'

## REBEL IN THE RANKS

A musical director was having a lot of trouble with one drummer. He talked and talked and talked with the drummer, but his performance simply didn't improve.

Rehearsal was under way and the exasperated conductor — before the whole orchestra — said, 'When a musician just can't handle his instrument and doesn't improve when given help, they take away the instrument, and give him two sticks, and make him a drummer.'

A stage whisper was heard from the percussion section:

'And if he can't handle even that, they take away one of his sticks and make him a conductor.'

## MUST BE AN AUSSIE CRICKETER!

I've been charged with murder for killing a man with sandpaper. To be honest, I only intended to rough him up a bit.

## GOLD-PLATED MISTAKE

Two mates were reminiscing about the party they'd been at last weekend.

'Great party that, last week, wasn't it?'

'Wow, yes, great food, great booze, great girls — and a posh house to boot.'

'Posh house? It was a suburban semi.'

'Never — they had a gold-plated toilet.'

'What? I can't remember that, you must have been really drunk.'

'No, honestly, I remember thinking — posh!'

The argument went backwards and forwards — yes, no, yes, no. Finally, they decided to prove once and for all who was correct so they looked up the address and went to the house.

A woman came to the door and one of the men said, 'Excuse me, we were at your party last weekend and we're having a difference of opinion, tell us please — have you, or have you not, got a gold-plated toilet? My mate here says yes but I disagree.'

The woman turned around and shouted to her husband, 'George, I've found the bastard that crapped in your tuba!'

## COWERING DOG

My dog was so traumatised by all the banging, screeching and wailing on Saturday night that she cowered behind the sofa and didn't come out until the whole racket was over.

From now on we're going to put her in the kitchen when we watch *Britain's Got Talent*!

My dad is obsessed with The Beatles, he's got all but one of their albums. I think he needs *Help!*

**Q:** Why does Batman wear a mask?
**A:** Because the citizens of Gotham aren't morons, like those idiots over in Metropolis.

I got invited to a party and was told to dress to kill. Apparently, a turban, beard and a backpack wasn't what they had in mind.

## JEHOVAH'S BREAD

Two women called at my door and asked what bread I ate. When I said white they gave me a lecture on the benefits of brown bread for 30 minutes.

I think they were those Hovis Witnesses.

'He has Van Gogh's ear for music.' — *Billy Wilder*

## SOME GROUCHO MOMENTS

'No, Groucho is not my real name. I'm breaking it in for a friend.'

'How do I feel about women's rights? I like either side of them.'

'A child of five could understand this. Fetch me a child of five.'

'Marry me and I'll never look at another horse!'

'If you find it hard to laugh at yourself, I would be happy to do it for you.'

'Marriage is the chief cause of divorce.'

'I never forget a face, but in your case, I'll be glad to make an exception.'

'I have had a perfectly wonderful evening, but this wasn't it.'

'I didn't like the play, but then I saw it under adverse conditions — the curtain was up.'

'If you don't read the newspaper, you are uninformed; if you do read the newspaper, you are misinformed.' — *Mark Twain*

## SOUND ARGUMENT

For the first time in many years, a friend of ours travelled from his rural town to the city to attend a movie. After buying his ticket, he stopped at the concession stand to buy some popcorn. Handing the attendant $1.50, my friend couldn't help but comment, 'The last time I came to the movie, popcorn was only 15 cents.'

'Well, sir,' the attendant replied with a grin, 'you're really going to enjoy yourself. We have sound now.'

### DUCK-LIKE

A circus owner walked into a bar to see everyone crowded around a table watching a little show. On the table was an upside-down pot and a duck tap-dancing on it.

The circus owner was so impressed that he offered to buy the duck from its owner. After some wheeling and dealing, they settled for $10,000 for the duck and the pot.

Three days later the circus owner runs back to the bar in anger. 'Your duck is a rip-off! I put him on the pot before a whole audience and he didn't dance a single step!'

'So?' asked the duck's former owner, 'did you remember to light the candle under the pot?'

### BIG BOOB JOB

Once there was this woman, who was, sad to say, very flat across the upper body. Year after year of seeing beautiful, large-breasted women walking away with handsome guys finally got to her. She decided that she would have large tits at any cost.

At first, she went to a breast treatment centre and asked for larger breasts. After several weeks, despite all the injections and fillers they had given her, her breasts were no larger. She despaired. She went everywhere, but everything she tried came to no avail.

So, she went home and cried and prayed for larger breasts. After several days of this, during one praying session, there was this sudden poof, and her fairy godmother appeared before her.

'Well, dearie, you want larger tits, do you?'

'Oh yes, oh yes, please Fairy Godmother, give me bigger

boobs. I beg you,' the woman implored.

'Okay, okay, calm down. I'll do it, if you promise to stop bothering me. Promise?' the fairy godmother asked.

'Yes, I promise!'

'Okay, then. Shish, swoosh, swash, liffiday-loffiday, balsshac, boom! There. Now, dearie, whenever anyone says "pardon" to you, your tits will grow one inch. Fine? Bye, dearie.' And with a flash and the smell of burnt hair, the fairy godmother left.

Of course, the woman wanted to try out her fairy godmother's spell immediately. She then ran out of her apartment and seeing some unlucky passer-by, collided with him and promptly fell to the ground.

'Oh, pardon me. I'm so sorry, are you all right?'

Zzzzuuuummmpp! Her boobs bulged forward an inch. 'No, I'm fine,' she laughed, as she ran back into her apartment. She inspected her breasts. Oh, they were actually one inch larger; in fact, exactly one inch. She decided to try again the next day.

At work, the following morning, she contrived to bump the manager and spill her coffee into her lap.

'Pardon me! Here, let me help clean you up,' the manager said. Zzzzuuuummmpp! Her tits jumped forward another inch. 'Oohhh, I'll clean up myself.'

She ran into the women's bathroom and gleefully examined her breasts. Two inches! 'I've got to celebrate.'

That night, she went to a posh Chinese restaurant. 'Aahh, I'll treat myself to the best. After all, I could easily beat out Dolly Parton by tomorrow. I'll be famous!'

As she sat there, a waiter passed by, carrying an armful of aromatic dishes. She stretched, delighting in the feel of her newfound breasts, and her arm banged into the waiter's midsection.

The waiter fell with an audible 'Oooffff!' sending dishes and sauces all over her. Grovelling, the waiter said to the lady, 'A thousand pardons . . .'

## BURGER TO DIE FOR

A bloke and his friend go to a little coffee shop in Herne Bay, and the guy orders a hamburger. The geezer behind the counter spits in his hands and rubs them against each other, grabs a chunk of ground beef from a dirty bowl with flies buzzing around, and spits on the grill. Then he puts the chunk of beef under his armpit to make a patty and throws the patty on the grill.

The guy ordering the hamburger looks at his friend and says, 'God damn, that is gross.'

The friend says, 'That's nothing, you should see how he makes the donuts.'

## TAKE A PICK

An infamous stud with a long list of conquests walked into his neighbourhood bar in Johnsonville and ordered a drink. The barman thought he looked worried and asked him if anything was wrong.

'I'm scared out of my mind,' the stud replied. 'Some pissed-off husband wrote to me and said he'd kill me if I didn't stop f---ing his wife.'

'So, stop,' the barman said.

'I can't,' the womaniser replied, taking a long swill. 'The prick didn't sign his name!'

## COMMUNICATION BYPASS

There was a nice lady who was a little old-fashioned. She was considering a week's vacation in sunny Florida at a particular campground, but she wanted to make sure of the accommodations first. Uppermost in her mind were toilet facilities, but she couldn't bring herself to write 'toilet' in a letter.

After considerable deliberation, she settled on 'bathroom commode', but when she wrote that down, it still sounded too forward, so she rewrote the letter to the campground, and referred to the 'bathroom commode' as the 'BC'. 'Does the campground have its own BC?' is what she actually wrote.

The campground owner was baffled by the euphemism, so he showed the letter around to several people at the campground, but they couldn't decipher it either. Finally, the campground owner concluded that she must be referring to the local Baptist Church, so he sat down and responded:

'Dear Madam,

'I regret very much the delay in answering your letter, but I now take pleasure in informing you that a BC is located nine miles north of the campground and is capable of seating 250 people at one time.

'I admit that it is quite a distance away if you are in the

habit of going regularly, but no doubt you will be pleased to know that a great number of people take their lunches along and make a full day of it. They arrive early and stay late!

'The last time my wife and I went was six years ago, and it was so crowded that we had to stand up the entire time we were there. It may interest you to know that right now there is a supper planned to raise money to buy more seats. The supper is going to be held in the basement of the BC.

'I would like to say that it pains me very much not to be able to go more regularly, but it is surely from no lack of desire on my part. As we grow older, it seems to be more of an effort, particularly in cold weather!

'If you do decide to come down to our campground, perhaps I could go with you to the BC the first time, sit with you, and introduce you to all the other folks. Remember we are widely known as a friendly community so come on down and we can enjoy the BC together.'

## DEFINITION OF MISERY

A man recently had his arm amputated and decided to kill himself by jumping off a building. When he was ready to jump, he saw a man with both arms amputated dancing around. He decided to find out why he was so happy.

The man told him, 'I'm not dancing. My ass is itching and I can't scratch it!'

## DOGGY DOES

A doctor, an architect and an attorney were dining at the country club one day, and the conversation turned to the subject of their respective dogs, which were apparently quite extraordinary. A wager was placed on who had the most intelligent dog.

The doctor offered to show his dog first, and called out to the parking lot, 'Hippocrates, come!' Hippocrates ran in and was told by the doctor to do his stuff. Hippocrates ran to the golf course and dug for a while, producing a number of bones. He dragged the bones into the country club and assembled them into a complete, fully articulated human skeleton. The doctor patted Hippocrates on the head and gave him a cookie for his efforts.

The architect was only marginally impressed, and called for his dog. 'Sliderule, come!' Sliderule ran in and was told to do his stuff. The dog immediately chewed the skeleton to rubble but reassembled the fragments into a scale model of the Taj Mahal. The architect patted his dog and gave him a cookie.

The attorney watched the other two dogs, and called, 'Bullshit, come!' Bullshit entered and was told to do his stuff. Bullshit immediately f---ed the other two dogs, stole their cookies, auctioned the Taj Mahal replica to the other club members for his fee and went outside to play golf.

# HOMEGROWN

Bit of a dodgy title for this chapter. Methinks most of the jokes depicting Kiwis were written by Australians. Naturally, they depict our alleged habit of having sex with our beloved farm animals. 'Sheep-shaggers' has long been an Australian jibe at us, as well as our perfect accent. Talk about the pot calling the kettle black, but we're grown up and can take it from the Ockers who are known to strangle the hell out of the English language.

## SHORT, INEVITABLE ONES

**Q:** What do you call a Kiwi with a hundred lovers?
**A:** A shepherd.

**Q:** How does every Kiwi joke start?
**A:** By looking over your shoulder.

**Q:** What's the difference between a smart Kiwi and a unicorn?
**A:** Nothing, they're both fictional characters.

**Q:** What do you call a Kiwi in the knockout stages of the World Cup?
**A:** A referee.

**Q:** Why was Chris Wood (Burnley) speeding?
**A:** To get three points.

**Q:** What time was it when the monster ate the New Zealand prime minister?
**A:** Eight P.M.

**Q:** Why does New Zealand have some of the fastest racehorses in the world?
**A:** Because the horses have seen what they do with their sheep.

**Q:** What time does Marina Erakovic go to bed?
**A:** Tennish.

**Q:** What do two Kiwis say after breaking up?
**A:** Let's just be cousins.

**Q:** Why do the Kiwis make better lovers than the Aussies?
**A:** Because Kiwis are the only ones who can stay on top for 45 minutes and still come second.

**Q:** What is a Kiwi's defence in court?
**A:** 'Honest your Honour, I was just helping the sheep over the fence.'

**Q:** How do Kiwis find sheep in long grass?
**A:** Delightful!

**Q:** Why wasn't Jesus born in Hamilton?
**A:** He couldn't find three wise men or a virgin.

## SENT UP A GUM TREE

An Australian went into a bar and sat next to a Kiwi who was chewing gum. The Kiwi chewing the gum asked the Aussie if they eat bread in Australia.

The Aussie said, 'Of course, we eat the inside of the bread and take the outside and recycle it, then make cereal with it for Kiwis.'

Then the Kiwi chewing on the gum asked if they ate bananas in Australia.

The Aussie replied, 'Well, of course, we eat the inside and recycle the rest and make smoothies for Kiwis.'

Then the Kiwi chewing the gum asked one more question: 'Do you have sex in Australia?'

The Aussie said, 'Yes, we use condoms for sex and when we're finished with them we recycle them and make gum for Kiwis.'

## HOT FOR DOGGIE

Two Kiwis are strolling down an Auckland street, when they see a stray dog licking its own testicles. One of the Kiwis turns to the other and says, 'I wish I could do that!'

His mate watches the dog for a moment, sighs longingly, and replies, 'Me too. But don't you think you ought to get to know him first?'

## SAUSAGE CAPER

Kiwis Darryl and Ken are planning to go out on a Saturday night, but only have 50 cents between them. Darryl has an idea. He takes the 50 cents off Ken, goes to a dairy and buys a sausage. Ken is really pissed off at first that Darryl spent their last money on a sausage, but Darryl lets him in on his plan.

'We're going to go into the next pub, order two pints, drink them and when it comes to paying, you go down on your knees, unzip my trousers, pull the sausage out and start sucking on it.'

So they go into the first pub and do exactly as Darryl suggested. The barmaid is disgusted by the sight and kicks the two out. Darryl says, 'See, it works — we didn't pay, did we?' As Darryl's plan seems to be working, they carry on doing it.

In the twelfth pub, both are quite drunk by now. Ken isn't looking too good. They have just finished their pints and Ken says, 'I can't do this any more, Darryl, my bloody knees are hurting badly . . .'

Darryl replies, 'No worries. I lost that bloody sausage in the third pub!'

## CHEAP AUCKLAND

Two men in a bar. One says, 'A girl I met in Auckland gave me a sexually transmitted disease.'

His mate replies, 'You were lucky — in Wellington you would have had to pay for it!'

## INTRODUCTIONS PLEASE!

Two Kiwis, two Aussies, two Welshmen and two Irishmen were marooned on a desert island.

The two Aussies got together and started a bank; the two Welshmen got together and started a choir; the two Irishmen got together and started a fight.

The two Kiwis never spoke to each other — they hadn't been introduced!

## SHEAR AND SHEAR ALIKE

A tour bus full of tourists stops by a farmer holding a sheep. One of them calls out, 'Are you shearing?'

The farmer yells back, in an unhappy tone, 'NO, f--k off and get your own!'

## NO BULL!

A tourist from the US was driving around New Zealand's South Island. He was a bit tired and thought he needed somewhere to stay the night before getting to Queenstown. Then out of the darkness ran a bull. He couldn't avoid it, drove into it and killed it. He was still able to drive the car, so feeling guilty he drove to the nearest farm house. He knocked on the door and the farmer answered.

The American said, 'I'm very sorry but I've killed your bull and would like to replace it.'

The farmer replied, 'No dramas, mate, go around the back and you'll find all the cows in the shed — go for your life!'

### CATCHING ON QUICK

An elephant, a penguin and a kiwi walk into a Central Otago pub. 'What's going on?' asks the bartender suspiciously. 'Is this supposed to be some kind of joke?'

### NICE ONE BRO

There was an Englishman, an Irishman and a Maori man all wanting to join the army. But they had to pass a test first.

The Englishman went in and the army recruitment guy asked, 'What would happen if one of your eyes got stabbed out?'

The Englishman said, 'I'll be half blind.'

The next question was, 'What would happen if both your eyes got stabbed out?'

The Englishman said, 'I'll be full blind.'

The army recruitment guy said, 'Good, you pass.'

Next the Irishman came in and the guy asked the same questions and the Irishman gave the same answers, so he passed too.

The Maori man was listening at the door for the answers so the army recruitment guy thought he'd change the questions. So he says to the Maori man, 'What would you do if one of your ears got cut off?'

The Maori man said, 'I'll be half blind.'

'What would you do if both your ears got cut off?'

The Maori man said, 'I'll be full blind.'

'Why's that?' asks the puzzled army recruitment guy.

And the Maori man says, 'Because I'll have no ears to hang my glasses on.'

**Q:** What's meals on wheels in Maori?
**A:** Kaitaia!

## NOW YOU'RE TALKING

**Q:** What is the definition of virgin wool in New Zealand?
**A:** The sheep that can run the fastest.

An Australian ventriloquist is touring New Zealand and one day he goes for a walk out of Gisborne where he is appearing. He's walking for a while when he approaches a little hamlet and sees a local stroking his dog on his verandah, so the ventriloquist asks the local if he can talk to the dog.

The local says, 'What are ya? The dog doesn't talk.'

The Aussie, ignoring the local, says to the dog, 'Is this your owner?'

'Yes,' says the dog.

The local is astounded and then the ventriloquist asks the dog whether he is well treated.

'Yes,' answers the dog. 'I get walked every day, sometimes twice, and am fed well. I also get to chase a ball, which is great fun.'

Then the ventriloquist spies a horse around the side of the house and he asks the local if he could speak to the horse too.

'Don't be silly,' scoffs the local, 'he doesn't talk.'

The ventriloquist walks up to the horse and says, 'Are you well treated by your owner?'

'Yeah,' replies the horse. 'I get regular runs along the beach. Get a swim in the water, am groomed every day and I get well fed.'

The local is dumbfounded. He never knew his dog and horse could speak.

The ventriloquist then asks if he could speak to his sheep eating grass near the horse.

Sweating and agitated, the local blurts, 'The sheep is a liar!'

### SAD WIREMU

Wiremu, a New Zealander, was in Australia to watch the upcoming Bledisloe Cup test and was not feeling well, so he decided to see a doctor.

'Hey doc, I don't feel so good, eh,' said Wiremu.

The doctor gave him a thorough examination and informed Wiremu that he had long-existing and advanced prostate problems and that the only cure was testicular removal.

'No way, doc,' replied Wiremu. 'I'm gitting a sicond opinion, eh!'

The second Aussie doctor gave Wiremu the same

diagnosis and also advised him that testicular removal was the only cure. Not surprisingly, Wiremu refused the treatment.

Wiremu was devastated, but with the Bledisloe Cup just around the corner he found an expat Kiwi doctor and decided to get one last opinion from someone he could trust. The Kiwi doctor examined him and said, 'Wiremu, cuzzy bro, you huv prostate suckness, eh.'

'What's the cure thin, doc?' asked Wiremu, hoping for a different answer.

'Wull, Wiremu,' said the Kiwi doctor, 'Wi're gonna huv to cut off your balls.'

'Phew, thunk god for thut!' said Wiremu, 'those Aussie bastards wanted to take my test tickets off me!'

## OOPS, WRONG WAY

There is a senior citizen driving on the highway. His wife calls him on his cell phone and in a worried voice says, 'Herman, be careful! I just heard on the radio that there is a madman driving the wrong way on the Southern Motorway near the Otara turnoff!'

Herman says, "I know, but there isn't just one, there are hundreds!'

**Q:** Did you hear about the two bald guys from Ashburton who put their heads together?
**A:** They made an arse out of themselves!

Man: I want to give myself to you.
Woman: Sorry, I don't accept cheap gifts.

A guy is sitting at a bar in Rangiora when a drunk dude walks up to him, calling his mother a whore. The first guy just ignores it and stays in his spot drinking his beer.

An hour goes by and the drunk comes back saying, 'Your mother is a whore!'

The first guy looks around the bar, sees people staring and says, 'Don't worry, everything is cool here,' and shrugs it off.

After a few more shots, the drunk walks up a third time and says, 'Your mother . . . is such . . . a whore!'

The guy finally gets mad, throws his fist on the table and says, 'You know what, Dad? Go home!'

**Q:** Who is the poorest person in the South Island?
**A:** The tooth fairy.

## WAIKATO TROUBLE

A man asks a woman: 'Haven't I seen you someplace before?'
The woman responds: 'Yeah, that's why I don't go to Hamilton any more.

## TURF LOVE

Bruce the Aussie builder was going through a house he had just built for the woman who owned it. She was telling him what colour to paint each room.

They went into the first room and she said, 'I want this room to be painted a light blue.'

The builder went to the front door and yelled, 'GREEN SIDE UP!'

When he went back into the house, she told him that the next room was to be bright red.

The builder went to the front door and yelled, 'GREEN SIDE UP!'

When he came back, the woman said, 'I keep telling you colours, but you go out the front and yell, "GREEN SIDE UP!" What is that for?'

The builder said, 'Don't worry about that, I've just got a couple of Kiwis laying the turf out front.'

## FRENCHIES FROM OZ

Jacinda Ardern, Prime Minister of New Zulland, is rudely awoken at 4 a.m. by the telephone.

'Jacinda, it's the Hilth Munister here. Sorry to bother you at this hour but there is an emergency! I've just received word thet the Durex fectory en Auckland has burned to the ground. It is istimated thet the entire New Zulland supply of condoms will be gone by the ind of the week.'

PM: 'Shut! The economy wull niver be able to cope with all those unwanted babies — wi'll be ruined!'

Hilth Munister: 'We're going to hef to shup some in

from abroad . . . Brutain?'

PM: 'No chence! The Poms will have a field day on thus one!'

Hilth Munister: 'What about Australia?'

PM: 'Maybe — but we don't want them to know thet we are stuck.'

Hilth Munister: 'You call Turnbull and tell hum we need one moollion condoms; 10 enches long and eight enches thuck! That way they'll know how bug us Kiwis really are!'

Jacinda calls Malcolm, who agrees to help the Kiwis out in their hour of need.

Three days later a plane arrives in Auckland full of boxes. A delighted Jacinda is invited to see the arrival of the Aussie largesse. She rushes out to open the boxes. She finds condoms: 10 unches long, eight unches thuck, all coloured green and gold. She then notices in small writing on each and ivery one:

MADE IN AUSTRALIA — SIZE: MEDIUM

## BIG BLUE'S ADVENTURE

Labourer Big Blue Murphy was at his mate Jimmy the Fish's training gym in Newtown, Wellington, bashing that which doesn't hit back — the punching bag.

Blue was a big bloke and while he was a regular at Jimmy's establishment, he wasn't making much headway getting rid of his pot belly. He knew that was because he was known to engage in a few beers at the Flying Jug bar in the Tramways Hotel.

He also figured that if he kept some of his weight on he

could still be handy in the regular Friday-night rumbles the Flying Jug is noted for.

So, he keeps bashing the punching bag that day when a foreign-sounding voice pipes up at his side.

'I hear you're the best fighter at this gym,' said the skinny Asian dude.

Blue said, 'Yeah, I'm pretty good, so what of it?'

The skinny Asian said he would like to challenge him to a fight. Blue agreed, asking for a stake of $50 to the winner. 'Handy beer money,' Blue thought, figuring he would easily beat 'the cocky little skinny bastard'.

So, into the gym they go and Jimmy the Fish acts as referee. He calls them out and cautions, with his eyes fixed on his mate Blue, about a fair fight.

Both fighters come out of their corners, Blue with his fists up Marquess of Queensberry-like, when all of a sudden, he gets tossed arse over tit onto the canvas. As he shook his head, trying to regain equilibrium, he asked the skinny Asian, 'What was that?!'

'Judo, Japan,' was his reply.

'Right,' thought Blue, 'so much for the Marquess of Queensberry.' He told Jimmy the Fish he was fine, and the two squared up again.

All of a sudden, Blue is arse over tit again and on his back on the canvas. As he beats Jimmy the Fish's count to 10, he asked the skinny Asian, 'What was that?!'

'Kung fu, China,' he replied.

So, they go at it again and suddenly Blue gets a chop to his neck and falls to the canvas again.

'Karate, Korea,' the skinny Asian said before Blue asked the question.

Blue was really getting a pounding, with kick-boxing from Thailand and jujitsu from Indonesia also decking him.

After the jujitsu drop, Blue, right pissed off, up and left the ring. The skinny Asian raised his right arm in victory to the dozen or so hoods and would-be boxers lining the ring.

Blue returned to the ring, and all of a sudden, the Asian was flat on his back on the canvas. As he lay there, getting counted out by Jimmy the Fish, he asked, 'What was that?!'

'Crowbar, Ministry of Works,' said Blue, raising his arm in victory.

## MAXI THE TAXI

Max the cab driver was waiting at Auckland Airport for a customer, when a big American opened the door of his Kingswood, and said, 'Howdy, pal. Can you take me to Takapoona?'

Max took a look at the checked-suited American and agreed. 'Yeah, hop in, and it's Takapuna with an emphasis on the U,' Max said.

'Whatever,' said the Yank.

So they drive from the airport and soon go over the Mangere Bridge.

'How long did it take to build this bridge?' the American asked.

Max replied that he didn't really know because there was a union dispute while building it. 'Maybe two years,' he guessed.

To this the passenger said, 'Back home in the States, a bridge like this would be up in less than a year.'

They drove on and they came to the new tunnel system at Waterview and the American asked, 'How long did it take to build these tunnels?'

Max didn't rightly know, but he bluffed and said 'about a year'.

The American said, 'Back home in the States, these tunnels would be built in about nine months.'

Max was getting annoyed with his passenger, so decided to go the long way to fleece him of a bigger fare, but he made the mistake of going past Eden Park.

The same question came from the American, who said, 'Back home in the States, that stadium would have been built in six months.'

Max drove down to Quay Street and pulled up for a ferry trip.

The American passenger was puzzled. 'What are we doing here?' he asked.

'You've got to get a ferry to Takapuna,' Max said.

At that the American looked over at the Harbour Bridge and said, 'What's wrong with that big bridge over there?'

Max looked over at the bridge and said, 'Jesus. That wasn't there yesterday!'

**Q:** What do Kiwis and sperm have in common?
**A:** Millions of them enter and only a couple of them actually work.

## LUNCHTIME BLUES

A Chinese man, a German and a Kiwi were working on a high-rise construction site. At lunchtime, they sat down together and opened their lunchboxes.

The Chinese man looked inside his and said, 'Ah, if I get dumpling again, I gonna jump off the building.'

The German looked inside his and said, 'Mann, if I get sauerkraut und pickle again, I vill jump off zee building too.'

The Kiwi looked inside his and said, 'Geez, if I get fush and chups again, I'm gonna jump off this building as well.'

The next day at lunchtime, they open their lunchboxes.

The Chinese man looked inside his and said, 'Ah, DUMPLINGS!' and jumped off the thirty-second floor and died.

The German looked inside his and said, 'Mann, SAUERKRAUT UND PICKLE!' and jumped off the thirty-second floor and died.

The Kiwi looked inside his and said, 'Bloody hell, FUSH AND CHUPS!' and jumped off the thirty-second floor and died.

At the funeral, the Chinese man's wife said, 'If I know he no like dumplings, I will have make something different.'

The German's wife said, 'If I know he doesn't like sauerkraut und pickle, I vould have made zompting divferent.'

Everyone looked at the Kiwi's wife. She said, 'Don't look at me, he made his own lunch.'

The Kiwis have solved their own fuel problems. They imported 50 million tonnes of sand from the Arabs and they're going to drill for their own oil.

Two Kiwis are riding horses along the fenceline of their property and find a sheep with its head stuck in the fence. One bloke jumps off his horse and, of course, as most Kiwis would, has his way with the sheep.

When he was finished he said to his mate, 'Right, your turn!'

His mate jumped off his horse and stuck his head in the fence.

**Q:** What do you call a Kiwi with a thousand lovers?
**A:** A shepherd.

## THAT'S TELLING HER

A Kiwi walks into his bedroom carrying a sheep in his arms and says, 'Darling, this is the pig I have sex with when you have a headache.'

His girlfriend is lying in bed and replies, 'I think you'll find that's not a pig but a sheep, you idiot.'

The Kiwi says, 'Shut up, I wasn't talking to you.'

## OUR HELEN

Back in the day when New Zealand's Prime Munister was Helen Clark, her husband Dr Davis liked to go for a daily jog near their home in Auckland. Every day, he'd jog past a hooker standing on the same street corner. He learned to brace himself as he approached her for what was almost certain to follow.

'Two hundred and fifty dollars!' she'd shout from the curb.

'No! Five dollars!' he would fire back, just to shut her up.

This ritual between him and the hooker became a daily occurrence. He'd run by and she'd yell, 'Two hundred and fifty dollars! and he'd yell back, 'No! Five dollars!'

One day, Helen decided she wanted to accompany her husband on his jog. As the jogging couple neared the working woman's corner, Dr Davis realised she'd bark her $250 offer and Helen would wonder what he'd really been doing on all his past outings. He figured he'd better have a darn good explanation for the 'Boss'.

As they jogged up towards the corner, he became even more apprehensive than usual. Sure enough, there was the hooker. He tried to avoid the prostitute's eyes as she watched the pair jog past.

Then, from her corner, the hooker yelled, 'See what you get for five bucks, you tight bastard?!'

## DREAM JOB HOAX

A Kiwi walks into a Sydney unemployment office. He marches straight up to the counter and says, 'Hi! I want to apply for the dole, I hate being on welfare and I'd much rather have a job but I've looked everywhere and just can't find one.'

The clerk behind the Centrelink desk says, 'Your timing is excellent. We just got a job opening from a very wealthy old man who needs a chauffeur/bodyguard for his twin

21-year-old nymphomaniac daughters. You'll have to drive them around in his Mercedes, but he'll supply all of your clothes. You'll have a three-bedroom apartment above the garage. Because of the long hours, meals will be provided. You'll be expected to escort his daughters on their frequent overseas holidays to Tahiti and the Bahamas. The starting salary is $250,000 a year.'

The Kiwi says, 'No way, mate, you gotta be bullshitting me!'

The Centrelink officer says, 'Yeah, well, you started it.'

## OVERCOME BY CHEMICALS

Two Kiwis are walking down a street in Sydney. One of the Kiwis happens to look in one of the shop windows and sees a sign that catches his eye: 'Suits $5.00 each, shirts $2.00 each, trousers $2.50 per pair.'

The Kiwi says to his mate, 'Look! We could buy a whole lot of those, and when we get back to New Zealund we could make a fortune. Now, when we go into the shop, you be quiet. Just let me do all the talking, 'cause if they hear our accent, they might not be nice to us, so I'll speak in my best Aussie accent.'

They enter the shop and the Kiwi says, 'I'll take 50 suits at $5.00 each, 100 shirts at $2.00 each and 50 pairs of trousers at $2.50 each. I'll back up my ute and–'

The owner of the shop interrupts. 'You're from New Zealund, aren't you?"

'Well, yes,' says the surprised Kiwi. 'How the hell did you pick that?'

The shop owner replies, 'This is a bloody dry cleaners, mate!'

## REGIONAL DIFFERENCES

Four women are driving down the North Island countryside together, each one from a different town: Pukekohe, Ohakune, Queenstown and Auckland. Shortly after the trip begins, the woman from Pukekohe pulls potatoes from her bag and throws them out the window.

'What are you doing?' asks the Ohakune woman.

'We have so many of these things in Pukekohe, I'm sick of looking at them.'

Later, the woman from Ohakune pulls carrots from her bag and tosses them out the window.

'What are you doing?' asks the gal from Queenstown.

'We have so many of these things in Ohakune, I'm sick of looking at them.'

Inspired, the woman from Queenstown opens the car door and kicks the Auckland woman out.

**Q:** How do you know if a Kiwi has been in the fridge?
**A:** Love bites on the lamb roast.

# KIDS

Kids are always funny. Your own children will have you cracking up at times with the innocent things they do or come up with. But all the smart answers the Little Johnnies give can have you thinking of the lost chances of your youth to 'tell the truth' to a pain-in-the-arse teacher or parent. Put-downs abound in this chapter and that little smartarse Johnny is still responsible for many. But what was a pleasing phenomenon when researching jokes about kids was that little Johnny was often outdone by smart-witted girls spouting their pearls of wisdom and providing plenty of mirth.

### COOL CAT!

Teacher: 'If I gave you two cats and another two cats and another two, how many would you have?'

Johnny: 'Seven.'

Teacher: 'No, listen carefully. If I gave you two cats, and another two cats and another two, how many would you have?'

Johnny: 'Seven.'

Teacher: 'Let me put it to you differently. If I gave you two apples, and another two apples and another two, how many would you have?'

Johnny: 'Six.'
Teacher: 'Good. Now if I gave you two cats, and another two cats and another two, how many would you have?'
Johnny: 'Seven!'
Teacher: 'Johnny, where in the heck do you get seven from?!'
Johnny: 'Because I've already got a freaking cat!'

## OH DEAR!

Contest in a girl's college: write a short story which contains religion, sex and mystery.
Winner's story: Oh God, I'm pregnant, I wonder who did it?'

## JIMMY THE GENIUS

One day, Jimmy got home early from school and his mum asked, 'Why are you home so early?'

He answered, 'Because I was the only one that answered a question in my class.'

She said, 'Wow, my son is a genius. What was the question?'

Jimmy replied, 'The question was: "Who threw the trash can at the principal's head?"'

## THIGHS THE LIMIT

Little Johnny travelled north to visit his friend during wintertime. His friend's mother saw Johnny shivering, so she said, 'Come here and put your hands between my thighs to warm them up.'

Johnny said, 'My ears are cold too.'

## LEGUMES AHOY

A teacher asked her students to use the word 'beans' in a sentence.

'My father grows beans,' said one girl.

'My mother cooks beans,' said a boy.

A third student spoke up, 'We are all human beans.'

## NASTY ONE-LINERS

Your mother is so fat, I took a picture of her last Christmas and it's still printing.

## YUM, YUM

A three-year-old boy sits near a pregnant woman.
Boy: 'Why do you look so fat?'
Pregnant woman: 'I have a baby inside me.'
Boy: 'Is it a good baby?'
Pregnant woman: 'Yes, it is a very good baby.'
Boy: 'Then why did you eat it?!'

## PROBLEM CHILD

Dad: 'Can I see your report card, son?'
Son: 'I don't have it.'
Dad: 'Why not?'
Son: 'I gave it to my friend. He wanted to scare his parents.'

## ANIMAL MAGIC

Teacher: 'Kids, what does the chicken give you?'
Student: 'Meat!'
Teacher: 'Very good! Now what does the pig give you?'
Student: 'Bacon!'
Teacher: 'Great! And what does the good old cow give you?'
Student: 'Homework!'

## NICE THINKING

A teacher sees that Johnny isn't paying attention, so she asks him, 'If there are three ducks sitting on a fence, and you shoot one, how many are left?'

'None,' says Johnny.

'Why?' asks the teacher.

'Because the shot scared them all off,' says Johnny.

'No, two, but I like how you're thinking,' says the teacher.

Johnny asks the teacher, 'If you see three women walking out of an ice-cream parlour, one is licking her ice cream, one is sucking her ice cream, and one is biting her ice cream, which one is married?'

'The one sucking her ice cream,' says the teacher.

'No, the one with the wedding ring,' says Johnny, 'but I like how you're thinking!'

## VENGEANCE

A policeman sees a little girl riding her bike and says, 'Did Santa get you that?'

'Yes,' replies the little girl.

'Well,' says the policeman, 'tell Santa to put a reflector light on it next year,' and fines her $5.

The girl looks up at the policeman and says, 'Nice horse you've got there, did Santa bring you that?'

The policeman chuckles and replies, 'He sure did!'

'Well,' says the little girl, 'next year, tell Santa the arse goes on the back of the horse and not on top of it.'

You mother is so fat that when she got on the scales it said, 'I need your weight not your phone number.'

**Q:** Why did the school kids eat their homework?
**A:** Because their teacher told them it was a piece of cake.

## SWEARING DEBUT

A seven-year-old and a four-year-old are in their bedroom.

'You know what?' says the seven-year-old, 'I think it's time we started swearing. When we go downstairs for breakfast, I'll swear first, then you.'

'Okay,' replies the four-year-old.

In the kitchen, when the mother asks the seven-year-old what he wants for breakfast, he answers, 'I'll have Coco Pops, bitch.'

A clip across the ear! And he's crying his eyes out.

The mother looks at the four-year-old and sternly asks, 'And what do you want?'

'Dunno,' he replies, 'but it won't be f---ing Coco Pops.'

## KICK-ABOUT

'Johnny, why did you kick your brother in the stomach?' exclaimed the angry mother.

'It was pure accident, Mum. He turned around.'

## FORGETFUL STORK

On his first visit to the zoo, a little boy stared at the caged stork for a long time and asked his dad, 'Why doesn't the stork recognise me?'

## TOILET TRAINING

A little girl is serving her father tea while her mother is out shopping. The mother comes home and the father says, 'Watch this!'

The little girl goes and serves the mother tea.

The mother responds, 'Did it ever occur to you that the only place she can reach to get water is the toilet?'

## FAINT PRAISE

Alfie was listening to his sister practise her singing. 'Sis,' he said, 'I wish you'd sing Christmas carols.'

'That's nice of you, Alfie,' she replied, 'but why?'

Alfie answered, 'Because then I'd only have to hear your voice once a year!'

## A LITTLE INSURANCE

A father passing by his teenage son's bedroom was astonished to see the bed was nicely made and everything was picked up. Then he saw an envelope propped up prominently on the pillow. It was addressed: 'Dad'. He opened the envelope and read the letter, with trembling hands . . .

'Dear, Dad.

'It is with great regret and sorrow that I'm writing to you. I had to elope with my new girlfriend, because I wanted to avoid a scene with Mum and you.

'I've been finding real passion with Stacy, and she is so nice, but I knew you would not approve of her because of her piercings, tattoos, tight motorcycle clothes, and because she is so much older than I am.

'But it's not only the passion, Dad. She's pregnant. Stacy said that we will be very happy. She owns a trailer in the woods and has a stack of firewood for the whole winter.

'We share a dream of having many more children. Stacy has opened my eyes to the fact that marijuana doesn't really hurt anyone. We'll be growing it for ourselves, and trading it with the other people in the commune, for all the cocaine and ecstasy we want.

'In the meantime, we'll pray that science will find a cure for AIDS, so Stacy can get better. She sure deserves it!

'Don't worry, Dad. I'm 15, and I know how to take care of myself. Someday, I'm sure we'll be back to visit, so you can get to know your many grandchildren.

'Love, your son, Joshua.

'P.S. Dad, none of the above is true. I'm over at Jason's house. I just wanted to remind you that there are worse things in life than the school report that's on the kitchen table. Call when it is safe for me to come home!'

## SAVED BY NO PILL

A fourth-grade teacher asks the class, 'Have any of you ever saved somebody's life?'

A little boy raises his hand, 'Yes, my little nephew's.'

'Wow, what a little hero you are! How did you do that, sweetie?' asks the teacher.

The little guy replies, 'I hid my sister's birth control pills!'

## GIVE IT TIME

A: 'I have the perfect son.'
B:'Does he smoke?'
A: 'No, he doesn't.'
B: 'Does he drink whisky?'
A: 'No, he doesn't.'
B: 'Does he ever come home late?'
A: 'No, he doesn't.'
B: 'I guess you really do have the perfect son. How old is he?'
A: 'He'll be six months old next Wednesday.'

## A BUM JOKE

Little Johnny likes to gamble. One day, his dad gets a new job, so his family has to move house.

Johnny's dad thinks, 'I'll get a head start on Johnny's gambling.' He calls his new teacher and says, 'My son Johnny will be starting your class tomorrow, but he likes to gamble, so you'll have to keep an eye on him.'

The teacher says, 'Okay,' saying she could handle it.

The next day, Johnny walks into class and hands the teacher an apple and says, 'Hi, my name is Johnny.'

She says, 'Yes, I know who you are.'

Johnny smiles and says, 'I bet you $10 you've got a mole on your bum.'

The teacher thinks that she will break his little gambling problem, so she takes him up on the bet. She pulls her pants down, shows him her bum, and there is no mole. That afternoon, Johnny goes home and tells his dad that he lost $10 to the teacher and explains why.

His dad calls the teacher and says, 'Johnny said that he bet you that you had a mole on your bum and he lost.'

The teacher says, 'Yeah, and I think I broke his gambling problem.'

Johnny's dad laughs and says, 'No, you didn't, he bet me $100 this morning that he'd see your arse before the day was over.'

### ASK A SILLY QUESTION . . .

Girlfriend: 'Am I pretty or ugly?'
Boyfriend: 'You're both.'
Girlfriend: 'What do you mean?'
Boyfriend: 'You're pretty ugly.'

### GOOD ON YA, GIRL!

Girl: 'Girls are better than boys.'
Boy: 'Yeah? Then why did God make boys first?'
Girl: 'Duh, you have to have a rough draft before the final copy.'

## CUTTING!

A mother said to her son, 'Look at that kid over there — he's not misbehaving like you do.'

The son replied, 'Maybe he has good parents then!'

**Q:** How do you know if you're a bogan?
**A:** You let your 15-year-old daughter smoke at the dinner table . . . in front of her kids.

## JOHNNY'S COLLARED

In class one day, Mr Johnson pulled Johnny over to his desk after a test and said, 'Johnny, I have a feeling that you have been cheating on your test.' Johnny was astounded and asked Mr Johnson to prove it.

'Well,' said Mr Johnson, 'I was looking over your test and the question was "Who was our first president?" and the little girl that sits next to you, Mary, put "George Washington", and so did you.'

'So, everyone knows that he was the first president,' said Johnny.

'Well, just wait a minute,' said Mr Johnson. 'The next question was "Who freed the slaves?" Mary put "Abraham Lincoln" and so did you.'

'Well, I read the history book last night and I remembered that,' said Johnny.

'Wait, wait,' said Mr Johnson. 'The next question was "Who was president during the Louisiana Purchase?" Mary put "I don't know" and you put "Me neither".'

## NEW AGE JESUS

My sister-in-law was teaching a Sunday school class. The topic for the day: Easter Sunday and the resurrection of Christ. 'What did Jesus do on this day?' she asked.

There was no response, so she gave her students a hint: 'It starts with the letter "R".'

One boy blurted out, 'Recycle!'

## IGNORANCE IS BLISS!

It is Christmas Day and a family is preparing dinner awaiting the arrival of the children's grandparents. Thomas, who is four, is running around looking for his new pair of grey socks. He ventures up to the washroom where his mother is putting make-up on. Not realising the boy is there, she yells 'Shit!' when she accidentally gets make-up in her eyes.

Never having heard the word before, Thomas asks her, 'Mummy, what does "shit" mean?'

The mother quickly replies, 'Shit is just another word for make-up dear.'

Thomas then asks his mother if she knows where his socks are and she tells him to go downstairs and ask his father. The boy's father is stuffing the turkey when he cuts his finger by mistake. He says, 'F--k!' Thomas asks him if he's seen his socks and the father tells him to go look in his sister's room. Before the boy leaves, he asks his father what 'f--k' means and the father says 'stuff'. 'Like stuffing a turkey.'

Thomas goes to his sister's room and finally finds his socks and puts them on just as the doorbell rings. He runs down the stairs, opens the door and greets his grandparents by saying, 'Hello, Grandma and Grandpa, Mummy is upstairs putting shit on her face and Daddy is in the kitchen f---ing the turkey!'

### PIECE OF PISS

A kindergarten pupil told his teacher he'd found a cat, but it was dead.

'How do you know the cat was dead?' she asked.

'Because I pissed in its ear and it didn't move,' answered the child innocently.

'You did WHAT?' the teacher exclaimed in surprise.

'You know,' explained the boy. 'I leaned over and went "psst" and it didn't move.'

### HEAVEN HELP US!

An exasperated mother, whose son was always getting into mischief, finally asked him, 'How do you expect to get into Heaven?'

The boy thought it over and said, 'Well, I'll run in and out and in and out and keep slamming the door until St Peter says, "For Heaven's sake, Dylan, either come in or stay out!"'

### DAD'S A BABY

One summer evening during a violent thunderstorm a mother was tucking her son into bed. She was about to turn off the light when he asked with a tremor in his voice, 'Mummy will you sleep with me tonight?'

The mother smiled and gave him a reassuring hug. 'I can't dear,' she said. 'I have to sleep in Daddy's room.'

A long silence was broken at last by his shaky little voice, 'The big sissy.'

## DRESSY BITCH!

It was time during the Sunday morning service for the children's sermon. All the children were invited to come forward. One little girl was wearing a particularly pretty dress and, as she sat down, the pastor leaned over and said, 'That is a very pretty dress. Is it your Easter dress?'

The little girl replied, directly into the pastor's clip-on microphone, 'Yes, and my mother says it's a bitch to iron.'

## ALL IN TRANSLATION

A little boy was doing his maths homework. He said to himself, 'Two plus five, that son of a bitch is seven.' 'Three plus six, that son of a bitch is nine.'

His mother heard what he was saying and gasped, 'What are you doing?'

The little boy answered, 'I'm doing my maths homework, Mum.'

'And this is how your teacher taught you to do it?' the mother asked.

'Yes,' he answered.

Infuriated, the mother asked the teacher the next day, 'What are you teaching my son in maths?'

The teacher replied, 'Right now, we are learning addition.'

The mother asked, 'Are you teaching them to say two plus two, that son of a bitch is four?'

After the teacher stopped laughing, she answered, 'What I taught them was, two plus two, THE SUM OF WHICH is four.'

### MOUTH OF BABES

One day the new entrants' teacher was reading the story *Chicken Little* to her class. She came to the part of the story where Chicken Little tried to warn the farmer. She read: '... and so Chicken Little went up to the farmer and said, "The sky is falling, the sky is falling."' The teacher paused and then asked the class, 'And what do you think the farmer said?'

One little girl raised her hand and said, 'I think he said, "Shit, a talking chicken!"'

### OH, SUGAR!

A certain little girl, when asked her name, would reply, 'I'm Mr Sugarbrown's daughter.' Her mother told her this was wrong, and that she must say, 'I'm Jane Sugarbrown.'

The vicar spoke to her in Sunday school, and said, 'Aren't you Mr Sugarbrown's daughter?'

She replied, 'I thought I was but mother says I'm not.'

### SMOOTH TALKER

A little girl asked her mother, 'Can I go outside and play with the boys?'

Her mother replied, 'No, you can't play with the boys, they're too rough.'

The little girl thought about it for a few moments and asked, 'If I can find a smooth one, can I play with him?'

### BOOB JOB!

A little girl goes to the barber's shop with her father. She stands next to the barber's chair, while her dad gets his hair cut, eating a snack.

The barber says to her, 'Sweetheart, you're going to get hair on your Twinkie.'

She says, 'Yes, I know, and I'm going to get boobs too.'

### RISING UP

The minister started his children's sermon with a question: 'Who knows what a resurrection is?

Without missing a beat, a young boy says, 'If you have one lasting more than four hours, call your doctor.'

### LITTLE SMARTARSE

A teacher wanted to teach her students about self-esteem, so she asked anyone who thought they were stupid to stand up.

One kid stood up and the teacher was surprised. She didn't think anyone would stand up so she asked him, 'Why did you stand up?'

He answered, 'I didn't want to leave you standing up by yourself.'

## JOHNNY GETS IT RIGHT

The Year 10 teacher asks Jessica, 'What part of the human body increases to 10 times its normal size when excited?'

Jessica responds, 'That's disgusting! I don't have to answer that question!'

So the teacher asks little Johnny, who responds, 'That's easy — the pupil of the eye.'

'That's correct, Johnny. Very good!' And turning to Jessica, she says, 'I've three things to say to you, young lady. First, you didn't do your homework. Second, you have a dirty mind. And third, you're in for a big disappointment!'

## VERY CLEVER

A teacher was testing her students' knowledge of opposite words. She asked, 'What is the opposite of go?'

A student answered, 'Stop.'

'Very good,' the teacher replied. 'What is the opposite of adamant?'

Another student said, 'Eveant.'

Q: What's the difference between a cranky two-year-old and a duckling?

A: One is a whiny toddler, and the other is a tiny waddler.

## MORON BY CLOCKWORK

A man arrives at the repair shop to pick up his watch.

Shop man: 'I haven't finished repairing it yet, just give me a few more minutes.'

Man: 'Sure, no problem.'

The man goes and stands right next to the shop man, who notices him but continues working. After a while, he can't take it any more.

Shop man: 'Why are you sticking so close to me invading my space?'

Man: 'I'm only doing what the sign outside your door says.'

Shop man: 'And what is that, may I ask?'

Man: 'It says, "Watch Repairs".'

John: 'Hey Rick, why are you standing below the tube light with your mouth open?'

Rick: 'Because the doctor told me to have a light dinner, but I don't think this is working.'

'When I was a kid I used to pray every night for a new bicycle. Then I realised that the Lord doesn't work that way so I stole one and asked Him to forgive me.' — *Emo Philips*

## THAT'S MY BOY!

We were an air force family, but our son couldn't grasp that fact. Anytime someone asked what his father did, he'd say, 'He's in the army.' I told him umpteen times, 'Stop telling people I'm in the army!'

It finally seemed to hit home because on the admittance form for kindergarten, under 'father's profession', the teacher wrote, 'He doesn't know what his father does, but he's not in the army.'

As a 13-year-old, online dating is a tough thing. Every time I meet someone new, they end up in jail.

### WRONG THING TO SAY, MUM

A mother and her seven-year-old child are in the grocery store. The young boy suddenly screams to a random woman, 'You're an ugly bitch!'

The mother grabs her son and says, 'I'm so sorry, I must have told him a thousand times to not judge people on how they look.'

### FAST LEARNER

'When I was a boy of 14, my father was so ignorant I could hardly stand to have the old man around. But when I got to be 21, I was astonished at how much the old man had learned in seven years.' — *Mark Twain*

Two kindergarten girls were talking outside. One said, 'You won't believe what I saw on the patio yesterday — a condom!'

The second girl asked, 'What's a "patio"?'

### LOVE MATCH

Little Billy asks his dad for a telly in his room. Dad reluctantly agrees. Next day, Billy comes downstairs and asks, 'Dad, what's "love juice"?'

Dad looks horrified and tells Billy all about sex. Billy just sits there with his mouth open in amazement. Dad says, 'So what were you watching?'

Billy says, 'Wimbledon.'

## MOTHER CAN'T WIN

There once was a five-year-old boy who enjoyed playing with his train set. One afternoon, his mother happened to be standing by the door listening to the boy play. She was shocked when she heard him saying, 'All right, all of you sons of bitches who want to get on the train, get on the train. And all of you sons of bitches who want to get off the train, get off the train. And all of you sons of bitches who want to change seats, change seats now 'cause the train's getting ready to leave. Whoo whooooo.'

The mother was just devastated, so she scolded her son and said to him, 'Now, son, I want you to go upstairs and take your nap, and when you get up, you can't play with your train set for two hours.'

So the boy took his nap and didn't even mention his train set for two hours. After the two hours were up, the boy asked his mother if he could play with his train set again. She said yes and asked him if he understood why he was punished. He nodded his head yes, and off he went. The mother stood by the door to listen to what her son would say. The boy sat down next to his train set and calmly said, 'Whoo whoooooo. All of you ladies and gentlemen who want to get on the train, get on the train. All of you ladies and gentlemen who want to get off the train, get off the train. And all of you sons of bitches who are pissed 'cause the train is two hours late, go talk to the bitch in the kitchen.'

## REAL STRANGER DANGER!

A little boy is leaving school at the end of the day. As he strolls along the footpath, a car pulls up to the curb, and a man winds down the window.

'Hey, kid, I've got candy in my car. Hop in and I'll give it to you.'

'No. I'm not going to.' The boy walks on. Further down the road, the car pulls over again.

'Hey there, kid, if you get in my car, I'll give you all this candy, and a big bottle of cola. How about it?'

'No way! Now leave me alone.' The boy walks on, quickening his pace. The car again pulls over beside him.

'Look, kid, I've got a puppy at home you'd love to see. Get in and I'll take you there. You can have all the candy and the cola on the way. What d'you say to that?'

The boy is getting agitated. He stops walking and leans down to the car window. 'Look, I don't care what you promise me, Dad. I'm NOT riding in your Lada!'

## COOKIE 'SIN'!

In a Catholic school cafeteria, a nun places a note in front of a pile of apples: 'Only take one. God is watching.'

Further down the line is a pile of cookies. A little boy makes his own note: 'Take all you want. God is watching the apples.'

# OLD GEEZERS

This isn't a chapter on the bodily calamities that often hit the three score and 10-plus oldies. That would be unfair. No, 'Old Geezers' generally provides jokes that rejoice in the naughty oldies that make fools of all and sundry — policemen/women are cases in point — and have great fun. The antics of the old jokesters almost want you to join them sooner rather than later.

## SCHOOL MATES

Have you ever been guilty of looking at others your own age and thinking, 'Surely I can't look that old?' Well, you'll love this one!

I was sitting in the waiting room for my first appointment with a new dentist. I noticed his dental diploma, which bore his full name. Suddenly, I remembered a tall, handsome, dark-haired boy with the same name had been in my secondary school class some 40-odd years ago. Could he be the same guy that I had a secret crush on, way back then? Upon seeing him, however, I quickly discarded any such thought.

This balding, grey-haired man with the deeply lined face was far too old to have been my classmate. After he examined my teeth, I asked him if he had attended Morgan Park Secondary School.

'Yes, yes, I did, I'm a Morganner!' he beamed with pride.

'When did you leave to go to college?' I asked.

'In 1965,' he answered. 'Why do you ask?'

'You were in my class!' I exclaimed.

He looked at me closely.

Then the ugly, old, bald, wrinkled, fat-arsed, grey-haired, decrepit bastard asked, 'What subject did you teach?'

## OLD GEEZER LESSON

An old geezer became very bored in retirement and decided to open a medical clinic in Ashburton. He put a sign up outside that said: 'Dr Geezer's clinic. Get your treatment for $500. If not cured, get back $1000.' Doctor Young, who was positive that this old geezer didn't know beans about medicine, thought this would be a great opportunity to make some easy money. So he went to Dr Geezer's clinic.

Dr Young: 'Dr Geezer, I have lost all taste in my mouth. Can you please help me?'

Dr Geezer: 'Nurse, please bring medicine from box 22 and put three drops in the patient's mouth.'

Dr Young: 'Aaah! This is petrol.'

Dr Geezer: 'Congratulations, you've got your taste back. That will be $500.'

Dr Young is annoyed and goes back after a couple of days spent figuring out how to recover his money.

Dr Young: 'I have lost my memory. I can't remember anything.'

Dr Geezer: 'Nurse, please bring medicine from box 22 and put three drops in the patient's mouth.'
Dr Young: 'Oh no you don't. That's petrol.'
Dr Geezer: 'Congratulations, you've got your memory back. That will be $500.'
Dr Young, after having lost $1000, leaves angrily and comes back after several more days.
Dr Young: 'My eyesight has become weak. I can hardly see anything.'
Dr Geezer: Well, I don't have any medicine for that, so here's your $1000 back,' giving him a $10 bill.
Dr Young: 'But this is only $10.'
Dr Geezer: 'Congratulations, you've got your vision back. That will be $500.'
Moral of the story: Just because you're 'Young' doesn't mean that you can outsmart an 'Old Geezer'.

## IMPORTANT AMUSEMENT

The wife and myself had come to Palmerston North to pick up a few things. We came out of Collinson & Cunningham's store and saw a cop writing a ticket for illegal parking right in front of us on the curb. So, we asked him nicely to give a couple of retirees a break. But he paid us no attention and kept writing.

Just loud enough for him to hear, my wife said, 'What a wanker.'

The cop looked up, stared at my wife, then started writing out another ticket.

I said, 'Honey, this guy probably just learned to read and

write, and he's so proud of himself, he's showing off.'

The cop tore off the second ticket and started on a third.

We kept making comments and he kept writing tickets till he was up to about half a dozen.

Finally, glaring at us, the cop left, and we walked on down the street. We didn't care about the tickets. We always take the bus into town, and anyway, that car was one of those obnoxious Remuera taxis.

Being retired, we always try to find ways to keep ourselves amused. We feel it's important.

## MEMORY LAPSE

There was an elderly couple who in their old age noticed that they were getting a lot more forgetful, so they decided to go to the doctor. The doctor told them that they should start writing things down so they didn't forget. They went home and the old lady told her husband to get her a bowl of ice cream.

'You might want to write it down,' she said.

The husband said, 'No, I can remember that you want a bowl of ice cream.'

She then told her husband that she wanted a bowl of ice cream with whipped cream. 'Write it down,' she told him, and again he said, 'No, no, I can remember — you want a bowl of ice cream with whipped cream.'

Then the old lady said she wanted a bowl of ice cream with whipped cream and a cherry on top. 'Write it down,' she told her husband, and again he said, 'No, I got it. You want a bowl of ice cream with whipped cream and a cherry on top.'

So, he goes to get the ice cream and spends an unusually long time in the kitchen, over 30 minutes. He comes out to his wife and hands her a plate of eggs and bacon.

The old lady stares at the plate for a moment, then looks at her husband and asks, 'Where's the toast?'

## SEVENTY-FIVE YEARS OF IGNORANCE

A very elderly couple is having an elegant dinner to celebrate their seventy-fifth wedding anniversary.

The old man leans forward and says softly to his wife, 'Dear, there is something that I must ask you. It has always bothered me that our tenth child Archibald never quite looked like the rest of our children. Now I want to assure you that these 75 years have been the most wonderful experience I could have ever hoped for and your answer cannot take all that away. But, I must know, did he have a different father?'

The wife drops her head, unable to look her husband in the eye, pauses for a moment and then confesses, 'Yes. Yes, he did.'

The old man is very shaken. The reality of what his wife was admitting hit him harder than he had expected. With a tear in his eye he asks, 'Who? Who was he? Who was the father?'

Again, the old woman drops her head, saying nothing at first as she tries to muster the courage to tell the truth to her husband. Then, finally, she says, 'You.'

## WHAT A SURPRISE

A 77-year-old man is having a drink in a Wellington bar. Suddenly, a gorgeous woman enters and sits down a few seats away. She is so attractive that the old bloke can't take his eyes off her. After a short while, the woman notices him staring and approaches him.

Before the man has time to apologise, the girl looks him deep in the eyes and says to him in a sultry tone, 'I'll do anything you'd like. Anything you can imagine in your wildest dreams. It doesn't matter how extreme or unusual it is, I'm game. But I want $100 and there's another condition.'

Completely stunned by the sudden turn of events, the man asks her what her second condition is.

'You have to tell me what you want me to do in just three words.'

The man takes a moment to consider the offer from the beautiful woman. He whips out his wallet and puts $100 in her hand. He then looks her squarely in the eyes and says slowly and clearly, 'Paint my house.'

## SCRIPTURE CONFUSION

An elderly woman had just returned to her home from an evening church service, when she was startled by an intruder. She caught the man in the act of robbing her home of its valuables and yelled, 'Stop! Acts 2:38. Repent and be baptised in the name of Jesus Christ, so that your sins can be forgiven.'

The burglar stopped in his tracks. The woman calmly

called the police and explained what she had done.

As the police officer cuffed the burglar to take him in, he asked him, 'Why did you just stand there? All the old lady did was yell a scripture to you.'

'Scripture?' replied the burglar, 'She said she had an axe and two 38s!'

## DEVIL'S KIN

One Sunday morning, Satan appeared before a small-town congregation. Everyone started screaming and running for the church door, trampling each other in a frantic effort to get away. Soon, everyone was gone, except for an elderly gentleman who sat there calmly.

Satan walked up to the man and said, 'Don't you know who I am?'

The man replied, 'Yep, sure do.'

Satan asked, 'Aren't you going to run?'

'Nope, sure ain't,' said the man.

Perturbed, Satan asked, 'Why aren't you afraid of me?'

The man calmly replied, 'Been married to your sister for over 48 years.'

## THAT'S TELLING HIM

A 70-year-old man asked his wife, 'Do you feel sad when you see me making eyes at younger women?'

'No, not at all.' replied the wife. 'Even dogs chase cars, doesn't mean they can drive them.'

## POISONED BROTH

My high school assignment was to ask a veteran about World War II. Since my father had served in the Philippines during the war, I chose him.

After a few basic questions, I very gingerly asked, 'Did you ever kill anyone?'

Dad got quiet. Then, in a soft voice, he said, 'Probably. I was the cook.'

## DECENT HINT

My 90-year-old dad was giving a talk at our local library about his World War II experiences. During the question-and-answer period, he was asked, 'How did you know the war was over?'

He replied, 'When they stopped shooting at me.'

## GREAT TASTE

I was in the bathroom brushing my teeth when my squad leader barged in. He was holding a toothbrush, which he proceeded to use to scrub underneath the rim of a toilet.

'What are you doing?' I asked.

'Having a laugh on the new guy,' he said with a grin.

'You do know that he could get ill from the bacteria on the toilet?'

His reply was quick and to the point: 'You didn't.'

As a hobby I started taking walks around the old clock tower. It's a great way to pass the time.

## THANKS GRAMPS

A young man who was an avid golfer found himself with a few hours to spare one afternoon. He figured that if he hurried and played very fast, he could get in nine holes before he had to head home.

Just as he was about to tee off, an old gentleman shuffled onto the tee and asked if he could accompany the young man as he was golfing alone. Not being able to say no, he allowed the old gent to join him. To his surprise, the old man played fairly quickly. He didn't hit the ball far but plodded along consistently and didn't waste much time. Finally, they reached the ninth fairway and the young man found himself with a tough shot.

There was a large pine tree right in front of his ball — and directly between his ball and the green. After several minutes of debating how to hit the shot, the old man finally said, 'You know, when I was your age, I'd hit the ball right over that tree.'

With that challenge placed before him, the youngster swung hard, hit the ball up, right smack into the top of the tree trunk and it thudded back onto the ground not a foot from where it had originally lain.

The old man offered one more comment: 'Of course, when I was your age, that pine tree was only three feet tall.'

## GROOVY GRANNY

A boy asks his granny: 'Have you seen my pills, they were labelled LSD?'

Granny replies: 'Bugger the pills, have you seen the dragons in the kitchen?'

## SILENT BUT VIOLENT?

An elderly couple is attending church. About halfway through, the wife leans over and whispers to her husband, 'I just let out a silent fart; what do you think I should do?'

He replies, 'Put a new battery in your hearing aid.'

## HEROES FROM THE TRON

Travelling through the country, an old couple drives into a gas station. The attendant asks the old man, 'Where you folks from? I know everybody in this town.'

The old man says, 'We're from Hamilton.'

Hard of hearing, the old lady nudges her husband, 'What did he say, Dad?'

The old man answers her, 'He asked us where we are from.'

'Oh,' replies the old woman.

The old man tells the attendant to fill up the tank and check the tyres. When that's all done, the attendant tells the old man, 'You know, the worst piece of ass I ever had was from Hamilton.'

The old lady nudges her husband once more and asks, 'What did he say, Dad?'

The husband replies, 'He thinks he knows you, Mum.'

## OBVIOUSLY ARGUMENTATIVE

A man and woman had been married for more than 60 years. They had shared everything. They had talked about everything. They had kept no secrets from each other, except that the little old woman had a shoe box in the top of her closet that she had cautioned her husband never to open or ask her about.

For all of these years, he had never thought about the box, but one day, the little old woman got very sick and the doctor said she would not recover. In trying to sort out their affairs, the old man took down the shoe box and took it to his wife's bedside.

She agreed that it was time that he should know what was in the box. When he opened it, he found two crocheted dolls and a stack of money totalling $95,000. He asked her about the contents.

'When we were to be married,' she said, 'my grandmother told me the secret of a happy marriage was to never argue. She told me that if I ever got angry with you, I should just keep quiet and crochet a doll.'

The old man was so moved, he had to fight back tears. Only two precious dolls were in the box. She had only been angry with him two times in all those years of living and loving. He almost burst with happiness.

'Honey,' he said, 'that explains the dolls, but what about all of this money? Where did it come from?'

'Oh,' she said. 'That's the money I made from selling the dolls.'

## WINDOW OF OPPORTUNITY

Last year, I replaced all the windows in my house with those expensive double-pane energy-efficient kind. But this week, I got a call from the contractor complaining that his work had been completed a whole year and I had yet to pay for them.

Boy, oh boy, did we go around! Just because I'm blonde, doesn't mean that I'm automatically stupid. So, I proceeded to tell him just what his fast-talking sales guy had told me last year. He said that in one year, the windows would pay for themselves.

There was silence on the other end of the line, so I just hung up, and he hasn't called back. Guess he was embarrassed.

## CRUSHED NUTS SUNDAE?

A little old man shuffled into an ice-cream parlour and pulled himself slowly, painfully, up onto a stool. After catching his breath, he ordered a banana split.

The waitress asked kindly, 'Crushed nuts?'

'No,' he replied, 'arthritis.'

## DUBIOUS BRAGGING

Three men were gathering one day to talk about how successful their sons were doing.

The first man says, 'My son has been doing so successfully as a lawyer he got a mansion and shares it with his friend.'

The second man says, 'My son has been so successful as a doctor that he bought a convertible and a private jet for his friend.'

The third man says, 'Well, my son hasn't been so "successful". In fact, I just learned he is gay and I've accepted that fact. I guess he must be doing well though because he lives in a mansion with his friend and owns a private jet and a convertible.'

### GETTING A CLOSER LOOK

Old lady: 'Officer, there is a man exposing himself in the next building.'
Officer: 'Okay, we'll be right over, madam.'
(Five minutes later at her apartment.)
Officer: 'Which way, madam?'
Old lady: 'This way officer, he's still shamelessly baring himself.'
Officer: 'Where is he, madam? I don't see a naked man.'
Old lady: 'Oh, you have to look through this telescope.'

### THE UNKINDEST CUT!

A poor little lonely old lady lived in a house with only her cat as a friend. One day, the lights went out as she sat knitting; she had been unable to pay the electric bill. So, she went up to the attic and got an old oil lamp from her childhood. As she rubbed it clean a genie appeared and allowed her three wishes.

'First, I want to be so rich I never have to worry about money again.'

'Second, I want to be young and beautiful again.'

'And last, I want you to change my little cat into a handsome prince.'

Poof!

As the smoke cleared, she saw she was surrounded

by big bags of coins, and that in the mirror was a young beautiful woman. She turned as the handsome prince walked in the door, held her in his arms and said, 'Now I'll bet you're sorry you took me to the vet for that little operation.'

## BODILY MIS-FUNCTIONS

Three old men are sitting on the porch of a retirement home.

The first says, 'Fellas, I got real problems. I'm 70 years old. Every morning at seven o'clock I get up and I try to urinate. All day long, I try to urinate. They give me all kinds of medicine but nothing helps.'

The second old man says, 'You think you have problems. I'm 80 years old. Every morning at eight I get up and try to move my bowels. I try all day long. They give me all kinds of stuff but nothing helps.'

Finally, the third old man speaks up, 'Fellas, I'm 90 years old. Every morning at seven I urinate. Every morning at eight, I move my bowels. Every morning at nine sharp I wake up.'

## MARRIAGE LINES

One day an older fella was in for a check-up. After his examination, his doctor was amazed.

'Holy cow! Mr Edwards, I must say that you are in the greatest shape of any 64-year-old I have ever examined!'

'Did I say I was 64?'

'Well, no, did I read your chart wrong?'

'Damn right, you did! I'm 85!'

'Eighty-five! Unbelievable! You would be in great shape if you were 25! How old was your father when he died?'

'Did I say he was dead?'

'You mean . . .'

'Damn straight! He's 106 and going strong!'

'My Lord! What a healthy family you must come from! How long did your grandfather live?'

'Did I say he was dead?'

'No! You can't mean . . .'

'Damn straight! He's 126, and getting married next week!'

'One hundred and twenty-six! Truly amazing, Mr Edwards. But gee, I wouldn't think a man would want to get married at that age!'

'Did I say he *wanted* to get married?'

## RUBBER THINGY

An old man gets onto a crowded bus and no one gives him a seat. As the bus shakes and rattles, the old man's cane slips on the floor and he falls.

As he gets up, a seven-year-old kid, sitting nearby, turns to him and says, 'If you put a little rubber thingy on the end of your stick, it wouldn't slip.'

The old man snaps back, 'Well, if your daddy did the same thing seven years ago, I would have a seat today.'

## SIMPLE ARITHMETIC

A middle-aged couple are discussing their plans.

'When I'm 80,' the man says to his wife, 'I plan on finding myself a pretty 20-year-old, and I'll have myself a real good time.'

The wife is a bit fazed, but thinks up a reply. 'When I'm 80, I plan on finding myself a handsome 20-year-old, and 20 goes into 80 a lot easier than 80 goes into 20!'

## BOASTFUL FELLOW

An old man goes to a church, and is making a confession.

Man: 'Father, I am 75 years old. I have been married for 50 years. All these years I have been faithful to my wife, but yesterday I was intimate with an 18-year-old.'

Father: 'When was the last time you made a confession?'

Man: 'I never have, I am Jewish.'

Father: 'Then why are telling me all this?'

Man: 'I am telling everybody . . .'

## DOG FOOD HEAVEN

Last week at The Warehouse I had a big bag of Happy Dog food in my cart, and as I passed a woman shopper she asked me if I had a dog. What did she think I had, a giraffe? Well, I'm retired and always on the lookout for fun, so I told her I didn't actually have a dog, but I was starting on the 'Happy Dog diet' again.

'It's really simple,' I said. 'You just keep your pockets full of Happy Dog chunks, and every time you feel your stomach rumble you just pop a couple in your mouth. It's nutritionally complete, has lots of fibre, and last time I lost five kilograms.'

A few more people had stopped and were listening by this time, and they all seemed mesmerised. When you live long enough to be retired, you realise people will believe anything if you make it interesting.

So I really cranked it up and said, 'Even though it worked great and I lost weight, I'm not sure it's a good idea, because last time I wound up in intensive care.'

The woman opened her eyes wide and asked, 'Were you poisoned by the dog food?'

'No,' I said. 'I ran into the street to sniff a golden retriever's butt and a motorcycle slammed into me.'

## GROWING OLD

First you forget names; then you forget faces; then you forget to zip up your fly; and then you forget to unzip your fly.

## GRIEVING WITH A BANG

A funeral director's phone call to a grieving wife: 'I realise we all grieve in our own way, ma'am, but the crematorium staff did not appreciate the fireworks you put in your late husband's pockets.'

## UNDIE ART

A doctor tells an old couple at his office he needs to get a stool sample, a urine sample and a blood test from the old man. Hard of hearing, the old man asks his wife what the doctor said.

The wife replies, 'He needs a pair of your underwear.'

# OLDIES BUT GOODIES

Remembering old jokes can often be a source of frustration. You know it was good when you heard it, but you can't remember it to impress your mates. Or worse, you recall how it went, but for the life of you, the laughter-inducing finale deserts you. This chapter is a personal choice one. Jokes you may remember hearing as a pimply-faced youth, still bringing a smile — as opposed to the goofy guffaw of all those years ago — like the one about the statues and the pigeons.

## HAPPY MEMORIES, PEOPLE

Although Oscar Wilde's life was not one of particular happiness, his sayings are often quoted for their wit and profound sense, as the following selection of his most memorable quotes and quips illustrates:

'Always forgive your enemies; nothing annoys them so much.'

'Be yourself. Everyone else is already taken.'

'All women become like their mother, that is their tragedy. No man does, and that is his.'

'With freedom, books, flowers and the moon, who could not be happy?'

'If you want to tell people the truth, make them laugh, otherwise they will kill you.'

'It is absurd to divide people into good and bad. People are either charming or tedious.'

'Education is an admirable thing, but it's well to remember from time to time that nothing that is worth knowing can be taught.'

'The public is wonderfully tolerant. It forgives everything except genius.'

'Some cause happiness wherever they go; others whenever they go.'

'A cynic is a man who knows the price of everything and the value of nothing.'

'You can never be overdressed or overeducated.'

'I don't want to go to Heaven. None of my friends are there.'

'Women are meant to be loved, not to be understood.'

'A good friend will always stab you in the front.'

'Anyone who lives within their means suffers from a lack of imagination.'

'You will always be fond of me. I represent to you all the sins you never had the courage to commit.'

'Life is far too serious a thing ever to talk seriously about.'

'There is only one thing in the world worse than being talked about, and that is not being talked about.'

'I am so clever that sometimes I don't understand a single word of what I am saying.'

'We are all in the gutter, but some of us are looking at the stars.'

'The truth is rarely pure and never simple.'

'Yes, I am a dreamer. For a dreamer is one who can only find his way by moonlight, and his punishment is that he sees the dawn before the rest of the world.'

## ROOM WITH A CRUCIFIX

Jesus walks into a hotel one night. He throws a bag of nails on the bar and asks the patron if he can put him up for the night!

## DODGY TIME ON RAOUL

Tom was a weatherman at the meteorological office in Wellington, when he was chosen to do a tour of duty on Raoul Island in the Kermadec group, north of New Zealand.

The Department of Conservation have officers stationed there, so he wouldn't be on his own. It's a pretty cool place but Tom had worries. He is a sociable sort of guy who has a new girlfriend, Mary, and he fears he will miss her and the good sex they have, being so isolated on Raoul. He was given a list of what to take for the three months he would be there. Good books, good torch and, strangely to Tom, a pair of gumboots.

When he got to Raoul, he asked a DoC bloke what the gumboots were needed for because his office had provided some tramping boots for him.

'Oh, the gummies are for your "extracurricular activities",' the DoC guy said. 'You find yourself getting quite lonely and frustrated here. We often go out and grab a ewe and have sex with it if we're feeling randy. The gumboots are for sticking the ewe's legs in to keep them still.'

Shocked, Tom said, 'You won't catch me doing that, I'm not that desperate.'

So Tom settled into life on Raoul Island. The workday was okay but trying to sleep at night was difficult. He missed Mary and he often succumbed to giving himself the odd 'five knuckle shuffle' in the darkness of his bed.

As the weeks went by, he found that activity frustrating because he struggled to remember what Mary looked like and his image of her often morphed into memories of former girlfriends. He began to wonder whether the DoC bloke's 'extracurricular activities' was worth a shot. He ummed and ahhed about it, before he got up, put his gumboots on, and crept out of his hut, making his way to the sheep.

Tom grabbed a ewe and it was easy enough to tether her in his gumboots, and he was away. He was having a surprisingly pleasant time of it, when suddenly he was flooded with the light from a dozen torches.

'You bastards,' Tom yelled. 'You were having me on. You don't have sex with sheep, do you? You made me look a fool.'

One of the DoC blokes said, 'Yes we do, but why did you pick such an ugly one!'

**Q:** When is a door not a door?
**A:** When it is ajar.

**Q:** What do you call the largest mammal in the world that lives in a palace?
**A:** The Prince of Wales, of course.

**Q:** What hangs on a man's thigh and wants to poke the hole it's often poked before?
**A:** A key.

**Q:** Who is the greatest chicken killer in Shakespeare?
**A:** Macbeth, because he did murder most foul.

**Q:** What's the similarity between a balloon floating in mid-air and a vagrant?
**A:** They both have no visible means of support.

**Q:** Why are young ladies and young men like arrows?
**A:** Because they are all aquiver in the presence of a beau.

'A clear conscience is usually the sign of a bad memory.'
— *Steven Wright*

### ASK A SILLY QUESTION . . .

While passing a house on a road, two salesmen spotted a very peculiar chimney. They asked a flaxen-haired young urchin standing near the house if it dragged well? Whereupon the aforementioned urchin gave them a stinging retort.

'Yes, it draws the attention of all the damned fools that pass on the road.'

When I lost my rifle, the army charged me $85. That's why in the navy, the captain goes down with the ship.

### PAINFUL LESSON

'Halt!' shouted our drill instructor. He had noticed that, for the umpteenth time, a recruit kept going to his right on a left command. Our instructor approached the directionally challenged marine and stomped on his left foot.

'Now,' he said, 'when I say "left", it's the one that hurts!'

'I didn't attend the funeral, but I sent a nice letter saying I approved of it.' — *Mark Twain*

'He loves nature in spite of what it did to him.'
— *Forrest Tucker*

### A FINE REVENGE

There are these two nude statues, man and woman, standing across from each other in a secluded park. A few hundred years after they've been put in place, an angel flutters down to them. A wave of his hand, and suddenly the statues have been given flesh, and they step down from their pedestals.

The angel says, 'I have been sent to grant the mutual request you both have made after hundreds of years of standing across from each other, unable to move. But be quick — you only have 15 minutes until you must become statues again.'

The man looks at the woman, and they both flush, and giggle, and run off into some underbrush. An intense rustling comes from the bushes, and seven minutes later, they both come back to the angel, obviously satisfied.

The angel smiles at the couple. 'That was only seven

minutes — why not go back and do it again?'

The former statues look at each other for a minute, and then the woman says, 'Why not? But let's reverse it this time — you hold down the pigeon, and I'll shit on it . . .'

**Q:** Did you hear about the fat, alcoholic transvestite?
**A:** All he wanted to do was eat, drink and be Mary.

'I have never killed a man, but I have read many obituaries with great pleasure.' — *Clarence Darrow*

'Sometimes I need what only you can provide: your absence.' — *Ashleigh Brilliant*

## WOMAN PUTS RHYME INTO WEDLOCK

The local news station was interviewing an 80-year-old lady because she had just got married for the fourth time. The interviewer asked her questions about her life, about what it felt like to be marrying again at 80, and then about her new husband's occupation.

'He's a funeral director,' she answered.

'Interesting,' the newsman thought. He then asked her if she wouldn't mind telling him a little about her first three husbands and what they did for a living.

She paused for a few moments, needing time to reflect on all those years. After a short time, a smile came to her face and she answered proudly, explaining that she had first married a banker when she was in her twenties, then a circus ringmaster when in her forties, and a preacher when in her sixties, and now — in her eighties — a funeral director.

The interviewer looked at her, quite astonished, and asked why she had married four men with such diverse careers.

She smiled and explained, 'I married one for the money, two for the show, three to get ready, and four to go.'

Two reasons why it's so hard to solve a redneck murder:
1. The DNA all matches.
2. There are no dental records.

### FOKKING HELL!

A World War II pilot is reminiscing before school children about his days in the air force.

'In 1942,' he says, 'the situation was really tough. The Germans had a very strong air force, I remember.' He continues, 'One day, I was protecting the bombers and suddenly, out of the clouds, these fokkers appeared.

At this point, several of the children giggle.

'I looked up, and right above me was one of them. I aimed at him and shot him down. They were swarming. I immediately realised that there was another fokker behind me.'

At this instant the girls in the auditorium start to giggle and boys start to laugh. The teacher stands up and says in a very prim manner, 'I think I should point out that "Fokker" was the name of the German-Dutch aircraft company.'

'That's true,' says the pilot, 'but these fokkers were flying Messerschmitts.'

## STAND UP TO BE DAMNED

A sobered-up drunk is at Sunday Mass listening to a long, boring sermon. Still feeling hungover and tired, he finally nods off to sleep, hoping no one will notice. The priest has been watching him all along and at the end of the sermon decides to make an example out of him.

'Whoever in this room would like a place in Heaven, please stand up,' he exclaims. The whole room stands up except of course the sleeping drunk.

Obviously displeased, the priest now says loudly, 'And he who would like to find a place in Hell, please STAND UP.'

The drunk, catching only the last part, groggily stands up only to find that he's the only one standing. Confused and embarrassed, he says, 'I don't know what we're voting on here, Father, but it sure seems like you and me are the only ones standing for it.'

A girl criticised my apartment so I knocked her flat.

## ONE-TRACK MIND

An Englishman was flying across the Pacific on Delta/Northwest and decided he had to go to the toilet. So, he got up and started walking down the aisle, but just as he passed the plane door it malfunctioned, opened and he was sucked out. Miraculously, he survived landing in the water and saw a tropical island nearby. He swam to it, certain that he would soon be rescued. However, 15 years passed and no one came to his rescue. Fortunately, there was a spring on the island and he survived on coconuts and fish.

Finally, one day, as he was drawing sand pictures at the beach, he sees a woman in a trim-fitting scuba outfit emerge from the ocean. She is beautiful! She says, 'Are you Fred Quimby?'

He says, 'Why, yes, I am.'

'Congratulations, I am from Rescue Inc., and we have been attempting to find you since you were lost. Now tell me, how long has it been since you've had a smoke?'

'Well, of course it's been about 15 years.'

So she reaches down the front of her wetsuit on the left side and pulls out a packet of Player's cigarettes.

'How in the world did you know that my favourite brand was Player's?' he asks.

'We have researched all of your preferences very carefully, Fred. We want to do a good job.'

So as Fred is taking a deep, satisfying drag on his cigarette, the rescuer says, 'And how long has it been since you've had a drink?'

'Well, that's 15 years too.'

So she reaches down inside the wetsuit on the other side and pulls out a bottle of Jack Daniel's.

'How did you know that Jack Daniel's was my favourite drink?' he asks.

'Well, Fred, as I said, we have looked into all of those things as well. Do you mind if I have a drink too?'

'No, of course not.' And they both put a couple away.

Then, as she starts to peel off the wetsuit, she says, 'And tell me, Fred, how long has it been since you've played around?'

'Don't tell me you've got a set of golf clubs in there too!'

The first civilian on the space shuttle was an English teacher. Now she's history.

### MAFIA BOZOS

The Mafia was looking for a new man to make weekly collections from all the private businesses that they were 'protecting'. Feeling the heat from the police, they decide to use a deaf person for this job; if he were to get caught, he wouldn't be able to tell the police what he was doing.

Well, on his first week, the deaf collector picks up more than $40,000. He gets greedy, decides to keep the money and stashes it in a safe place. The Mafia soon realises that their collection is late and sends some of their hoods after the deaf collector.

The hoods find the deaf collector and ask him where the money is. The deaf collector can't communicate with them, so they drag the guy to an interpreter.

'Ask him where da money is.'

The interpreter signs, 'Where's the money?'

The deaf man replies, 'I don't know what you're talking about.'

'He says he doesn't know what you're talking about,' says the interpreter.

One of the hoods pulls out a .38 and places it in the ear of the deaf collector. 'NOW ask him where the money is.'

Again the interpreter signs, 'Where's the money?'

The deaf collector replies, 'The $40,000 is in a tree stump in Central Park.'

The interpreter's eyes light up and he says to the hood, 'He says he still doesn't know what you're talking about and doesn't think you have the balls to pull the trigger.'

## BETTING MAN

There was this guy who went into a bar. He went up to the barman and said, 'Bartender, are you a bettin' man?'

The bartender replied, 'Certainly! I'm ALWAYS a bettin' man!'

To which the man said, 'I'll bet you $50 that I can lick my right eye.'

The barman thought about this for a while and finally agreed to the bet. The man reached up and pulled out his glass right eye and licked it. The bartender groaned and begrudgingly gave the man his $50, telling him to leave his bar.

A week or so later, the same man appeared in the bar. He went up to the barman and said, 'Bartender, are you still a bettin' man?'

The bartender replied, 'Certainly! I told you I'm ALWAYS a bettin' man!'

To which the man said, 'I'll bet you $100 that I can bite my left eye.'

Well, the barman thought he had him on this one. There was no way that he had two glass eyes, so the bartender agreed. The man reached up to his mouth, pulled out his dentures and clicked them on his left eye. The bartender moaned and paid the man his $100, telling him to get out of his bar.

A week or so later, the same man ventured into the bar again. He went up to the barman and said, 'Bartender, are you still a bettin' man?'

The bartender said, although with a little caution this time, 'Certainly! I told you I'm ALWAYS a bettin' man!'

To which the man said, 'Give me a shot of whiskey.'

The bartender poured the man a shot and he drank it down. Slamming the glass on the bar, he said, 'I'll bet you $500 that you can spin me around on this bar stool and I can piss in that glass right where it lays and not miss a drop.'

Well, the barman's eyes lit up. Here was one time that he was certain that he would win! 'Agreed!' he cried. Coming out from behind the bar, he grabbed onto the man's bar stool and spun it as hard as he could.

Well, the man just let loose and piss flew everywhere! Not so much as one drop even came close to the glass and the bartender was soaked.

When he was done, the bartender was laughing and laughing and holding out his hand. The man pulled out his wallet and gave him his $500. But the barman was puzzled and as he was wiping off his face, he asked the man, 'Why did you bet me $500 that you could piss in that shot glass on the bar when you had to have known there wasn't any possible way to do it?'

The man just smiled and told him, 'You may have won $500 off me, but I bet that guy over in the corner $10,000 that I could piss all over you and your bar and you would just laugh!'

## WALLPAPER AFICIONADO

This man is suffering from extreme headaches so he goes to his doctor.

Man: 'Doctor, I seem to be having these bad headaches and nothing I do seems to cure them.'

Doctor: 'Well, one thing I always do to relieve my headaches is put my head between my wife's breasts and go prrrrrrrrrr with my lips.'

Man: 'Thanks, doc, I think I'll try it.'

Two weeks pass and the man goes back to his doctor.

Doctor: 'Well, have your headaches cleared up?'

Man: 'They sure have. I tried what you said. And by the way I love the wallpaper in your home!'

## HOLY CONDOM!

Three women are having lunch, discussing their husbands.

The first says, 'My husband is cheating on me, I just know it. I found a pair of stockings in his jacket pocket, and they weren't mine!'

The second says, 'My husband is also cheating on me, I just know it. I found a condom in his wallet, so I poked it full of holes with my sewing needle!'

The third woman fainted.

## WOULD YOU ADAM AND EVE IT?!

God one day decided he ought to check in with Adam to see how things were going.

'Adam, how are things going?'

Adam replies that he considers himself quite fortunate

to be living in such a beautiful and peaceful place, but he did have a couple of questions to ask, if the Lord didn't mind, of course.

'No problem,' said the Lord, 'ask away.'

'Well, Lord, I was wondering why you made Eve so beautiful? Not that I'm complaining, mind you.'

'Adam, I made Eve so beautiful so that you would like her.'

'Oh, well, yes, I do like her very much. Thank you, Lord. You made her so beautiful, but why is it then that you made her so stupid?'

'Well, Adam, I had to make sure she liked you too!'

## CHEAP SCAPE

Two men are occupying booths in a public toilet, when one calls to the other, 'There is no toilet paper over here — do you have any over there?'

The second man replies, 'No, sorry, I don't seem to have any, either.'

The first man then asks, 'Well, do you have a magazine or newspaper?'

The second man says, 'No, sorry!'

The first man pauses, then inquires, 'Do you have change for a 20?'

## OFFICER IGNORANCE

A young subaltern was posted to a British army detachment in the desert. On his tour of the facility with the master sergeant, he noticed a group of camels.

'What are those for?'

'The men use them when they want to have sex . . .'

'Don't say another word, sergeant. That is the most disgusting thing I have ever heard. Get rid of those camels immediately.'

'Yes, sir.'

A few weeks went by and the young officer began to get rather horny. He called the sergeant over and asked, 'Where are the camels we used to have?' The sergeant replied that he had sold them to a Bedouin that camped nearby. 'Take me to them, please.'

The officer and the sergeant went over to the Bedouin camp and found the camels. The officer told the sergeant to leave him alone with the camels, then picked out the most attractive one, and proceeded to have sex with it.

On the way back to the camp, the officer asked, 'Sergeant, do the men actually enjoy sex with the camels?'

The sergeant looked at the officer in astonishment and exclaimed, 'I don't know. They use them to ride into town where the girls are.'

## GORILLA IN HEAT

A certain zoo had acquired a very rare species of gorilla. Within a few weeks, the gorilla, a female, became very ornery, and difficult to handle. Upon examination, the zoo veterinarian determined the problem: she was in heat. But what to do? There was no male of this species available.

While reflecting on their problem, the zoo administrators noticed Mike, a janitor responsible for cleaning the animals' cages. Now Mike, it was rumoured, possessed ample ability to satisfy any female, and he wasn't very bright. So the zoo administrators thought they might have a solution. Perhaps they could entice Mike to satisfy the female gorilla.

So he was approached with a proposition: would he be willing to screw the gorilla for 500 bucks? Mike replied that he might be interested, but would have to think the matter over.

The following day, Mike announced that he would accept their offer, but only under three conditions.

'First,' he said, 'I don't want to have to kiss her; and second, I want nothing to do with any offspring that may result from this union.'

The zoo administrators quickly acceded to these conditions, but what could be the third?

'Well,' said Mike, 'you've gotta give me another week to come up with the 500 bucks.'

### 'ALL THAT MALARKEY'

An English POW is in a German hospital with multiple serious injuries. The doctor comes into his room and says, 'The news iss bad. Ve are going to have to amputate your left leg.'

The Brit replies, 'Right, then. War is hell and all that malarkey. But could you ask your commandant if he wouldn't find it too much of a bother to drop it over my beloved homeland when he goes on his next bombing mission?'

Off goes the doctor, and with the commandant's permission, they fulfil his request.

A few days later, the doctor returns into his room and says, 'More bad news. Ve are going to have to amputate your other leg.'

The Brit replies, 'Right, then. War is hell and all that malarkey. Could you ask your commandant if he wouldn't mind terribly if he could drop it over my beloved homeland when he goes on his next bombing mission?'

Off goes the doctor, and again his request is fulfilled.

Another week passes, and the doctor returns to his room and says, 'Achh! More bad news. Ve are going to have to amputate your right arm.'

The Brit replies, 'Right, then. War is hell and all that malarkey. Please do ask your commandant if he could find the time to drop it over my beloved homeland on his next bombing mission?'

Sure enough, it is done.

More time passes, and the doctor once again returns and says, 'Ze news, she does not get any better. Ve are going to have to amputate your other arm.'

The Brit replies, 'Right, then. War is hell and all that malarkey. It would warm my heart dearly if the commandant could drop it over my beloved homeland on his next bombing mission.'

The doctor goes off and returns with an agitated look on his face. 'The commandant says NO, he vill not do ziss for you. He thinks you are trying to escape.'

## BOB BOBBING ALONG

A limbless man sat on the side of a lake every day. He had no hands and no legs. One day, he was crying when a woman was walking by and saw that he was upset, so she asked if he was okay. He replied, 'No.'

The woman said, 'Well, what's wrong?'

The limbless man said, 'I've never been hugged by anyone ever.'

So the woman, out of kindness, hugged the man. 'Are you okay now?' she asked.

'No,' the man replied. So again the woman asked him what was wrong. He answered, 'I've never been kissed before.'

The woman eagerly gave him a peck on the lips and asked, 'Are you okay now?'

The man shook his head sadly. So the woman asked him what was wrong for the third time. The man said, 'I've never been f---ed.'

The woman looked at him, picks him up, throws him in the lake, and says, 'Now you are!'

## ERRANT KISSER

'Do you ever wake up, kiss the person sleeping beside you, and feel glad that you are alive? I did and apparently I will not be allowed on this airline again . . .'

# POLITICS

Donald Trump has had the misfortune to be lampooned and laughed at almost every day since his 2016 election. But this is brought about by the man himself. He continues to confound his critics (and allies, it has to be said) with some withering stupidity spouting either from his mouth or his Twitter account. But the man suffering a constant bad hair day is not the only politician to cop it in this chapter. George W. cops plenty, and Bill Clinton and his old friend Monica get in on the act too. Politics bring cynics to the fore and these cynics have some great lines, some of which are ensconced in this chapter.

## TRUMP PROTEST PLACARDS

A billboard entitled Trump-Pence 2020 with the line: 'Just kidding. They'll be in prison.'

A Russian spy, a sexual predator and a billionaire walk into a bar. Bartender says: 'What can I get you, Mr President?'

Who would have guessed that a reality TV star with no government experience or knowledge, six bankruptcies, five kids from three different marriages, 11 charges of sexual

assault, and 4000-plus lawsuits, could be so bad at being President?
(That was from a citizen by the name of Bruce Bacon.)

A sign that says: Can we just admit we may have taken this 'anyone can grow up to be President' thing just a bit too far?

A picture of Trump at a lecture. 'Sad man gives speech he didn't write on issues he doesn't understand to organisation he doesn't like for reasons he can't explain.'

The 45th President is depicted as an orange ice block with the words 'orange on the outside, white on the inside, has frequent meltdowns and has a stick up his arse'.

## TRUMP ON PARADE

A friend of the Donald — maybe a golfing buddy — told him that he had a fantastic dream the other night: 'There was a really, really big, huge parade in Washington celebrating Trump. Hundreds of thousands, perhaps millions, lined the parade route, and cheered and cheered when Donald went past. It was the biggest celebration Washington had ever seen. Really huge!'

The Donald was very impressed and said, 'That's really great! The best! By the way, how did I look? Was my hair okay?'

'I don't know. The casket was closed.'

## NAUGHTY BILL

Bill Clinton and the Pope both died on the same day. Due to a minor clerical error, the Pope went to Hell, while Clinton went to Heaven. When the Pope arrived in Hell, everyone realised the mistake. Due to an issue with the union, they couldn't swap the two until the next day and the Pope had to spend the night in Hell, while Clinton spent the night in Heaven.

The next day, the paperwork got worked out. On his way up to Heaven, the Pope ran into Clinton. Clinton asked the Pope, 'How was your night in Hell?'

'Very educational,' responded the Pope. 'I've learned a lot from the experience, but now I'm glad I'm going to Heaven. I've been waiting all my life to meet the Virgin Mary.'

'Ooh, sorry,' said Clinton, 'you should have been there yesterday.'

**Q:** What did Clinton say when asked if he had used protection?
**A:** 'Sure, there was a guard standing right outside the door.'

When asked if they would have sex with Bill Clinton, 86 per cent of women in Washington DC said, 'Not again.'

It was so cold today, a Democrat had his hands in his own pockets!

## AMERICAN CORRUPTION

Three contractors are bidding to fix a broken fence at the White House. One is from Chicago, another from Tennessee and the third is from Minnesota. All three go with a White House official to examine the fence.

The Minnesota contractor takes out a tape measure and does some measuring, then works some figures with a pencil. 'Well,' he says, 'I figure the job will run to about $900: $400 for materials, $400 for my crew, and $100 profit for me.'

The Tennessee contractor also does some measuring and figuring, then says, 'I can do this job for $700: $300 for materials, $300 for my crew, and $100 profit for me.'

The Chicago contractor doesn't measure or figure, but leans over to the White House official and whispers, '$2700.'

The official, incredulous, says, 'You didn't even measure like the other guys! How did you come up with such a high figure?'

The Chicago contractor whispers back, '$1000 for me, $1000 for you, and we hire the guy from Tennessee to fix the fence.'

'Done!' replies the government official.

## DEEP DOO-DOO

A little boy goes to his dad and asks, 'What is politics?'

The dad says, 'Well, son, let me try to explain it this way: I'm the breadwinner of the family, so let's call me capitalism. Your mother, she's the administrator of the money, so we'll call her the government. We're here to take care of your needs, so we'll call you the people. The nanny, we'll consider her the working class. And your baby brother, we'll call him the future. Now, think about that and see if that makes sense.'

The little boy goes off to bed thinking about what his dad had said. Later that night, he hears his baby brother crying, so he gets up to check on him. He finds that the baby has soiled his diaper. The little boy goes to his parents' room and finds his mother sound asleep. Not wanting to wake her, he goes to the nanny's room. Finding the door locked, he peeks in the keyhole and sees his father in bed with the nanny. He gives up and goes back to bed.

The next morning, the little boy says to his father, 'Dad, I think I understand all about politics now.'

The father says, 'Good, son, tell me in your own words what you think politics is all about.'

The little boy replies, 'Well, while capitalism is screwing the working class, the government is sound asleep, the people are being ignored and the future is in deep shit.'

## GEORGE W. TALE

One day, the Pope was in the US and after a rough week of meeting archbishops and other religious figures, he decided to go see the Galveston shore in Texas. When he arrives in his popemobile, he sees a man struggling for his life against a shark. Upon a closer look, he notices that it is John Kerry.

Horrified, he starts to call for help when a speedboat pulls up alongside Mr Kerry, with George W. Bush and

Dick Cheney on board. Dick Cheney leans over and pulls him out. Then George W. Bush and Dick Cheney begin to beat the shark to death with baseball bats. The two men notice the Pope and land the boat on the beach.

The Pope says to the men, 'I know that there has been a lot of attention and a lot of strife in this election, but I can see that you and your opponent respect each other and would help each other in your hour of need. You have my blessings.' The Pope then drives away.

Bush asks, 'Who was that?'

'That was the Pope, Mr President, he is all-knowing and in touch with God. Leader of the Catholic Church,' says Cheney.

Bush says, 'Well, that's all neat and fine, but he doesn't know anything about shark fishing. How's the bait holding up?'

**Q:** What do you call a lawyer with an IQ of 100?
**A:** Your Honour.

**Q:** What do you call a lawyer with an IQ of 50?
**A:** Senator.

Parliament does some strange things. They put a high tax on liquor and then raise the other taxes that drive people to drink.

## MARINES CRACK IT

After numerous rounds of 'We don't know if Osama is still alive' before he was killed in his Pakistan hiding hole, Osama himself decided to send Ted Kennedy a letter in his own handwriting to let him know he was still in the game.

Kennedy opened the letter which appeared to contain a single line of coded message, 370HSSV-0773H. Kennedy was baffled, so he emailed it to John Kerry.

Kerry and his aides had no clue either, so they sent it to the FBI.

No one could solve it at the FBI, so it went to the CIA, then to the NSA.

With no clue as to its meaning, the FBI finally asked Marine Corps Intelligence for help.

Within a few seconds, the Marine Corps cabled back with this reply: 'Tell Kennedy he's holding the message upside down.'

Did you hear about Monica Lewinsky becoming a Republican? The Democrats left a bad taste in her mouth.

## ONE-LINE MADNESS

A liberal is just a conservative that hasn't been mugged yet.

**Q:** What's the difference between baseball and politics?
**A:** In baseball, you're out if you're caught stealing.

They say St Patrick drove the snakes out of Ireland. I wonder if he could do that for Congress.

I don't approve of political jokes . . . I've seen too many of them get elected.

The consensus after the election is that 100 per cent of Americans think 50 per cent of Americans have lost their minds.

America is a country which produces citizens who will cross the ocean to fight for democracy but won't cross the street to vote.

A fine is a tax for doing wrong. A tax is a fine for doing well.

Politicians and nappies have one thing in common. They should both be changed regularly, and for the same reason.

My favourite mythical creature? The honest politician.

Don't steal. That's the government's job.

Trump should not have said 'shit-hole countries'. The correct term is 'turd-world countries'.

Have you heard about the Osama bin Laden celebratory drink? It's two shots and a splash of water!

## PICK A POCKET

I went into a Liberal clothing store to purchase some pants. When I started trying on a few pairs, I noticed that all the pockets except one were visibly removed. I stopped an assistant and asked him if anyone complained.

He said, 'No, Liberals always want a hand out.'

I asked what happened to the other pockets.

'They don't go to waste: Conservatives use them to line theirs.'

## PROS AND CONS

If con is the opposite of pro, then isn't Congress the opposite of progress?

## SOUTHERN CHARM

A kid from Mississippi is on Harvard campus for the first time. He stops a student and asks, 'Excuse me, can you tell me where the library is at?'

The Harvard student replies, 'At Harvard, you don't end a sentence with a preposition.'

The kid said, 'Sorry about that. Can you tell me where the library is at, asshole?'

## BUSH A THICKET

George W. Bush and his presidential running mate, Dick Cheney, were talking, when George W. said, 'I hate all the dumb jokes people tell about me.'

Wise old Cheney, feeling sorry for his boss, said, sage-like, 'Oh, they are only jokes. There are a lot of stupid people out there. Here, I'll prove it to you.'

Cheney took George W. outside and hailed a taxi. 'Please take me to 29 Nickel Street to see if I'm home,' said Cheney.

The cab driver, without saying a word, drove them to Nickel Street, and when they finally got out, Cheney looked at George W. and said, 'See! That guy was really stupid!'

'No kidding,' replied George W., 'there was a pay phone just around the corner. You could have called instead.'

### THAT MAN TRUMP

A man dies, goes to Heaven, and sees St Peter. There are many clocks surrounding him, so the man asks, 'What are these clocks for?'

St Peter replies, 'These are lie clocks — they tick once for every lie you tell. Here we have Mother Teresa's clock. She has never lied so the clock has not moved. Honest Abe has only lied twice in his life, so it has only ticked twice.'

The man then asks, 'So where is Donald Trump's clock?'

St Peter replies, 'Oh, that's in Jesus' office — he's using it as a ceiling fan!'

When somebody calls you gay, say, 'I'm straighter than the pole your mother dances on.'

### BLAME GAME

A woman in a hot-air balloon is lost, so she shouts to a controller on the ground, 'Excuse me, I promised a friend I would meet him, but I don't know where I am.'

'You are at 31 degrees, 14.57 minutes north latitude and 100 degrees, 49.09 minutes west longitude,' he replies.

'You must be a Democrat,' she says.

'I am. How did you know?'

'Because everything you told me may be technically correct, but the information is useless, and I am still lost. Frankly, you have been no help,' she says.

'You must be a Republican,' the controller says.

'Yes. How did you know?'

'You have risen to where you are due to a lot of hot air, you made a promise you couldn't keep, and you expect me to solve your problem. You're in exactly the same position you were in before we met, but somehow, now this is my fault.'

## HUSTINGS STING

The former mayor of Timaru recounted some funny stories about his time in office. One happened while he was running for re-election. He was in a bar in Stafford Street and paid for a woman's drink. She thanked him but wondered why a stranger had bought her a beer.

'I'm running for mayor,' he told her, 'and I want your vote.'

'You got it,' she said, grabbing her glass. 'Anyone's better than the jerk who's in there now.'

## COLLECTIVE JERKS

A pride of lions, a gaggle of geese . . . and here's how we might give collective nouns to the following groups:

- a brat of boys
- a giggle of girls
- a stagger of drunks
- a tedium of accountants
- a stitch of doctors
- a whine of losers
- a jerk of politicians

## PLONKERS UNITED

Little wonder that the printed form of newspapers is struggling around the world, when you read these misadventures in headline writing:

'City Unsure Why the Sewer Smells'

'Case of Innocent Man Freed After Spending 18 Years in Prison Proves Texas System Works'

'British Left Waffles on Falklands'

'At Last Singer Etta James Dies'

## TRUMP AND THE RIDDLE

President Trump had just finished another round of golf at Trump National Golf Club in Virginia. As the President's golf cart rolls down the fairway, his caddy turns to him.

'Mr President, may I share a riddle with you?'

'Sure, go ahead,' Trump nods.

'Who is my father's son but is not my brother?'

Trump throws his small hands in the air. 'I have no idea.'

'Mr President, the answer is me!' the caddy exclaims.

Trump gasps with excitement. 'What a tremendous riddle! I will use it tonight to open my cabinet meeting and impress them bigly.'

Later that night, Trump enters the Cabinet Room in the West Wing with bravado. He sits down at the long table surrounded by his cabinet secretaries and advisors and tilts his chin up.

'Ladies and gentlemen, I have a great riddle for you tonight, believe me. Here it goes: Who is my father's son but is not my brother?'

The room goes dead silent. Everybody is frantically staring at each other looking baffled. Trump hits his little fist on the table and leans back.

'Well, I hate to be braggadocious about it but I knew you guys wouldn't get it. He's my goddamned caddy!'

## ONE-NIL TO BARACK

Donald Trump and Barack Obama ended up at the same barber's shop. As they sat there, each being worked on by a different barber, not a word was spoken. The barbers were each afraid to start a conversation, for fear that it would turn nasty. As the barbers finished their shaves in silence, the one who had Trump in his chair reached for the aftershave.

But Donald was quick to stop him, jokingly saying, 'No thanks. My wife, Melania, will smell that and think I've been in a brothel.'

The second barber turned to Barack and said, 'How about you, Mr Obama?'

Barack replied, 'Go right ahead, my wife, Michelle, doesn't know what the inside of a brothel smells like.'

## STEVIE CHALLENGES TRUMP

President Trump is attending a golf-related celebrity event and finds himself in the presence of the musician Stevie Wonder — who was the first one to 'break the ice'.

'Very nice to meet you, Mr President. I have it on good authority that you deem yourself to be quite an accomplished golfer. I myself am a keen golfer.'

Never one to be humble, his Haughtiness seizes the opportunity to big-note himself as a ravenous grizzly bear would pluck salmon from a raging waterfall.

'You're welcome. Yes, I am one of the greatest golfers there is. I own several golf courses and hope to build several more. Of course, you know Greg Norman is a good friend of mine — a very good friend of mine. But tell me, how can you play golf when you are blind and can't see anything?'

In his humble fashion, Stevie Wonder replies, 'Well, Mr President. Part of my entourage involves a very loyal caddy who stands on the green right behind the next hole and calls out to me. Just as I can visualise music notes, I can visualise where the next hole is — with astonishing accuracy, I might add. In fact, I feel so confident that I propose you and I engage in a round of golf and I will even put $500,000 of my own money on the table as a wager. Are you willing to accept my challenge, Mr President?'

The President can barely contain his excitement, thinking to himself, 'I can't believe it — here is a man who was a legend back when Obama was a schoolboy in Kenya — whose skin is darker — AND he's blind! This will be more fun than taking candy from babies!'

He ever-so-proudly announces, 'Yes, I accept your challenge. In fact, I will even stump up one million dollars of tax-pa– my own money! When do you want to play against me?'

Slowly waving his head around and beaming a sincere smile, Stevie Wonder replies, 'Any night you wish, Mr President, any night you wish.'

## IMAM NAILS IT

A priest and a rabbi are arguing over the meaning of a word. They cannot seem to get anywhere, and finally the rabbi says to the priest, 'Look, Father, we aren't getting anywhere with this, maybe we need a different perspective — let's ask the imam!'

The priest agrees and they go to the mosque. 'Please, Reverend Imam,' says the priest, 'we've been arguing all day long over this. Maybe you can help us!'

'Help you with what?' the imam asks.

'Help us answer this question,' says the rabbi. 'What is the difference between an accident and a mistake?'

The imam thinks for a moment, goes and studies the

Qur'an, and returns. 'Well, gentlemen,' he says, 'I can best explain it this way: Donald Trump is walking down a street when a car careens out of control and ploughs into him, turning him into sidewalk pizza. That is an accident.'

The two men nod. 'Continue,' says the priest.

'Well, then the President is walking down the same street, and a car is approaching . . . the driver recognises Trump, he hits the brake and manages to avoid striking him . . . And *that*, gentlemen . . . is a mistake!'

## NATIVITY SCENE

A bunch of Ku Klux Klan members are out having beers and talking about how much they love the President. They decide to break onto the White House lawn on Christmas Eve to surprise their hero with a nativity scene that represents Trump's presidency.

So they make a sign that says: 'The Donald Trump Presidency Commemorative Creche'. They argue for days over what it should look like, but eventually all agree that it should have no blacks, no Jews and no immigrants.

Everything, eventually comes together and they set up their ultimate 'Make America Great Again' scene on Christmas Eve on the White House lawn.

The White House wakes up on Christmas morning to a sign on the lawn that says 'The Trump Presidency Commemorative Creche' and a nativity scene made up of nothing but a jackass surrounded by sheep.

## EXTRACTING THE URINE

The Trump entourage, wife, Vice President and all, were on a campaign junket in an upper midwestern wintery, snowy city. After a rousing speech, Trump returned to his suite. Standing, he paused proudly looking out of the suite to the balcony, when he noticed that written in yellow in the snowdrift outside was: 'Trump is an ass.'

Exploding into a rage, Trump called his Secret Service people to immediately get a sample of the 'yellow snow', and find out whose urine it was. The Secret Service jumped into action taking samples and pictures. The Secret Service returned shortly. Trump jumped up angrily and demanded an immediate report.

The Secret Service agent, a little crestfallen, said, 'Mr President, we know whose urine was used in the message.'

'Whose was it!' demanded Trump.

The agent responded, 'The urine is VP Pence's sir.'

Trump flew into another rage.

The agent, even more wilted, said, 'Mr President, there's more information.'

'What the hell could be worse?' replied Trump.

The agent replied, 'The handwriting was Melania's!'

## BREZHNEV DIM, TRUMP HUMBLE?

Brezhnev, a former ruler of Russia, was thought to be none too bright. There is an anecdote about him. Once, he comes to address a big Communist Party meeting, and starts, 'Dear Comrade Imperialists–'

The whole hall perked up. 'What did he say?'

Brezhnev tried again . . . 'Dear Comrade Imperialists–'

Well, by now the hall was in pandemonium — was he trying to call them Imperialists? Then, an advisor walked over to the podium and pointed to the speech for Brezhnev.

'Oh,' he muttered, and started again, 'Dear Comrades, Imperialists are everywhere.'

There was a famous anecdote that the reason Brezhnev's speeches ran to six hours is because he read not only the original, but the carbon copy. In fact, there was a report near the end of Brezhnev's life that he went down to south Russia to deliver a speech on science, and accidentally gave the wrong speech — on culture — and didn't even know it until it was over. Now to Trump, who is outrageously vain and, well, dishonest with his pronouncements. Here are a few pearls . . .

'Number one, I have great respect for women. I was the one that really broke the glass ceiling on behalf of women, more than anybody in the construction industry.'

'My IQ is one of the highest — and you all know it! Please don't feel so stupid or insecure; it's not your fault.'

'My fingers are long and beautiful, as, it has been well documented, are various other parts of my body.'

'The beauty of me is that I'm very rich.'

'One of the key problems today is that politics is such a disgrace. Good people don't go into government.' (He must have said this when he was least expecting to win.)

'I will build a great wall — and nobody builds walls better than me, believe me — and I'll build them very inexpensively. I will build a great, great wall on our southern border, and I will make Mexico pay for that wall. Mark my words.'

'I'm also honoured to have the greatest temperament that anybody has.' (With that temperament, he once said, 'Why can't we use nuclear weapons?')

**On women again, consistently:**

'I have tremendous respect for women.'

'I think the only difference between me and the other candidates is that I'm more honest and my women are more beautiful.'

**Finally, Trump being humble:**

'I think I am actually humble. I think I'm much more humble than you would understand.'
'I surround myself with the best people. I know the best people.'
'I only hire the best people.'

(Heckler: Except Mike Flynn, Sean Spicer, Reince Priebus, Anthony Scaramucci, Paul Manafort, Roger Stone, Corey Lewandowski, Michael Caputo, Betsy DeVos, Steve Bannon, George Papadop–)

## DELHI DEMO

A driver was stuck in a traffic jam on the road outside Parliament in Delhi. Suddenly, a man knocks on the window. The driver rolls down the window and asks, 'What's going on?'

'Terrorists have kidnapped all the Indian politicians in Parliament, and they're asking for a $100 million ransom. Otherwise, they're going to douse them all in petrol and set them on fire. We're going from car to car, collecting donations.'

'How much is everyone giving, on average?' the driver asks.

The man replies, 'Roughly two litres.'

## EGYPTIAN HANDSHAKE

Way back in the late 1990s, George W. Bush wants to secure his second term as President, so orders his staff to undertake research about other world leaders to find some useful information.

HIs staff looks around and sees that Hosni Mubarak of Egypt wins every election in the last 25 years with 99 per cent support. They think this is remarkable and contact his aides to ask about the story of such consistent success.

The Egyptians don't talk much but they agree to help.

'Just call us a week before the elections and let us inside the Federal Elections HQ. And don't disturb us for 48 hours prior to the announcement of official results.'

The Americans agree. Time passes and two Egyptian guys come a week before the elections as agreed and start working. Final day comes, polls close and the official result is declared: 99 per cent Hosni Mubarak.

## BARACK BLANKED

President Obama walks into the Bank of America to cash a cheque. As he approaches the cashier, he says, 'Good morning, ma'am, could you please cash this cheque for me?'

Cashier: 'It would be my pleasure, sir. Could you please show me your ID?'

Obama: 'Truthfully, I did not bring my ID with me as I didn't think there was any need to. I am President Barack Obama, the President of the United States of America!'

Cashier: 'Yes, sir, I know who you are, but with all the regulations and monitoring of the banks because of impostors and forgers, I must insist on seeing ID.'

Obama: 'Just ask anyone here at the bank who I am and they will tell you. Everybody knows who I am.'

Cashier: 'I am sorry, Mr President but these are the bank rules and I must follow them.'

Obama: 'I am urging you, please, to cash this cheque.'

Cashier: 'Look, Mr President, here is an example of what we can do. One day, Tiger Woods came into the bank without ID. To prove he was Tiger Woods he pulled out his putter and made a beautiful shot across the bank into a cup. With that shot, we knew him to be Tiger Woods and cashed his cheque. Another time, Andre Agassi came in without ID. He pulled out his tennis racquet and made a fabulous shot that landed the tennis ball in my cup. With that shot, we cashed his cheque. So, Mr President, what can you do to prove that it is you, and only you, as the President of the United States?'

Obama (standing there for some time, thinking and thinking): 'Honestly, my mind is a total blank . . . there is nothing that comes to my mind. I can't think of a single thing. I have absolutely no idea what to do and I don't have a clue.'

Cashier: 'Will that be large or small bills, Mr President?'

## DEFINITIONS . . .

**Socialism:** You have two cows and you give one to your neighbour.

**Communism:** You have two cows; the government takes both and gives you some milk.

**Fascism:** You have two cows; the government takes both and sells you some milk.

**Nazism:** You have two cows; the government takes both and shoots you.

**Bureaucracy:** You have two cows; the government takes both, shoots one, milks the other and throws the milk away.

**Traditional capitalism:** You have two cows. You sell one and buy a bull. Your herd multiplies and the economy grows. You sell them and retire on the income.
**An American corporation:** You have two cows. You sell one, and force the other to produce the milk of four cows. Later, you hire a consultant to analyse why the cow dropped dead.
**A French corporation:** You have two cows. You go on strike because you want three cows.
**A Japanese corporation:** You have two cows. You redesign them so they are one-tenth the size of an ordinary cow and produce twenty times the milk. You then create a clever cow cartoon image called *Cowkimon* and market them worldwide.
**A German corporation:** You have two cows. You re-engineer them so they live for 100 years, eat once a month, and milk themselves.
**A British corporation:** You have two cows. Both are mad.
**An Italian corporation:** You have two cows, but you don't know where they are. You break for lunch.
**A Russian corporation:** You have two cows. You count them and learn you have five cows. You count them again and learn you have 42 cows. You count them again and learn you have two cows. You stop counting cows and open another bottle of vodka.
**A Swiss corporation:** You have 5000 cows, none of which belong to you. You charge others for storing them.

**A Chinese corporation:** You have two cows. You have 300 people milking them. You claim full employment, high bovine productivity, and arrest the newsman who reported the numbers.

**An Iraqi corporation:** Everyone thinks you have lots of cows. You tell them that you have none. No one believes you and they bomb your ass. You still have no cows, but at least now you are part of a democracy . . .

**Counterculture:** 'Wow, dig it, like there's these two cows, man, grazing in the hemp field. You gotta have some of this milk!'

**Surrealism:** You have two giraffes. The government requires you to take harmonica lessons.

**Fatalism:** You have two doomed cows . . .

**Hong Kong capitalism:** You have two cows. You sell three of them to your publicly listed company, using letters of credit opened by your brother-in-law at the bank, then execute a debt/equity swap with an associated general offer so that you get all four cows back, with a tax deduction for keeping five cows. The milk rights of six cows are transferred via a Panamanian intermediary to a Cayman Islands company secretly owned by the majority shareholder, who sells the rights to all seven cows' milk back to the listed company and proceeds from the sale are deferred. The annual report says the company owns eight cows, with an option on one more. Meanwhile, you kill the two cows because the feng shui is bad.

**An Arkansas corporation:** You have two cows. That one on the left is kinda cute.
**An Indian corporation:** You have two cows. You worship them.
**An Australian corporation:** You have two cows. Business seems pretty good. You close the office and go down to the pub to celebrate.
**A New Zealand corporation:** You have two cows and you shoot them both because they have *Mycoplasma bovis*.

Q: What's the difference between the Constitutions of the USA and the USSR? Both of them guarantee freedom of speech.
A: Yes, but the Constitution of the USA also guarantees freedom after the speech.

## STALIN'S SECRETARY

A secretary is standing outside the Kremlin as Marshal Zhukov leaves a meeting with Stalin, and she hears him muttering under his breath, 'Murderous moustache!'

She runs in to see Stalin and breathlessly reports, 'I just heard Zhukov say "Murderous moustache!" Stalin dismisses the secretary and sends for Zhukov, who comes back in.

'Who did you have in mind with "Murderous moustache!"?' asks Stalin.

'Why, Iosif Vissarionovich, Hitler, of course!'

Stalin thanks him, dismisses him, and calls the secretary back. 'And who did *you* think he was talking about?'

'My opinions may have changed, but not the fact that I'm right.' — *Ashleigh Brilliant*

## COMPARING NOTES

In a prison, two Soviet inmates are comparing notes. 'What did they arrest you for?' asks the first. 'Was it a political or common crime?'

'Of course, it was political. I'm a plumber. They summoned me to the district Party committee to fix the sewage pipes. I looked and said, "Hey, the entire system needs to be replaced." So they gave me seven years.'

'Don't be humble. You're not that great.' — *Golda Meir*

## BALLS TO GOVERNMENT

The Pentagon said they had too many generals running around, so they decided to get rid of some of them. They offered $10,000 in severance pay for each inch of their body to be measured however they chose.

The air force general went first. He said he wanted to be measured from his head to his toe. He was 69 inches. He received $690,000.

Next up was the army general. He wanted to be measured from the tip of his finger to the tip of his other finger. It was 80 inches. He received $800,000.

The two generals were very happy with their earnings.

Finally, the marine general came up. He said he wanted to be measured from the tip of his dick to the tip of his balls.

The man said, 'Sir, do you know how much the other

generals received?'

The general said no.

'Sir, they received $690,000 and $800,000 respectively. Are you sure that is what you want measured?'

The general said, 'Just do it!'

The man dropped the general's pants and measured his dick. When he went for the general's balls, they weren't there. The man said, 'Sir, where are your balls?'

The general said, 'I left them back in Vietnam.'

Don't steal, don't lie and don't cheat. The government hates competition.

### PIG OF A PICKLE

Bill Clinton and his driver were cruising along a country road one evening when a pig ran in front of the car. The driver tried to avoid it but couldn't and the pig was killed. The President tells his driver to go up to the farmhouse and explain to the owners what had happened. About an hour later, the driver staggers back to the car with his clothes in total disarray. He's holding a bottle of wine in one hand, a cigar in the other and smiling happily.

'What happened?' asked the President.

'Well,' the driver replied, 'the farmer gave me the wine, his wife gave me the cigar, and their beautiful daughter made mad passionate love to me.'

'My God, what did you tell them?' asked the President.

The driver replied, 'I'm Bill Clinton's driver, and I just killed the pig.'

## HILLARY CHEERS UP

Hillary Clinton isn't taking the loss to Trump very well. So I said to her, 'Cheer up! At least you won't have to work at the same desk that Monica spent so much time under.'

George W. Bush went to see the doctor to get the results of his brain scan. The doctor said, 'Mr President, I have some bad news for you. First, we have discovered that your brain has two sides: the left side and the right side.'

Bush interrupted, 'Well, that's normal, isn't it? Doesn't everybody have two sides to their brain?'

The doctor replied, 'That's true, Mr President. But your brain is very unusual because on the left side there isn't anything right, while on the right side there isn't anything left.'

'One of the lessons of history is that nothing is often a good thing to do and always a clever thing to say.' — *Will Durant*

Winston Churchill is probably best remembered for his rousing 'We shall fight on the beaches . . . we shall never surrender' speech during the Second World War. Here are some other gems of his oratory:

'Diplomacy is the art of telling people to go to hell in such a way that they ask for directions.'

'Fear is a reaction. Courage is a decision.'

'A nation that forgets its past has no future.'

'The positive thinker sees the invisible, feels the intangible and achieves the impossible.'

'If you are not a liberal at 20 you have no heart. If you are not a conservative at 40, you have no brain.'

'Socialism is a philosophy of failure, the creed of ignorance, and the gospel of envy, its inherent virtue is the equal sharing of misery.'

'There is nothing a government can give you that it hasn't taken from you in the first place.'

'The best argument against democracy is a five-minute conversation with the average voter.'

'Success is going from failure to failure without loss of enthusiasm.'

'The main vice of capitalism is the uneven distribution of prosperity. The main vice of socialism is the even distribution of misery.'

'However beautiful the strategy, you should occasionally look at the results.'

'You don't make the poor richer by making the rich poorer.'

'A lie gets halfway around the world before the truth has a chance to get its pants on.'

'A good speech should be like a woman's skirt. Long enough to cover the subject and short enough to create interest.'

'A pessimist sees the difficulty in every opportunity. An optimist sees the opportunity in every difficulty.'

'If Britain must choose between Europe and the open sea, she must always choose the open sea.'

'One man with conviction will overwhelm a hundred who have only opinions.'

'In the course of my life, I have often had to eat my words, and I must confess that I have always found it a wholesome diet.'

'Life is fraught with opportunities to keep your mouth shut.'

'An appeaser is one who feeds a crocodile, hoping it will eat him last.'

'Life can either be accepted or changed. If it's not accepted it must be changed. If it can't be changed then it must be accepted.'

'We contend that for a nation to try and tax itself into prosperity is like a man standing in a bucket and trying to lift himself up by the handle.'

'I would rather argue against a hundred idiots than have one agree with me.'

Although some of the preceding quotes are more witty than funny, Churchill was certainly a winner with the classic put-down throughout his long political life, such as the time he was accosted by the Conservative Lady Astor who said, 'Mr Churchill you are drunk.' Churchill responded with, 'Tomorrow I'll be sober but you'll still be ugly.' Or his withering assessment of his political rival Clement Attlee: 'A modest little person, with much to be modest about.' Or when he received a call from the Lord Privy Seal while sitting on the toilet and he told the aide who gave him the message, 'Tell him I can only deal with one shit at a time.'

**Q:** What did Barack say to Michelle when he got down on one knee?
**A:** 'I don't want to be Obama myself.'

**Q:** What is the difference between Bill Clinton and former Manchester United striker Wayne Rooney?
**A:** Clinton could score.

## GENEROUS TO A FAULT

A Republican and a Democrat were walking down the street when they came to a homeless person. The Republican gave him his business card and told him to stop by for a job. He then took $20 out of his pocket and handed it to him.

The Democrat was impressed, and when they came to another homeless person, he decided it was his turn to help. So he reached into the Republican's pocket and gave the homeless man $50.

'History teaches us that men and nations behave wisely once they have exhausted all other alternatives.' — *Abba Eban*

## RISKY UNDERTAKING

Donald Trump goes on a fact-finding visit to Israel. While he is on a tour of Jerusalem he suffers a heart attack and dies.

The undertaker tells the American diplomats accompanying him, 'You can have him shipped home for $50,000, or you can bury him here, in the Holy Land, for just $100.'

The diplomats go into a corner and discuss for a few minutes. They come back to the undertaker and tell him they want the Donald shipped home.

The undertaker is puzzled and asks, 'Why would you spend $50,000 to ship him home, when it would be wonderful to be buried here and you would spend only $100?'

The American diplomats reply, 'Long ago a man died

here, was buried here, and three days later he rose from the dead. We just can't take the risk.'

'Reader, suppose you were an idiot. And suppose you were a member of Congress. But I repeat myself.' — *Mark Twain*

'Trump said Democrats want illegal immigrants to "infest" our country. He used the word "infest". Like his German grandfather infested our country. No job, no English. He crawled in on his stomach and infested the country with a bunch of Trumps.

'This is not a popular policy — 67 per cent of Americans oppose it. Even Melania released a statement saying she hates to see families separated. Partly because it makes her jealous. "Why can't I get separated?"'

## LITTLE RONNIE'S BOOKS

'I heard bad news on the way over here: the Ronald Reagan Presidential Library was just destroyed by fire, and, tragically, both books were a total loss. Worse yet, he wasn't finished colouring the second one. — *Gore Vidal*

## POLITICAL PARROT

A Russian man loses his pet parrot. He looks everywhere, all around the neighbourhood, in the park, everywhere. He just can't find the parrot. Finally, he goes around to the local KGB office, and tells the desk officer his problem.

The desk officer is a little puzzled. 'Look comrade, I'm sorry you lost your pet, but this is the KGB. We don't handle missing animal reports.'

'Oh, I know that,' says the man. 'I just wanted you to know, if you do happen to find my parrot — I don't know where he could have picked up his political ideas.'

## TAKE YOUR CUE!

Two Russians are standing in a very long line for vodka.

The first one says, 'This line is too long. We must always wait for everything. I am going to go to the Kremlin and shoot Gorbachev.'

After about an hour, he returns.

The second Russian asks him, 'Well, did you shoot him?'

'No, the line was too long.'

'I voted Remain in the EU, not just for political reasons but because my mum's moved to Spain and I want her to stay there.'

A little girl asked her father, 'Do all fairy tales begin with once upon a time?'

'No,' replied her father, 'some begin with — "If I am elected".'

## INSIDER TRASHING

Two politicians were having a heated debate. Finally, one of them jumped up and yelled at the other, 'What about the powerful interest that controls you?'

And the other politician screamed back, 'You leave my wife out of this!'

# RELIGION

Back in the day, the great Irish comedian Dave Allen, he with the missing finger and the constant smoking, used to poke the borax mercilessly at the Catholic Church to great acclaim. Perhaps the acclaim didn't necessarily come from the Catholic Church, or the Vatican City, but it did from us secular, agnostic, irreligious bodies. This chapter is more obliging to the Catholic Church. Every weird and wonderful religion gets a dose of humour poked its way, including the Catholics. Religion offers plenty of avenues for humour and we've got a doozy chapter here to enjoy.

## TONGUE-TIED

Every 10 years, the monks in the monastery are allowed to break their vow of silence to speak two words.

Ten years go by and it's one monk's first chance. He thinks for a second before saying, 'Food bad.'

Ten years later, he says, 'Bed hard.'

It's the big day, a decade later. He gives the head monk a long stare and says, 'I quit.'

'I'm not surprised,' the head monk says. 'You've been complaining ever since you got here.'

## THANKS, SKIPPY

A devout Australian cowboy lost his favourite Bible while he was mending fences out on the range. Three weeks later, a kangaroo walked up to him carrying the Bible in its mouth. The cowboy couldn't believe his eyes. He took the precious book out of the kangaroo's mouth, raised his eyes heavenward and exclaimed, 'It's a miracle!'

'Not really,' said the kangaroo. 'Your name is written inside the cover.'

## SHORT-CHANGED

A little boy wanted $100 badly and prayed for two weeks but nothing happened. Then he decided to write a letter to the Lord requesting the $100. When the postal authorities received the letter addressed to the Lord, USA, they decided to send it to President Clinton. The President was so impressed, touched and amused that he instructed his secretary to send the little boy a $5 bill, as this would appear to be a lot of money to a little boy. The little boy was delighted with the $5, and sat down to write a thank-you note to the Lord. It said:

'Dear Lord,

Thank you very much for sending me the money.

However, I noticed that for some reason you had to send it through Washington DC, and as usual, those jerks deducted $95.'

If anyone needs an ark, I happen to Noah guy.

## SAINTLY LARRY

Religion is generally a forbidden topic for everyone at work, except for Larry. Recently, after he steered yet another conversation towards the subject, a co-worker whispered to me, 'That Larry — he always has to put his two saints in.'

## FUTURE SIGNAL

A priest and a pastor are standing by the side of a road holding up a sign that reads 'The end is near! Turn around now before it's too late!'

A passing driver yells, 'You guys are nuts!' and speeds past them. From around the curve, they hear screeching tyres — then a big splash.

The priest turns to the pastor and says, 'Do you think we should just put up a sign that says "Bridge Out" instead?'

## BUM STARE

We were reading *The Wisdom of King Solomon* in my Sunday-school class. An illustration showed King Solomon ordering a child to be cut in half, as one woman sobbed and another watched uncaringly. Pointing to the heartless woman, a young boy said, 'I hope she ends up with the part that has the butt on it.'

## ANGEL WITH A HEART

Three guys are fishing when an angel appears. The first guy says, 'I've suffered from back pain for years. Can you help me?' The angel touches the man's back, and he feels instant relief.

The second guy points to his thick glasses and begs for a cure for his poor eyesight. When the angel tosses the lenses into the lake, the man gains 20/20 vision.

As the angel turns to the third fellow, he instantly recoils and screams, 'Don't touch me! I'm on compo!'

'Why should we take advice on sex from the Pope? If he knows anything about it, he shouldn't!' — *George Bernard Shaw*

## REEFTON REPRIEVE

Howard dies and waits in line for judgement. He notices that some souls go right into Heaven, while Satan throws others into a burning pit. But every so often, instead of hurling a poor soul into the fire, the devil tosses it aside.

Curious, Howard asks Satan, 'Excuse me, but why are you tossing those ones aside instead of flinging them into hell with the others?'

'They're from Reefton,' Satan replies. 'They're too wet to burn.'

'I sometimes think that God in creating man somewhat overestimated his ability.' — *Oscar Wilde*

## DALAI LAMA DILEMMA

So, I called up the spiritual leader of Tibet, and he sent me a large goat with a long neck. Turns out I phoned dial-a-llama.

**Saved by Mammon**

A Jew, a Muslim, a Catholic and a Mormon are shipwrecked on a small desert island. They have very little food and water, and the situation is perilous.

The Muslim finds a corner of the beach, prostrates himself, and prays to Allah for succour. The Mormon finds a different corner and prays fervently to God. The Catholic heads for a palm tree, sits down, and begins reciting the Rosary non-stop, her beads miraculously having survived the wreck. The Jew continues hanging out by the shore, picking up a shell now and then, and occasionally skipping rocks.

After a while, the Muslim, Mormon and Catholic realise that the Jew's just idly staring off into the distance, whistling a little tune, instead of doing everything possible to get them saved. They confront the Jew, and the Catholic says, 'Hey, you jerk! We're all doing the best we can to get a little divine intervention here! How about you help us cover your base, eh?'

The Jew just smiles for a moment. Then she says, 'Well, over the past 10 years, I've donated about $2 million to the Jewish Federation.'

The Catholic, outraged, replies, 'So what? What does that have to do with anything?'

The Jew answers, 'Don't worry. They'll find me.'

**SAINTLY JOSIE**

Josie wasn't the best pupil at Sunday school. She often fell asleep and one day while she was sleeping, the teacher asked her a question.

'Who is the creator of the universe?'

Joe was sitting next to Josie and decided to poke her with a pin to wake her up. Josie jumped and yelled, 'God almighty!' The teacher congratulated her.

A little later, the teacher asked her another question, 'Tell me who is our Lord and Saviour?' Joe poked Josie again and she yelled out, 'Jesus Christ!' The teacher congratulated her again.

Later on, the teacher asked, 'What did Eve say to Adam after their twenty-sixth child?' Joe poked Josie again and she shouted, 'If you stick that thing in me again, I'll snap it in half and stick it up your arse!'

## ST PETER IN A PICKLE

On their way to get married, a young Catholic couple are killed in a car accident. The couple found themselves sitting outside the Pearly Gates waiting for St Peter to process them into Heaven. While waiting, they began to wonder: could they possibly get married in Heaven? When St Peter showed up, they asked him.

St Peter said, 'I don't know. This is the first time anyone has asked. Let me go find out,' and he left.

The couple sat and waited, and waited. Two months passed and the couple were still waiting. While waiting, they began to wonder what would happen if it didn't work out: could you get a divorce in Heaven?

After yet another month, St Peter finally returned, looking somewhat bedraggled. 'Yes,' he informed the couple, 'You can get married in Heaven.'

'Great!' said the couple. 'But we were also wondering, what if things don't work out? Could we also get a divorce in Heaven?

St Peter, red-faced with anger, slammed his clipboard onto the ground.

'What's wrong?' asked the frightened couple.

'OH, COME ON!' St Peter shouted. 'It took me three months to find a priest up here! Do you have any idea how long it'll take me to find a lawyer?'

## TIMELESS

A man is talking to God. 'God, how long is a million years?'

God answers, 'To me, it's about a minute.'

'God, how much is a million dollars?'

'To me, it's a penny.'

'God, may I have a penny?'

## MARIA LEGS IT!

Maria, a devout Catholic, got married and had 15 children. After her first husband died, she remarried and had 15 more children. A few weeks after her second husband died, Maria also passed away.

At Maria's funeral, the priest looked skyward and said, 'At last, they're finally together.'

Her sister sitting in the front row said, 'Excuse me, Father, but do you mean she and her first husband, or she and her second husband?'

The priest replied, 'I mean her legs.'

## BLIND MAN'S BLUFF

Mother Superior tells two new nuns that they have to paint their room without getting any paint on their clothes.

One nun suggests to the other, 'Hey, let's take all our clothes off, fold them up, and lock the door.'

So they do this, and begin painting their room. Soon they hear a knock at the door. They ask, 'Who is it?'

'Blind man!'

The nuns look at each other and one nun says, 'He's blind, so he can't see. What could it hurt?' So they let him in.

The blind man walks in and says, 'Hey, nice tits. Where do you want me to hang the blinds?'

## DAMNED IF YOU DO . . .

I was walking across a bridge near the university in Dunedin one day, and I saw a man standing on the edge, about to jump. I ran over and said, 'Stop. Don't do it.'

'Why shouldn't I?' he asked.

'Well, there's so much to live for!'

'Like what?'

'Are you religious?'

He said, 'Yes.'

I said, 'Me too. Are you Christian or Buddhist?'

'Christian.'

'Me too. Are you Catholic or Protestant?'

'Protestant.'

'Me too. Are you Anglican or Baptist?'

'Baptist.'

'Wow. Me too. Are you Baptist Church of God or Baptist Church of the Lord?'

'Baptist Church of God.'

'Me too. Are you original Baptist Church of God, or are you Reformed Baptist Church of God?'

'Reformed Baptist Church of God.'

'Me too. Are you Reformed Baptist Church of God, Reformation of 1879, or Reformed Baptist Church of God, Reformation of 1915?'

He said, 'Reformed Baptist Church of God, Reformation of 1915.'

I said, 'Die, heretic scum,' and pushed him off.

## MIRACLE MAN

The Pope and Jesse Jackson were out fishing one day. At one stage the Pope's hat blew off and landed on the water.

Jesse leaves the boat and, lo and behold, is able to walk on the water and retrieve the Pope's hat.

The next day, the headlines said: 'Jesse can't swim'.

## THREE GREAT RELIGIOUS TRUTHS

1. Jews do not recognise Jesus as the Messiah.
2. Protestants don't recognise the Pope as the leader of Christianity.
3. Baptists do not recognise each other at the liquor store or the gay bar.

**Q:** Why should you always take two Baptists when you go fishing?
**A:** If you only take one, he'll drink all your beer!

## SEX TALK

What do a whore, a nymphomaniac and a Jewish American princess say after sex?

The whore says, 'That's all.'

The nymphomaniac says, 'That's all?'

The Jewish American princess says, 'Beige. I think we'll paint the ceiling beige.'

**Q:** How do you know you are at a Mormon wedding?
**A:** The mother of the bride is pregnant.

**Q:** How many Jewish mothers does it take to change a light bulb?
**A:** None. Don't bother. I'll just sit here alone in the dark.

## NASTY PIECE OF MANKIND

A bus full of ugly people had a head-on collision with a truck. When they died, God granted all of them one wish.

The first person said, 'I want to be gorgeous.' God snapped his fingers and it happened.

The second person said the same thing and God did the same thing.

This went on and on throughout the group.

God noticed that the last man in line was laughing hysterically. By the time God got to the last 10 people, the last man was laughing and rolling on the ground. When the man's turn came, he laughed and said, 'I wish they were all ugly again.'

### BISH THE CHAUFFEUR

Bishop T. D. Jakes is returning to Texas after a speaking engagement. When his plane arrives, there is a limousine there to transport him to his home in Dallas. As he prepares to get into the limo, he stops and speaks to the driver. 'You know,' he says, 'I am almost 50 and I have never driven a limousine. Would you mind if I drove it for a while?'

The driver says, 'No problem.'

Bishop T. D. Jakes gets into the driver's seat, and they head off down the highway.

A short distance away sits a rookie state trooper operating his first speed trap. The long black limo goes by him doing 70 in a 55 mph zone. The trooper pulls out, easily catches the limo, and gets out of his patrol car to begin the procedure.

The young trooper walks up to the driver's door, and when the glass is rolled down, he is surprised to see who is driving. He immediately excuses himself, goes back to his car, and calls his supervisor. He tells the supervisor, 'I know we are supposed to enforce the law, but I also know that important people are sometimes given certain courtesies. I need to know what I should do because I have stopped a very important person.'

The supervisor asks, 'Is it the Governor?'

The young trooper says, 'No, he's more important than that.'

The supervisor says, 'Oh, so it's the President.'

The young trooper says, 'No, he's even more important than that.'

The supervisor finally asks, 'Well, then, who is it?'

The young trooper says, 'I think it's Jesus, because he's got T. D. Jakes for a chauffeur!'

### COMPUTER WHIZZ

Jesus and Satan are having a competition on who can finish an essay first. One, two, three go!

Jesus starts and takes his time while Satan is typing up a storm. Satan is typing so fast that the power goes out and both computers are shut off.

They start back up, and Jesus states that he is done with the essay. Startled, Satan asks how he wrote that fast.

Jesus turns to him and simply says, 'Jesus saves.'

**Q:** Why did the dyslexic agnostic with insomnia stay up all night?

**A:** She was wondering if there really is a dog.

### ROCK ON

One fine day, a priest, a rabbi and a high priestess decide to all go fishing. They reach the boat, and off they go.

One hour later, the high priestess says, 'I think I forgot the food!' She steps off the boat, walks across the water, gets the picnic basket, and walks back!

As they are eating, the priest thinks, 'What a display. Jeez, where does she get off walkin' on the water?'

Right then, the rabbi says, 'Oye! I forgot the drinks.' He steps right off the boat, and walks across the water to get the drinks.

By this time, the priest is very frustrated! He excuses himself, and as the priest steps out of the boat, he falls into the water and sinks.

The high priestess turns to the rabbi and says, 'You think we should have told him about the rocks?'

## BLASPHEMING BARMAN

A drunk staggers out of a bar and runs into two priests. He goes over to the first priest and says, 'Dude, I'm Jesus Christ!' And the priest says, 'No son, you're not.'

So the drunk goes over to the second priest and says, 'Man, I'm Jesus Christ!' Then the priest says, 'No son, you're not.'

Finally, the drunk has had enough and says, 'Here, I'll prove it.'

He walks back into the bar with both priests and the bartender looks up and sees the drunk and says, 'Jesus Christ, you're back AGAIN?'

## PAVING THRILL

Two nuns were riding their bicycles down the street.

The first nun says, 'I've never come this way before.'

The second nun says, 'Yeah, it's the cobblestones!'

**Q:** What do you call a sleepwalking nun?
**A:** A roamin' Catholic.

## GETTING IN EARLY

'What's wrong, Bob?' asked the pastor.

'I need you to pray for my hearing,' said Bob.

The pastor put his hands on Bob's ears and prayed. When he was done, he asked, 'So how's your hearing?'

'I don't know,' said Bob. 'It isn't until next Tuesday.'

**Q:** What do you call an Amish guy with his hand in a horse's mouth?
**A:** A mechanic.

## CURSED ARE THE MOWERS

Gary was having a garage sale. A minister bought a lawn mower but returned it a few days later, complaining that it wouldn't run.

'It'll run,' said Gary. 'But you have to curse at it to get it started.'

The minister was shocked. 'I have not uttered a curse in 30 years.'

'Just keep pulling on the starter rope — the words will come back to you.'

## JUST BULLSHIT

Before beginning the service, our pastor read aloud a note he'd been handed moments earlier.

'It says here that I should announce that there will be no B.S. tomorrow morning,' he said.

He tucked the piece of paper into a pocket and added, 'I'm hoping they mean "Bible Study".'

## MASS-IRE

Scene: Sunday Mass. I turned to greet an older woman.
Woman: 'My! You have the most beautiful skin.'
Me: 'Oh, thank you.'
Woman: 'If I were younger, I'd hate you.'

## THAT'S ALRIGHT THEN

En route to church to make his first confession, my nervous seven-year-old grandson asked me what he could expect.

'Confession is where you tell all the bad things you've done to the priest,' I told him.

He looked relieved. 'Good. I haven't done anything bad to the priest.'

## GOD'S A SWINGER

When our minister and his wife visited our neighbour, her four-year-old daughter answered the door.

'Mum!' she yelled towards the living room. 'God's here, and he brought his girlfriend.'

## A TIMBUKTU TO-DO

At last, the long-awaited finale of the televised poem competition had arrived. The Pope, who was a keen lyricist and writer of poems, had to everyone's surprise entered the competition. He immediately announced that he would only be reciting poems about personal spiritual experiences. Despite this limitation, it turned out he was gifted with words and he had made it all the way to the final.

His opponent was the favourite to win: a Harvard linguistics professor at the top of his career and with a mind as sharp as a knife's edge. The Harvard professor was up first. He was informed of the rules: 'Two minutes to come up with a poem, and it must involve Timbuktu.' The clock started, and when the time was up, the Harvard professor approached the microphone:

'On my way through desert sand
'Met a lonely caravan
'Men on camels, two by two
'Destination: Timbuktu.'

The crowd went wild. The commentators waxed lyrical. This was without a doubt the best poem of the competition. The Harvard professor had done it again!

But as the crowd settled down, their spirits sank. As far as anyone knew, the Pope had never been to Timbuktu. How could the Pope have a personal spiritual experience with such a word?

The elderly Pope was walked to the stage and informed of the same rules: 'Two minutes to come up with a poem, and it must involve Timbuktu.'

The clock was started, but after only a short pause for thought the Pope stopped it. Everybody in the competition had used all the provided time, and as the Pope approached the microphone a sigh rippled through the audience. Was he withdrawing from the competition? Would it all end in anti-climax? No, to everybody's surprise, the Pope started to recite his poem based on personal spiritual experience:

'Me and Tim to Brisbane went
'Met some ladies, cheap to rent.
'They were three and we were two,
'So I bucked one, and Tim bucked two.'

**Q:** How does Moses make his tea?
**A:** Hebrews it.

## TAKING THE PISS

Three Christian boys live in a church. One day the boys say, 'Pastor! Pastor! We have done no bad deed.'

The pastor replies, 'Very good. Now each of you are granted one bad deed.'

One boy comes back and says, 'Pastor! Pastor! I broke a car window.'

The pastor tells him, 'Go to the back, pray, and drink some holy water.'

The second boy comes back saying, 'Pastor! Pastor! I punched a woman in the face.'

The pastor replies, 'Go to the back, pray, and drink some holy water.'

The third boy comes in and says, 'Pastor! Pastor! I peed in the holy water!'

The lord said unto John, 'Come forth and receive eternal life', but John came fifth and won a Teasmade.

## PRETZEL LOGIC

Two nuns are doing their grocery shopping. As they pass the cooler full of beer, one nun says longingly to the other one, 'A cold beer would go down great tonight!'

'Indeed,' the other nun replies, 'but how can we show up with beer at the checkout counter?'

'Don't worry, I have a plan,' the first nun answers. 'Grab a six-pack.'

The cashier is indeed surprised when she sees the beer, but the first nun is ready with an explanation.

'We use the beer to wash our hair,' she says. 'At the convent, we call it "Catholic shampoo".'

Without hesitation the cashier bends down, grabs a package of pretzels, and throws it in one of the nuns' grocery bags, saying, 'The curlers are on the house.'

**Q:** Who was the smallest man in the Bible?
**A:** King David, because he was only 12 inches tall as he was a ruler.

**Q:** Why did all the hippies go to church on the first day of Lent?
**A:** They heard it was 'Hash Wednesday'.

**Q:** Did you hear about the Buddhist who refused Novocaine during a root canal?
**A:** His goal: transcend dental medication.

**Q:** Why did God create alcohol?
**A:** So ugly people could have sex, too.

## LAX RECORD KEEPING

The biggest swindler in the world dies and finds himself before the Pearly Gates and St Peter, who says, 'Come on in man!'

Confused, the swindler questions, 'I thought I would be going to Hell for all of the bad things I did?'

St Peter replies, 'Oh, we don't keep records here, it's too much work!'

The swindler goes in and is once again surprised to see tons of beautiful girls whipping themselves.

He asks St Peter, 'Why are they doing that?'

St Peter answers, 'Ah, those are all of our virgins. They just found out we don't keep records, too!'

Yo mama so old she was in Year Three with Moses.

## POINTLESS ARGUMENT

An elderly Mormon visits his doctor and asks if he'll live to be a hundred.

'Do you smoke or drink?' asks the doctor.

'Those things have never and will never touch my lips,' says the man.

'Do you gamble, drive fast cars, and fool around with women?'

'Nope, don't believe in doing any of that, either.'

'Well then,' says the doctor, 'what do you want to live to be a hundred for?'

## JESUS SHOWING OFF

Jesus and St Peter are golfing. St Peter steps up to the tee on a par three and hits one long and straight. It reaches the green.

Jesus then tees up. He slices it. It heads over the fence into traffic on an adjacent street. Bounces off a truck, onto the roof of a nearby shack and into the rain gutter, down the drainpipe and onto a lily pad at the edge of a lake.

A frog jumps up and snatches the ball in his mouth. An eagle swoops down, grabs the frog. As the eagle flies over the green, the frog croaks and drops the ball. Right in the hole.

St Peter looks at Jesus, exasperated. 'Are you gonna play golf?' he asks. 'Or are you just gonna f--k around?'

## ATTA BOY, TIGER

The Pope met with the College of Cardinals to discuss a proposal from Shimon Peres, the former leader of Israel.

'Your holiness,' said one of the cardinals, 'Mr Peres wants to determine whether Jews or Catholics are superior, by challenging you to a golf match.'

The Pope was greatly disturbed, as he had never held a golf club in his life.

'Not to worry,' said the cardinal, 'we'll call America and talk to Jack Nicklaus. We'll make him a cardinal, and he can play Shimon Peres — we can't lose!'

Everyone agreed it was a good idea. The call was made and, of course, Jack was honoured and agreed to play.

The day after the match, Nicklaus reported to the Vatican to inform the Pope of his success in the match.

'I came in second, your Holiness,' said Nicklaus.

'Second?' exclaimed the surprised Pope. 'You came in second to Shimon Peres?!'

'No,' said Nicklaus, 'second to Rabbi Woods.'

'What have you been reading, the Gospel according to St Bastard?' — *Eddie Izzard*

Moe: 'My wife got me to believe in religion.'
Joe: 'Really?'
Moe: 'Yeah. Until I married her, I didn't believe in Hell.'

### DREAM GENIE

This guy was out playing his weekly round of golf when he hit a shot into the trap off the eleventh green. So he pulls out his sand wedge and takes a swing at the ball only to hit something metallic underneath. Being curious, he digs away the sand only to find what looks like Aladdin's lamp. It's kind of dirty, so he takes out his golf towel to clean it off.

All of a sudden, poof!, a genie appears from the lamp and says, 'Sir, you have freed me from the lamp. For this I will grant you three wishes!'

The man thinks for a moment and says, 'You know, I have everything I could possibly want. Give the wishes to someone else.' He quickly putts out and leaves for the twelfth tee.

The genie is flabbergasted. 'To think that someone in this world could feel so fulfilled that he could pass up not just one but three wishes! I know what I'll do. To reward him, I'll grant him three things without him knowing. Now, let's see. What does every man want? Money. He will have all the money he can use. Power. Every man wants that. And what else? Sex. All that he wants.'

A couple of weeks later the man is heading towards the eleventh green and there is the genie — sunning himself in the trap.

Genie: 'Hey. How's it going?'

Man: 'Couldn't be better. Last week I raised over $1,000,000 and gave the most spellbinding and effective talk of my life. It looks like I'm gaining more influence among my peers and superiors. Things are great.'

Genie: 'If you don't mind me asking, how's your sex life?'

Man: 'It's great. I've had two women in the last two weeks.'

Genie (looking puzzled): 'Only TWO women? That's not very good!'

Man: 'It is if you're a priest in a small parish!'

## ANGEL'S INDIGNITY

From time to time, people have wondered about the reason for an angel on the top of the Christmas tree.

Well, it seems that one particular Christmas, Santa was rushed and harried trying to get ready for his annual trip to deliver gifts to the world's children. He told Mrs Claus to wake him at 5 a.m. and to have his breakfast ready with a lunch to take along. He then went to his workshop and told the elves to have all the presents packed in the sleigh and the reindeer harnessed at 5.30 a.m.

At 5.30 the following morning he awoke and jumped out of bed furious with Mrs Claus for not waking him on time. His mood worsened when he realised she had fixed neither his breakfast nor his afternoon meal. Then he ran out to his sleigh only to find that the elves, drunk from partying all night, had no presents packed and the reindeer were running loose in the pasture.

About this time, a little angel walked by dragging a large Christmas tree. Santa tried to ignore her since his mood was so foul, but the angel spoke up and said, 'Santa what should I do with this Christmas tree?'

And that is why there is an angel on the top of the Christmas tree.

## HOLIDAY 'FUN'

Adolf Hitler was very keen on the occult, so he went to a fortune teller hoping that the woman could tell him how long he would live.

After careful charting, she said, 'I can't predict the exact date of your death, but I do know that you will die on a Jewish holiday.'

'And which holiday will this be?' he asked.

'It does not matter,' she replied. 'Any day that you die will be a Jewish holiday.'

## SORE POINT!

A priest and a rabbi operated a church and a synagogue across the street from each other. Since their schedules intertwined, they decided to go in together to buy a car. So they did. They drove it home and parked it in the street between their establishments.

A few minutes later, the rabbi looked out and saw the priest sprinkling water on their new car. It didn't need a wash, so he ran out and asked the priest what he was doing.

'I'm blessing it,' the priest replied.

The rabbi said, 'Oh,' then ran back into the synagogue. He reappeared a few minutes later with a hacksaw, ran to the car and cut off the last two inches of the exhaust pipe.

## GOD PROVIDES

During a particularly wet winter, flood waters rise so high in Greymouth that the army is brought in to help evacuate all the residents. One man stays behind, however, and when the water is waist-high, two army blokes in a boat motor past his house, checking for people left behind.

'We're evacuating the town because of the flood. Jump in the boat and we'll carry you to safety.'

But the man says, 'No, don't bother; I've led a pious life,

and the Lord will save me.'

The men in the boat shrug their shoulders and motor away. Later, when the water level has driven the man onto his roof, another boat appears.

'Haven't you heard the town has been evacuated? Come on, we'll save you.'

But the man sends them away, saying, 'No, no, the Lord will save me!'

The water level keeps rising until the man is standing on his chimney and barely keeping his head above water, and a helicopter, doing a final check, appears overhead. It drops a rope, and the loudspeaker says, 'Grab the rope and we'll bring you to safety.'

But the man waves the helicopter away, once again saying, 'No, no, the Lord will save me!'

But the water level keeps rising, and he drowns.

When he gets to Heaven, he is completely bewildered. He asks God, 'God, why didn't you save me?'

And God says, 'Well, I sent you two boats and a helicopter!'

### OH MOSES!

Moses, returning from the mountain, spoke to his people:

'The good news is we got them down to 10.'

'The bad news is that adultery is still one of them.'

### HAVE MERCY

A man is driving down a deserted stretch of highway, when he notices a sign out of the corner of his eye. It says,

'SISTERS OF MERCY HOUSE OF PROSTITUTION 10 MILES.'

Thinking it was just a figment of his imagination, he drives on without a second thought. Soon, he sees another sign, which says, 'SISTERS OF MERCY HOUSE OF PROSTITUTION 5 MILES', and realises that these signs are for real.

When he drives past a third sign saying, 'SISTERS OF MERCY HOUSE OF PROSTITUTION NEXT RIGHT', his curiosity gets the better of him and he pulls into the drive.

On the far side of the parking lot is a sombre stone building with a small sign next to the door reading, 'SISTERS OF MERCY'. He climbs the steps and rings the bell.

The door is answered by a nun in a long black habit who asks, 'What may we do for you, my son?'

He answers, 'I saw your signs along the highway, and was interested in possibly doing business.'

'Very well, my son. Please follow me.'

He is led through many winding passages and is soon quite disoriented. The nun stops at a closed door, and tells the man, 'Please knock on this door.'

He does as he is told and this door is answered by another nun in a long habit and holding a tin cup. This nun instructs, 'Please place $50 in the cup, then go through the large wooden door at the end of this hallway.'

He gets $50 out of his wallet and places it in the second nun's cup. He trots eagerly down the hall and slips through the door, pulling it shut behind him.

As the door locks behind him, he finds himself back in the parking lot, facing a fourth sign: 'GO IN PEACE, YOU HAVE JUST BEEN SCREWED BY THE SISTERS OF MERCY.'

### FRUSTRATION INC.

Three married couples, aged 20, 30 and 40 years old, want to join the Orthodox Church of Sexual Repression in Taumarunui. Near the end of their initial interview, the cleric informs them that before they can be accepted they will have to pass one small test. They will have to abstain from all sex for a month. They all agree to try.

One month later, they are having their final interview with the cleric. He asks the 40-year-old couple how they did.

'Well, it wasn't too hard. I spent a lot of time in the workshop and she has a garden, so we had plenty of other things to do. We did okay,' the husband said.

'Very good, my children. You are welcome in the church. And how well did you manage?' he asked the 30-year-old couple.

'It was pretty difficult,' the husband answered. 'We thought about it all the time. We had to sleep in different beds and we prayed a lot. But we were celibate for the entire month.'

'Very good, my children. You are welcome in the church. And how about you?' he asked the 20-year-old couple.

'Not too good, I'm afraid,' replied the husband. 'We did

okay for the first week,' he said sheepishly. 'By the second week, we were going crazy with lust. Then one day during the third week my wife dropped a head of lettuce, and when she bent over to pick it up, I . . . I weakened and took her right there.'

'I'm sorry, my son, you are not welcome in the church.'

'Yeah, and we're not too welcome in the local New World any more, either.'

## EBONY OR IVORY

Adam and Eve are wondering whether they are black or white.

Eve says, 'Why don't you go and ask God?'

So Adam goes into the Garden of Eden and shouts out to God, 'Are we black or white?'

A big booming voice bellows out, 'YOU ARE WHAT YOU ARE.'

He immediately goes back to Eve and tells her that they are white.

'How do you know?' asks Eve.

'Because he said, "You are what you are",' Adam replied.

'Why does that mean we are white?' asked Eve.

'Because if we were black he would have said, "You is what you is".'

**Q:** What do you call a cheap circumcision?
**A:** A rip-off.

# DARK AND RISQUÉ

Not so much dark, but definitely risqué. Fifteen years ago, this writer got the job of editing two issues of email jokes, when the email was in its early days. For some reason, the advent of the medium resulted in jokes being winged around. We tapped into them through *The World's Best Emails* and *The World's Very Best Emails*, which were published almost 20 years ago. Those books were no-holds-barred. They were racist, sexist and every form of bad taste you could imagine. Readers were warned to park their politically correct thoughts to get a good laugh and the books proved to be successful. Now, in 2018, things have changed. No longer is it deemed appropriate to be as aggressively non-PC as we were back in the day. Having said that, we have had to break the rules occasionally, but anyone who read the email books would acknowledge the present copy is very mild in comparison. Mind you, this intro was written before editing. Maybe I'll be in for a surprise and the odd compromise!

## UNFORTUNATE WORD

I was at my bank today waiting in a short line. There was just one lady in front of me, an Asian woman, who was trying to exchange yen for dollars. It was obvious she was a little irritated.

She asked the teller, 'Why it change? Yesterday, I get two hunat dolla of yen. Today I only get hunat eighty? Why it change?'

The teller shrugged his shoulders and said, 'Fluctuations.'

The Asian lady says, 'Fluc you white people too!'

## MONKEY BAR

A girl realised she had grown hair between her legs. She got worried and asked her mum about that hair.

Her mum calmly said, 'That part where the hair has grown is called your monkey. Be proud that your monkey has grown hair.'

The girl smiled. At dinner, she told her sister, 'My monkey has grown hair.'

Her sister smiled and said, 'That's nothing — mine is already eating bananas.'

**Q:** Why is Santa Claus' sack so big?
**A:** He only comes once a year.

## BEE MISHAP

Beverly had decided she would learn to play golf, so she signed up and took lessons. After six months of diligent effort, she was ready to play 18 holes with three of her friends.

Out on the course, she was stung by a bee. Fearing an allergic reaction, she hurried back to the clubhouse to find the pro.

'I've been stung by a bee! What shall I do?'

'Where were you stung?'

'Between the first and second hole!'

'Beverly, we really need to work on your stance . . .'

## SOME BIG DADDY

Dad: 'Say "Daddy".'
Toddler: 'Mummy!'
Dad: 'Come on, say "Daddy"!'
Toddler: 'Mummy!'
Dad: 'Fuck you! Say "Daddy"!'
Toddler: 'Fuck you! Mummy!'
Mum: 'Honey, I'm home!'
Toddler: 'Fuck you!'
Mum: 'Who taught you to say that?'
Toddler: 'Daddy!'
Dad: 'Son of a bitch . . .'

## DODGY GUY

I was walking round town yesterday and passed by a gun store. Intrigued, I entered to find that everything was 50 per cent off. I didn't know that back to school sales had already started.

## YELLOW LIE?

Monica Lewinsky walks into the dry cleaners. The old man behind the counter is hard of hearing and doesn't understand her request, so he says, 'Come again.'

Monica responds, 'No, this time it's mustard.'

There is an overweight guy who is watching TV. A commercial comes on for a guaranteed weight loss of 10 pounds in a week. So the guy, thinking what the hell, signs up for it. Next morning, an incredibly beautiful woman is standing at his door in nothing but a pair of running shoes with a sign about her neck that reads, 'If you can catch me, you can have me.'

As soon as he sees her, she takes off running. He tries to catch her, but is unable. This continues for a week, at the end of which, the man has lost 10 pounds. After this, he tries the next weight-loss plan, 15 pounds in a week.

The next morning, an even more beautiful woman is standing at the door, in similar condition. The same happens with her as the first woman, except he almost catches her. This continues for a week, at the end of which he, as suspected, weighs 15 pounds less.

Excited about this success, he decides to do the master

programme. Before he signs up, he is required to sign a waiver and is warned about the intensity of this plan. Still he signs up to lose 25 pounds.

The next morning, waiting at the door, is a hulking 300-pound muscle man with nothing but a pair of running shoes, a raging erection, and a sign around his neck that says, 'If I catch you, you're mine!' The man lost 34 pounds.

PMS jokes aren't funny. Period.

## POPE

Three good Kiwi blokes, Gary, Doug and Paddy, had been workmates, drinking mates and footie buddies for a long time. To mark their friendship, they did something different together every year — going to the Trentham races, going to an All Black test at Eden Park, watching a cricket test at the Basin Reserve, spending a week on the Gold Coast lairing it up and getting sunburnt in the many outside bars they got pissed in.

So, the year after the Gold Coast trip, they decided to push the boat out and go to Rome. As always, wives or female partners were not invited, because the three mates didn't want their mojo muffled.

A long, drunken flight was enjoyed by the threesome. Two days after visiting damn near all the bars in the centre of Rome, they spent five minutes looking at the Colosseum from a nearby bar, walked up the Spanish Steps and collapsed into another bar at the top out of exhaustion, and decided to go to the Vatican.

Standing among the thousands of the faithful in front of St Peter's Basilica to hear the Pope preach to the masses, naturally enough, they got bored and wandered off back into the city to find a bar or three, where they got even more pissed than they normally did. They were having a ball knocking back Peroni and chasing that with an assortment of spirits of all colours.

When the three were turfed out of a bar after being refused more drinks owing to their oafish, alcoholic state, they staggered back towards their hotel. It was then that they saw an even drunker guy lying in a gutter. Recognising a kindred spirit, they went up to help him out. But they got a hell of a shock when they turned him over. It was the Pope and he was dead.

'We need to ring the cops,' said sensible Doug, but perhaps the even more sensible Gary suggested they could make some good money out of this.

'What we do is, keep quiet about it, get hold of the London bookies and place a $20 bet on the death of the Pope. They take bets for all sorts of silly things and I bet they'll give us a price.'

So all three picked bookies to ring first thing in the morning London time after which they would all meet in the bar of their hotel at 10 a.m. to celebrate their winnings.

At 10 a.m. the next day they were ensconced in the bar, all having their choice of 'hair of the dog'. They sat in the corner and Gary, who had dealt with Ladbrokes, said he got a good price and made $30,000; Doug, who had contacted Mecca, also said he got a good price and made $35,000.

They were mightily excited and demanded Paddy's tale.

Paddy had placed a bet with with the TAB, but he looked anything but happy.

'What's the matter,' said Doug. 'Don't keep us in suspense.'

Paddy, looking miserable, said, 'I got nothing. I put a quinella on with the Archbishop of Canterbury.'

## POOR RECEPTION

A woman decides to get a porno movie, so she goes to the video store and picks one with a fairly dirty title. When she plays the movie, the screen gets fuzzy and nothing is going on. When she calls the store about the movie, they ask her what the title was, and she says, 'Head Cleaner.'

## TATT'S NICE

It was Christmas Eve. A woman came home to her husband after a busy day of shopping in Lambton Quay. Later on that night when she was getting undressed for bed, he noticed a mark on the inside of her leg.

'What's that?' he asked.

'I visited the tattoo parlour today,' she said. 'On the inside of one leg I had them tattoo "Merry Christmas", and on the inside of the other one they tattooed "Happy New Year".'

Perplexed, he asked, 'Why did you do that?'

'Well,' she replied, 'now you can't complain that there's never anything to eat between Christmas and New Year!'

## FLOUR REGRETS

A black boy walks into the kitchen where his mother is baking and accidentally pulls the flour over onto his head.

He turns to his mother and says, 'Look, Mama, I'm a white boy!'

His mother smacks him and says, 'Go tell your Daddy what you just said!'

The boy finds his father and says, 'Look, Daddy, I'm a white boy!'

His daddy gives him a severe scolding and says, 'Now, what do you have to say for yourself?'

The boy replies, 'I've only been a white boy for five minutes and I already hate you black people!'

## TRUMP TANKED

Trump, Putin and Blair were going for a walk when a giant came up to them. He told them to bring a human killing machine from their country so as to not die from his wrath.

First came Blair with a small pistol. The giant told him to put it up his ass.

Then came Putin with an AK-47. The giant told him to do the same.

Surprisingly, Putin was crying and laughing at the same time.

'Why are you crying?' demanded the giant.

'Because of the pain.'

'Then why are you laughing?' the giant growled.

'Because Trump's bringing a tank!' howled Putin.

I want to die peacefully in my sleep, like my grandfather. Not screaming and yelling like the passengers in his car.

## WHAT A GAS

Your Halloween costume came in the mail today. I opened it. It was a rooster mask and a bag of lollipops. Going as a cocksucker again!?

## PARROT PUCKERED OUT

A husband suspected his wife was cheating on him. He explained his situation to a pet shop owner who replied, 'I have a parrot that will let you know daily what goes on in your house. The bird has no legs, so he holds onto his perch with his penis.'

Reluctantly, the husband brought the bird home. At the end of the first day, the man asked the bird, 'Did anything happen today?'

The parrot said, 'Yes, the milkman came over.'

The man asked, 'What did he do with my wife?'

The bird said, 'I don't know. I got hard and fell off the perch.'

## VIRGIN ON RIDICULOUS

Kid 1: 'Hey, I bet you're still a virgin.'
Kid 2: 'Yeah, I was a virgin until last night.'
Kid 1: 'As if.'
Kid 2: 'Yeah, just ask your sister.'
Kid 1: 'I don't have a sister.'
Kid 2: 'You will in about nine months.'

### HARDLY TENNYSON

A guy and girl had a sex poem competition.

Guy: 'Two times two is four, four plus five is nine. I can put mine in yours, but you can't put yours in mine.'

Girl: 'Two times two is four, four plus five is nine. I know the length of yours, but you won't know the depth of mine.'

Save your breath. You'll need it to blow up your date.

You're so ugly, the last time you got a piece of arse was when your hand slipped through the toilet paper.

### JOB WELL DONE

A man and a woman were having sex. After they were done, the man asks the woman, 'Are you a nurse?'

The woman answers, 'Yes. How did you know?'

The man replies, 'Because you took care of me so well.'

Then the woman asks the man, 'Are you an anaesthetist?'

He says proudly, 'Yes. How do you know that?'

The woman answers, 'Because I didn't feel a thing.'

**Q:** What's an Australian's idea of foreplay?

**A:** You awake?

**Q:** What's a Tasmanian's idea of foreplay?

**A:** You awake, Mum?

## THE MIDDLE MAN

A woman walks into a tattoo parlour in Woodville and tells the artist she would like two tattoos: one of Robert Redford on her left upper thigh, and one of Paul Newman on her right thigh.

After hours of work the tattoo artist is finished and holds a mirror in between the woman's legs for her to view.

The woman says, 'I don't know if these really look like Paul and Robert, and I'm not payin' for this if it isn't right!'

She tells the tattoo artist she will go just outside the business and ask someone walking down the street if they know who the two men are on her thighs. If they answer correctly, she would pay.

She soon sees a man walking down the street, so she pulls up her skirt and asks him, 'Can you tell me who the man on my right thigh and the man on my left thigh are?'

The man replies, 'I dunno, but the one in the middle certainly looks like Willie Nelson.'

Taylor Swift has 500 songs about guys leaving her and none about blow-jobs. Do you see where I'm going with this?

The adult shop boss turned up from his lunch break and asked his assistant how things went while he was away.

The assistant said, 'Well, I sold one white dildo, one black one and I sold your Thermos flask for $165.

## SILENCE IS GOLDEN

Two deaf people got married. During the first week of marriage, they found they were unable to communicate in the bedroom when the lights were off because they couldn't see each other using sign language. After several nights of fumbling around and misunderstandings, the wife decides to find a solution.

'Honey,' she signs, 'why don't we agree on some simple signals? For instance, at night, if you want to have sex with me, reach over and squeeze my right breast one time. If you don't want to have sex, reach over and squeeze my left breast one time.'

The husband thinks this is a great idea and signs back to his wife, 'Great idea, now if you want to have sex with me, reach over and pull on my penis one time. If you don't want to have sex, reach over and pull on my penis 50 times.'

## COOL BLUFF DRIVER

A man gets on a bus, and ends up sitting next to a very attractive nun. Enamoured with her, he asks if he can have sex with her. Naturally, she says no, and gets off the bus. The man goes to the bus driver and asks him if he knows of a way for him to have sex with the nun.

'Well,' says the driver, 'every night at eight, she goes to the cemetery to pray. If you dress up as God, I'm sure you could convince her to have sex with you.'

The man decides to try it, and dresses up in his best God costume. At eight, he sees the nun and appears before her.

'Oh, God!' she exclaims. 'Take me with you!'

The man tells the nun that she must first have sex with him to prove her loyalty. The nun says yes, but tells him she prefers anal sex. Before you know it, they're getting down to it, having nasty, grunty, loud sex. After it's over, the man pulls off his God disguise.

'Ha, ha!' he says, 'I'm the man from the bus!'

'Ha, ha!' says the nun, removing her costume, 'I'm the bus driver!'

## WONDER TOOL

When the rust remover WD-40 was introduced in the early 1960s it became a firm favourite. But what was the copywriter of a newspaper advertisement promoting the product thinking back in 1964? The ad reads:

'Do you have TIGHT NUTS or A RUSTY TOOL? Then use WD-40 in the MAN SIZE PRESSURE PACK. STANDS 9 inches high 1 and a half inches DIAMETER [complete with red knob]

'Makes old tools like new again

'Tools slide in and out with ease

'Lubricates dry passageways

'Makes screwing a pleasure

'Gives better penetration

'BUY SOME TRY SOME

'WD-40 . . . It's good stuff

Keep a spare pack in your car for emergencies.'

## YOU ASKED FOR IT!

A substitute for a Catholic priest is hearing confessions. He is confused about what to recommend as a confessor's penance after doing a sexual favour for her boss. He sticks his head out of the confessional and asks a nearby altar boy what the father gives for a blow-job.

The altar boy responds, 'Usually a Snickers and a ride home.'

## POINT PERCY AT THE GLASS

A Russian is strolling down the street in Moscow and kicks a bottle lying in the street. Suddenly, out of the bottle comes a genie. The Russian is stunned and the genie says, 'Hello master, I will grant you one wish, anything that you want.'

The Russian begins thinking, 'Well, I really like drinking vodka.' Finally, the Russian says, 'I wish to drink vodka whenever I want, so make me piss vodka.'

The genie grants him his wish. When the Russian gets home, he gets a glass out of the cupboard and pisses into it. He looks at the glass and it's clear. Looks like vodka. Then he smells the liquid. Smells like vodka. So he takes a test and it is the best vodka that he has ever tasted.

The Russian yells to his wife, 'Olga, Olga, come quickly.'

She comes running down the hall and the Russian takes another glass out of the cupboard and pisses into it. He tells her to drink, that it is vodka.

Olga is reluctant but goes ahead and takes a sip. It is the best vodka that she has ever tasted. The two drink and party all night.

The next night, the Russian comes home from work and tells his wife to get two glasses out of the cupboard. He proceeds to piss in the two glasses. The result is the same, the vodka is excellent and the couple drink until the sun comes up.

Finally, Friday night comes around and the Russian tells his wife to grab one glass from the cupboard and they will drink vodka.

She gets the glass but asks him, 'Boris, why do we only need one glass?'

Boris raises the glass and says, 'Because tonight, my love, you drink from the bottle!'

**Q:** Can you name three football clubs that contain swear words?
**A:** Arsenal, Scunthorpe and F--ing Man United.

**Q:** What's the difference between a bucket of shit and a West Ham United fan?
**A:** The bucket.

## WONKY ARROWS

Once upon a time there was an archery contest. The first archer, wearing a long cape covering his face, lines up in position. He takes a deep breath and fires an arrow which finds the bullseye. Then he takes off his cape and screams, 'I AM . . . ROBIN HOOD!' The crowd cheers.

The second archer in a cape lines up in position. He fires his arrow which hits the bullseye and cuts Robin Hood's arrow into two. He takes off his cape and screams, 'I AM . . . WILLIAM TELL!' The crowd cheers.

Finally, a third man in a cape lines up in position. He fires his arrow but it goes all wrong. It flies past the crowd and kills the king. Then the man takes off his cape and screams, 'I AM . . . SORRY!'

## GENEROUS GRANDPA

A teenager, his father and his grandfather go out to play a round of golf. Just before the son is ready to tee off, this fine-looking woman walks up carrying her clubs. She says her partner didn't show and asks if she can join them. The guys say sure, since she is quite a beautiful woman.

The lady turns to the three of them and says, 'I don't care what the three of you do, cuss, smoke, chew, spit, fart or whatever. Just don't try to coach me on my game.'

The guys say okay and ask if she would like to tee off first. All eyes are on her ass as her skirt rides up when she bends over to place the ball. She then proceeds to knock the hell out of the ball right up the middle.

She starts pounding these guys, getting par on every hole. They get to the eighteenth and she has a 12-foot putt for par. She turns around and says, 'You guys have done a great job at not trying to coach me on my game. I've never shot par before, and I'm going to ask your opinions on this putt. Now, if any of your opinions help me make the putt, I will give that guy a blow-job he will never forget.'

The guys think, 'What a deal!'

The kid walks over, eyes up the putt for a couple of

minutes, and finally says, 'Lady, aim that putt six inches to the right of the hole. The ball will break left 12 inches from the hole and go in the cup.'

The father walks up and says, 'Don't listen to the youngster. Aim 12 inches to the right and the ball will break left two feet from the hole and fall into the cup.'

The grandpa looks at both of them in disgust, walks over and picking up the ball, drops it into the cup, unzips his fly and says, 'That's a gimme.'

'IT'S A BOY!' I shouted. 'A BOY, I DON'T BELIEVE IT, IT'S A BOY!' And with tears streaming down my face I swore I'd never visit another Thai brothel!

**Q:** What do you get when you cross a chicken and a vacuum?
**A:** A cocksucker.

## SUPERIOR SERVICE

The Abbot of an abbey was out in the nearby city running errands when he saw a woman of questionable character say to a passer-by, 'Twenty bucks for a blow-job,' at which point the passer-by and the woman promptly went down the next alley, where they went out of view.

The Abbot was perplexed, for the very same thing occurred at another street corner in the city. He was walking down a footpath, when another woman, much the same as the first, stated to another passer-by, 'Twenty bucks for a blow-job,' at which point the two rapidly went into a nearby alley, where the Abbot couldn't see what was going on.

Still not knowing what a 'blow-job' was, the Abbot left the city as naive as he was upon entering it.

Back up the hill, the Abbot was still contemplating what a blow-job was, so he went to see the Mother Superior at the adjacent convent.

'Mother Superior,' he asked, 'what's a blow-job?'

'Twenty bucks, same as downtown!'

## TIGER'S PAR PERFORMANCE

It was the wedding night for a young couple and the groom wanted everything to be just perfect. He arranged to stay in the honeymoon suite of a plush hotel, and he and his new bride eagerly jumped into the heart-shaped bed to make love for the first time (at least for him).

After making wild and passionate love for a considerable length of time, they both reached the climactic moment simultaneously, slipping into a state of utmost relaxation. At this point, the groom reaches for the telephone.

'What on earth do you think you're doing?' asks the young bride.

'Well, I wanted everything to be perfect, so I thought I should call room service for a bottle of their finest champagne,' came the reply.

'Well, I used to date Tiger Woods and when Tiger and I finished making love we would wait 10 minutes and make love again,' the young groom was informed.

'If that's what you are used to, I will be glad to comply . . .'

And 10 minutes or so later, the young couple was making wild and passionate love again. At the culmination of this second lovemaking session, the young groom reaches for the phone once again . . .

'What on earth do you think you're doing?' asks the young bride.

'Like I said before, I want this to be a special occasion, so I was going to call room service for that bottle of champagne.'

'Well, Tiger and I used to relax for 15 minutes or so, and then make love a third time,' came her reply.

So, once again, not wanting to disappoint his young bride, the groom relaxed a bit and finally was capable of making love a third time.

After this third wild and passionate and somewhat time-consuming session, the couple finally reached the climactic moment and returned to a relaxed state. Once again, the groom reaches for the phone . . .

'What on earth do you think you're doing?' asks the young bride.

'Calling Tiger Woods to find out what's par for this hole!'

## WILLY YEARNING!

There was this guy who really took care of his body. He lifted weights and jogged six miles every day. One morning he looked in the mirror and was admiring his body and noticed that he was suntanned all over, with the exception of his penis, which he decided to do something about. So, he went to the beach, completely undressed and buried himself in the sand, except for his penis, which he left sticking out.

Two little old ladies were strolling along the beach, one using a cane. Upon seeing the thing sticking out of the sand, one began to move it around with her cane, remarking to the other little old lady, 'There really is no justice in this world.'

The other lady said, 'What do you mean?'

The first old lady said, 'Look at that . . . When I was 20, I was curious about it; when I was 30, I enjoyed it; when I was 40, I asked for it; when I was 50, I paid for it; when I was 60, I prayed for it; when I was 70, I forgot about it, and now that I'm 80, the damn things are growing wild — and I'm too old to squat!'

## GAME A WHOLE FAMILY CAN ENJOY!

In a small Wairarapa town, almost everybody was excited about the wedding that was coming up, but at the last moment, the groom called it off. A puzzled local wanted to know why.

Out-of-towner: 'Why did you call off the wedding so suddenly?'

Former groom: 'I just found out last night that she's a virgin.'

Out-of-towner: 'But why is that so bad?'

Former groom's father, leaping to his son's defence: 'Hell, if she's not good enough for her own family, she ain't good enough for my son!'

## IF AT FIRST YOU DON'T SUCCEED!

One night, as a couple lay down for bed, the husband gently taps his wife on the shoulder and starts rubbing her arm.

The wife turns over and says, 'I'm sorry honey, I've got a gynaecological appointment tomorrow.'

The husband, rejected, turns over and tries to sleep. Later, he rolls back over and taps his wife again. This time he whispers in her ear, 'Do you have a dentist's appointment tomorrow too?'

## THAT'S TELLING IT SON

An old man takes his grandson fishing in a local pond one day. After 20 minutes of fishing, the old man fires up a cigar.

The young boy asks, 'Grandpa, can I have a cigar?'

The old man asks, 'Son, can your dick touch your asshole?' The young boy says no. 'Then you can't have a cigar.'

Another 20 minutes passes, and the old man opens a beer.

The young boy asks, 'Grandpa, can I have a beer?'

The old man asks, 'Son, can your dick touch your asshole?' The young boy says no. 'Well, then, you can't have a beer.'

Another 20 minutes passes, and the young boy opens a bag of potato chips.

The old man asks, 'Son, can I have some of your chips?'

The boy asks, 'Well, Grandpa, can your dick touch your asshole?'

The old man says, 'It sure can.'

The boy says, 'Well, good, then go f--k yourself, these are my chips.'

## FLIGHT OF FANCY

Three women were on a flight, when suddenly the captain announced, 'Please prepare for a crash landing.'

The first lady put on all her jewellery. Surprised by this, the other ladies questioned her actions. The first lady replied, 'Well, when they come to rescue us, they will see that I am rich and will rescue me first.'

The second woman, not wanting to be left behind, began to take off her top and bra. 'Why are you doing that?' the other ladies questioned. 'Well, when they come to rescue us, they will see my great tits and will take me first.'

The third woman, who was African, not wanting to be outdone, took off her pants and panties. 'Why are you doing that?' the other ladies questioned. 'Well, they always search for the black box first.'

# SPORTING LIFE

Sport has a broad brush for humour. There's a great one about an Old Firm football match in Glasgow between the two big teams, Rangers and Celtic. It's cleverly written, so we don't know which side the protagonists are supporting, in case that offends the odd reader. Other football jokes take the mickey out of Arsenal, for some understandable reason! As sport evokes plenty of angst, it also gives plenty of options for humour. As the late great Liverpool manager Bob Paisley said, 'Some people think sport is about life or death. It's not. It's more important than that.' Many take that as gospel, but they'd be the sort who couldn't take a joke. The more relaxed would have their wits about them to see the funny side of most events.

## CAREER DAY

It's career day in primary school where each student talks about what their dad does. Little Johnny is last, and finally the teacher calls on him to talk about his dad.

Johnny comes to the front of the class. 'My daddy is a dancer at a gay bar. He takes off his clothes for other men, and if they pay him enough money, he goes into the alley and performs sexual acts on them.'

The teacher is shocked, and she calls for an early recess for the rest of the class.

She sits down with Johnny and asks him if this is really true about his dad. Johnny says, 'No, but I was too embarrassed to say he played for Arsenal.'

## GOOD SPORT

A Tottenham supporter thought he might amuse himself by scaring every Gunners supporter he saw strutting down the street in an obnoxious Arsenal jersey. He would swerve his van as if to hit them, then swerve back just missing them.

One day while driving along, he saw a priest. He thought he would do a good deed, so he pulled over and asked the priest, 'Where are you going, Father?'

'I'm going to say Mass at St Francis' Church, about two miles down the road,' replied the priest.

'Climb in, Father. I'll give you a lift!'

The priest climbed into the passenger seat, and they continued down the road.

Suddenly, the driver saw an Arsenal supporter walking down the street, and he instinctively swerved as if to hit him. But, as usual, he swerved back onto the road just in time.

Even though he was certain that he had missed the guy, he still heard a loud thud. Not knowing where the noise came from, he glanced in his mirrors but still didn't see anything.

He then remembered the priest, and he turned to him and said, 'Sorry, Father, I almost hit that Gunners supporter.'

'That's okay,' replied the priest. 'I got him with the door.'

## LIVER BIRD FOR HER

A primary school teacher explains to her class that she is an Arsenal supporter. She asks her students to raise their hands if they were Arsenal supporters, too. Not really knowing what an Arsenal supporter was, but wanting to be like their teacher, hands explode into the air. There is, however, one exception. A girl named Mary has not gone along with the crowd. The teacher asks her why she has decided to be different.

'Because I'm not an Arsenal fan.'

'Then,' asks the teacher, 'what are you?'

'I'm proud to be a Liverpool supporter,' boasts the little girl.

The teacher is a little perturbed now, her face slightly red. She asks Mary why she is a Liverpool supporter.

'Well, my dad and mum are Liverpool supporters, and I'm a Liverpool fan, too!'

The teacher is now angry. 'That's no reason,' she says loudly. 'What if your mum was a moron, and your dad was a moron, what would you be then?'

A pause, and a smile. 'Then,' says Mary, 'I'd be an Arsenal supporter.'

## JUST A TOSSER!

Legendary Arsenal defender Tony Adams walks into a sperm donor bank in London . . .

'I'd like to donate some sperm,' he says to the receptionist.

'Certainly, sir,' she replies. 'Have you donated before?'

'Yes,' replies Tony, 'you should have my details on your computer.'

'Oh, yes, I've found your details,' says the receptionist, 'but I see you're going to need help. Shall I call your wife for you?'

'Why do I need help?' asks Tony.

The receptionist replies, 'Well, it says on your record that you're a useless wanker . . .'

## WELL BRED

Three Auckland fans were bemoaning the sorry state of their football team.'

'I blame the general manager,' said the first fan. 'If he signed better players, we'd be a great team.'

'I blame the players,' said the second fan. 'If they made more of an effort, we'd score some goals.'

'I blame my parents,' said the third. 'If I'd been born in Wellington, I'd be supporting a decent team.'

**Q:** How do you make a tissue dance?
**A:** Put a little boogie in it.

## LEFT-HANDER

A husband and wife were golfing when suddenly the wife asked, 'Honey, if I died would you get married again?'

The husband said, 'No, sweetie.'

The woman said, 'I'm sure you would.'

So the man said, 'Okay, I would.'

Then the woman asked, 'Would you let her sleep in our bed?'

And the man replied, 'Yeah, I guess so.'

Then the wife asked, 'Would you let her use my golf clubs?'

And the husband replied, 'No, she's left-handed.'

**Q:** Why were the swimming elephants thrown out of the Olympics?

**A:** Because they couldn't keep their trunks up!

## HEAVEN FORBID

Two old men, Don and Bob, sit on a park bench feeding pigeons and talking about rugby.

Don turns to Bob and asks, 'Do you think there's rugby in Heaven?'

Bob thinks about it for a minute and replies, 'I dunno. But let's make a deal. If I die first, I'll come back and tell you if there's rugby in Heaven, and if you die first, you do the same.'

They shake on it and sadly, a few months later, poor Don passes on.

Soon afterward, Bob sits in the same park feeding the pigeons by himself and hears a voice whisper, 'Bob.'

Bob responds, 'Don. Is that you?'

'Yes, it is, Bob,' whispers Don's ghost.

Bob, still amazed, asks, 'So, is there rugby in Heaven?'

'Well,' says Don, 'I've got good news and bad news.'

'Gimme the good news first,' says Bob.

Don says, 'Well, there is rugby in Heaven.'

Bob says, 'That's great! What news could be bad enough to ruin that?'

Don sighs and whispers, 'You're fullback on Friday.'

## DRAM BEFORE BATTLE

Glaswegian Jimmy was going to a football match for the first time in ages — what with being on the run, caught and ending in Barlinnie Prison for far too long. It was the Old Firm derby, Rangers versus Celtic.

Now they're big events, so Jimmy decided he needed a few drams before confronting the crowds at the match. After one or two, plus another one or two, Jimmy was ready. Unfortunately, he had drammed far too long and was late getting to the ground and took the first turnstile he came to just as the match kicked off.

He got up onto the standing terraces behind one of the goals, and muscled his way through the throngs to get a good possie. It was then that Jimmy realised a possibly fatal error. He was at the wrong end, which could spell trouble. He hoped he was not recognised as a long-time supporter of the other lot.

The match went on and after about 20 minutes the team whose end he was at scored. All around him went ballistic and started singing '1–0, 1–0, 1–0' while pointing at the opposition fans at the other end of the ground. Jimmy just put on a sickly grin by way of 'celebration' but he was in abject misery.

Half-time came and Jimmy was sighing with relief that he'd so far got away with being in enemy territory. But his relief was premature. A big hand came down on his shoulder and a big, big guy said, 'Hey you, go get me a Bovril — and another for my mate here,' motioning to another hairy big bugger next to him.

Jimmy readily agreed, 'Yeah, yeah, sure.'

But his hopes of a little window of peace vanished when the first bloke said, 'Take your shoes off.'

Jimmy didn't know why but reluctantly did so and began hobbling in holey socks to the Bovril bar.

He returned to the giant twosome and delivered the Bovril and then saw his shoes, which were filled to the brim with shit.

'Put them on,' the first big guy said.

So Jimmy squished his feet into the shit-filled shoes, which led to a wide circle around him as the fans drew away from the stench. Abject misery was a gross understatement now and he remained that way till the end of the match which ended 1-all. His team scored in the last minute. He stayed mute as the fans at the other end went wild with joy. The Old Firm match had finished all square.

As Jimmy squelched his way out of the ground, he was keen to get to the nearest pub to down a couple more drams of the good stuff and clean his shoes out.

Waddling down the road away from the ground, Jimmy was stopped by a bloke with a microphone.

'Excuse me sir, I'm from the BBC and we're doing a survey about whether violence at football matches is ruining the game and is it getting worse.'

Jimmy looked at the man and said into the microphone, 'There will always be football violence as long as they're shitting in our shoes and we're pissing in their Bovril.'

## STOLEN, DEAR WATSON

Sherlock Holmes and Dr Watson went on a camping trip. After a good meal and a bottle of wine, they laid down for the night, and went to sleep.

Some hours later, Holmes woke and nudged his faithful friend. 'Watson, look up at the sky and tell me what you see.'

Watson replied, 'I see millions and millions of stars.'

'What does that tell you?'

Watson pondered for a minute. 'Astronomically, it tells me that there are millions of galaxies, and potentially billions of planets. Astrologically, I observe that Saturn is in Leo. Horologically, I deduce that the time is approximately a quarter past three. Theologically, I can see that God is all-powerful and that we are small and insignificant. Meteorologically, I suspect that we will have a beautiful day tomorrow. What does it tell you?'

Holmes was silent for a minute, then spoke. 'It tells me that someone has stolen our tent.'

**Q:** Why did the witches' team lose the baseball game?
**A:** Their bats flew away.

**Q:** What's the difference between England and a teabag?
**A:** A teabag could stay in the World Cup for longer.

## SCUBA MANOEUVRES

Paddy and Murphy are having a pint in the pub, when some scuba divers come on the TV.

Paddy says, 'Murphy, why is it them deep sea divers always sit on the side of the boat with them air tanks on their backs, and fall backwards out of the boat?'

Murphy thinks for a minute, then says, 'That's easy. It's 'cause if they fell forwards, they'd still be in the friggin' boat!'

You know you're getting fat when you say you're fat in front of your team-mates and nobody corrects you.

## ODDS AND EVENS

A Kiwi and an Aussie went fishing one afternoon and decided to have a couple of cold beers.

After a while, the Aussie says to the Kiwi, 'If I was to sneak over to your house and make wild passionate love to your wife while you were at work, and she got pregnant and had a baby, would that make us related?'

The Kiwi, after a great deal of thought, says, 'Well, I don't know about related, but it sure would make us even.'

The one thing I've learned from the World Cup is that Europe still hasn't mastered the haircut.

## NICE ONE, OLD MAN

'Poor old fool,' thought the well-dressed gentleman as he watched an old man fish in a puddle outside a pub. So he invited the old man inside for a drink.

As they sipped their whiskies, the gentleman thought he'd humour the old man and asked, 'So how many have you caught today?'

The old man replied, 'You're the eighth.'

## MY LAST HARLEY RIDE

While riding my Harley in the forests near Gisborne, I had to swerve to avoid a deer and landed in a ditch, severely banging my head. Dazed and confused, I crawled out of the ditch to the edge of the road, when a shiny new convertible pulled up driven by a very beautiful woman, who asked, 'Are you okay?'

As I looked up, I noticed she was wearing a low-cut blouse with cleavage to die for. 'I'm okay I think,' I replied as I pulled myself up to the side of the car to get a closer look.

She said, 'Get in and I'll take you home so I can clean and bandage that nasty scrape on your head.'

'That's nice of you,' I answered, 'but I don't think my wife will like me doing that.'

'Oh, come now, I'm a nurse,' she insisted. 'I need to see if you have any more scrapes and then treat them properly.'

Well, she was really pretty and very persuasive. Being sort of shaken and weak, I agreed, but repeated weakly, 'I'm sure my wife won't like this.'

We arrived at her place which was just a few miles away in the swankiest part of Gisborne and, after a couple of cold beers and the bandaging, I thanked her and said, 'I feel a lot better but I know my wife is going to be really upset so I'd better go now.'

'Don't be silly,' she said with a smile, while unbuttoning her blouse and exposing the most beautiful set of boobs I've ever seen. 'Stay for a while. Your wife won't know anything. Where is she?'

'Still in the ditch with my Harley, I guess.'

### INTELLIGENT WINNER

Justify, the winner of the Triple Crown in Kentucky, turns down an invitation to the White House to meet President Trump.

Asked why, he said, 'If I wanted to see a horse's arse, I would've finished second.'

### HEADLINE BRILLIANCE

Football in Britain is like rugby in New Zealand. They are mad for it and there is barely a day when a big screaming headline about football doesn't adorn the back pages — particularly those of the tabloids. The only things that tip football off the back pages are the Open golf championship, a cricket victory, and if Andy Murray does well at Wimbledon. The rest is football, football, football, and listed are some absolutely fantastic headlines.

### SUPER CALEY GO BALLISTIC CELTIC ARE ATROCIOUS

Somehow it was *The Sun* that came up with this great headline following the shocking result between Scottish minnows Inverness Caledonian Thistle and the mighty Celtic in 2000. A spoonful of sugar, anybody?

### NEW CHEQUE FOR CZECH CECH

The reference is to Chelsea goalkeeper Petr Cech, from the Czech Republic, receiving a pay rise for signing a new contract with the Stamford Bridge outfit.

### OLD LADY UNABLE TO MASTER BATE AT HOME

This bit of genius was in reference to Italian team Juventus — nicknamed the Old Lady — who were unable to beat Belarusian side FC Bate in a Champions League game back in 2008.

### KEEGAN FILLS SCHMEICHEL'S GAP WITH SEAMAN

This was Sky Sports' headline following the news that Manchester City (managed by Kevin Keegan) had signed David Seaman in order to replace the departing Dane Peter Schmeichel.

### YOUNG BOYS WANKDORF ERECTION RELIEF

Young Boys are a Swiss football club who had recently finished the construction — or erection — of their brand-new stadium, entitled the Stade de Suisse Wankdorf Stadium.

### FUCKS OFF TO BENFICA

This headline wrote itself when the news came out that a player named Argélico Fucks decided to sign for Portuguese club Benfica from Brazilian side Palmeiras. Genuinely.

## THIS SPORT IS STUPID ANYWAY

The *New York Post* decided to go with this childish headline when the USA crashed out of the 2010 World Cup. Clearly, they don't care about football, I hear you say. I'm not convinced. Just days before, the same newspaper celebrated the 1–1 draw with England by writing the headline 'US Wins 1–1'.

## SPURS HUNTING FOR YOUNG BOYS

Again, we're back to Swiss team Young Boys, and Spurs obviously refers to English team Tottenham Hotspur. This headline was to mark an upcoming Champions League game.

## THESE ARE THE WORLD CHAMPIONS

On the day of the World Cup final in 1950, Rio newspaper *O Mundo* released their morning issue showing a photo of the Brazil national team below the headline: 'THESE ARE THE WORLD CHAMPIONS'. Unfortunately, Uruguay had different ideas and subsequently won the World Cup final 2–1. Brazil were hosts.

## SWEDES 2, TURNIPS 1

This was another *Sun* headline — surprise, surprise — which was written in relation to the disastrous Euro 92 performance by England as they crashed out of the competition to Sweden 2–1. Then England manager Graham Taylor's head was superimposed on a turnip and printed for the world to see.

## OOH ARNIE!

During a Pro Am, when the professionals play local worthies before a proper tournament, Arnold Palmer's partner asked, 'Well, Arnold, what do you think of my game?'

'It's okay,' said Arnie, 'but I prefer golf!'

**Q:** What do you get if you see a Leeds United fan buried up to his neck in sand?

**A:** More sand.

## A DISH BUT NO QUICHE

During graduate school, I tutored a football player in Psychology 101. After the session, my supervising professor asked me if I was interested in the student, since he was a good-looking athlete.

'No, I'm not,' I assured him.

'Yeah, you probably prefer men who eat quiche,' he joked.

'Actually, I prefer men who can spell quiche,' I replied.

## LOYAL FAN

Looking down the stairs at a football game, a fan spots an open seat on the 50-yard line. He asks the man sitting next to it if the seat is taken.

'No,' he replies. 'I used to take my wife to all the games, but ever since she passed away, I've gone alone.'

'Why don't you invite a friend?'

'I can't. They're all at the funeral.'

## BACK NINE BLUES

Fred comes home from his usual Saturday golf game. 'What a terrible day,' he tells his wife. 'Harry dropped dead on the tenth tee.'

'Oh, that's awful!' she says.

'You're not kidding,' says Fred. 'For the whole back nine, it was hit the ball, drag Harry, hit the ball, drag Harry . . .'

## IMPORTANCE OF INACCURACY

A golfer called one of the caddies and said, 'I want a caddy who can count and keep the score. What's three and four and five add up to?'

'Eleven, sir,' said the caddy.

'Good, you'll do perfectly.'

**Q:** What should you do if you're golfing near lightning?
**A:** Hold your 2-iron in the air, because not even God can hit a 2-iron.

## CHOICES, CHOICES

A wife walked into the bedroom and found her husband in bed with his golf clubs.

Seeing the astonished look on her face, he calmly said, 'Well, you said I had to choose, right?'

'We didn't lose the game; we just ran out of time.' — *Vince Lombardi*

## YUMMY BLACK CAVIAR

Two female teachers took a group of students from Years 1, 2 and 3 for a field trip to Trentham Racecourse. When it was time to take the children to the toilet, it was decided that the girls would go with one teacher and the boys would go with the other.

The teacher assigned to the boys was waiting outside the men's toilet when one of the boys came out and told her that none of them could reach the urinal. Having no choice, she went inside, helped the little boys with their pants, and began hoisting them up one by one, holding on to their 'wee-wees' to direct the flow away from their clothes and shake them dry.

As she lifted one boy up, she couldn't help but notice that he was unusually well endowed. Trying not to show that she was staring at his equipment, the teacher said, 'You must be in Year 3?'

'No, ma'am,' he replied. 'I'm riding Black Caviar in the next race, but I really appreciate your help.'

Seven wheelchair athletes have been banned from the Paralympics after they tested positive for WD-40.

## TIMELY TIP

Just a reminder to those who looted electrical goods in last year's Auld Firm riots in Glasgow . . . your one-year manufacturer's warranty runs out soon.

In the first few days of the Olympics the Romanians took gold, silver, bronze, copper and lead.

Sailing results are in, Great Britain took gold, the United States took silver and Somalia took a middle-aged couple from Weymouth.

## WAITAKERE 2024

In an attempt to influence the members of the International Olympic Committee on their choice of venue for the games in 2024, the organisers of Waitakere's bid have already drawn up an itinerary and schedule of events. A copy has been leaked and is reproduced below.

**Opening Ceremony**

The Olympic flame will be ignited by a petrol bomb thrown by a native of the city (preferably from the New Lynn area), wearing the traditional balaclava. The flame will be contained in a large chip van situated on the roof of the stadium.

**The Events**

In previous Olympic games, Waitakere's competitors have not been particularly successful. In order to redress the balance, some of the events have been altered slightly to the advantage of local athletes.

**100 Metres Sprint**

Competitors will have to hold a video recorder and microwave oven (one in each arm), and on the sound of the starting pistol, a police dog will be released from a cage 10 yards behind the athletes.

**100 Metres Hurdles**
As above but with added obstacles, like car bonnets, hedges, gardens, fences, walls etc.

**Hammer Throw**
Competitors in this event may choose the type of hammer claw, sledge etc. The winner will be the one who can cause the most grievous bodily harm to members of the public within the time allowed.

**Fencing**
Entrants will be asked to dispose of as much stolen silver and jewellery as possible in 5 minutes.

**Men's 50 km Walk**
Unfortunately, this will have to be cancelled as the police cannot guarantee the safety of anyone walking the streets of Waitakere City.

**Gymnastics**
Will now be held in an abandoned meat works, and will include carcass vaulting and swinging from meat hooks.

**Rhythmic Gymnastics**
All competitors will be graded on their ability to sway drunkenly to Metallica.

**Relay**
Involves four competitors removing an appliance of their choice from a house in New Lynn and getting back to Titirangi using at least four stolen cars.

**Wrestling**
The rules will now specify that competitors must be topless and jelly will be involved.

**Baseball**
Requires contestants to line up with steel baseball bats. The medal will be awarded to the last man standing.

**Discus**
Will be decided by which contestant can get a hubcap off a Holden and throw it to his mate the fastest.

**Rowing**
The 500-metre scull will be changed to the 500-litre scull and promises to be the most hotly contested event. Many, many, many athletes are currently in training.

## MACDONALD'S STRANGE FARM

Two Florida State football players, Bubba and Tiny, were taking an important exam. If they failed, they would be on academic probation and not allowed to play in the big game the following week. The exam was 'fill in the blank' and the last question read, 'Old MacDonald had a —.'

Bubba was stumped — he had no idea what to answer,

but he knew he needed to get this one right to be sure he passed. Making sure the teacher wasn't watching, he tapped Tiny on the shoulder. 'Tiny, what's the answer to the last question?'

Tiny laughed, then looked around to make sure the professor hadn't noticed. He turned to Bubba and said, 'Bubba, you're so stupid. Everyone knows that Old MacDonald had a FARM.'

'Oh yeah,' said Bubba, 'I remember now.'

He picked up his No. 2 pencil and started to write the answer in the blank. Then he stopped. Tapping Tiny on the shoulder again, he whispered, 'Tiny, how do you spell farm?'

'You are really dumb, Bubba. that's so easy,' hissed Tiny, 'farm is spelled E-I-E-I-O.'

## ACE KILLING!

Two Mexican detectives were investigating the murder of Juan Gonzalez.

'How was he killed?' asked one detective.

'With a golf gun,' the other detective replied.

'A golf gun? What's a golf gun?'

'I don't know. But it sure made a hole in Juan.'

## STICK IN THE MUD

At a resort, a bloke walks up to an older fellow who is sitting in the sun, sipping iced tea.

The younger guy says — 'Hey, you gonna just sit around all day? How about you join me for a round of golf?'

'Nah,' the older fellow replies, 'tried it once, didn't like it.'

'Well, then,' the younger fellow asks, 'how about a swim? It might be just as refreshing as your iced tea there.'

'Nah,' the older fellow responds, 'tried it once, didn't like it. But if you're game for tennis, my son will be here soon and is usually up for a game or two — you might want to play with him.'

The younger fellow replies, 'Your only child, I presume?'

**Q:** Did you hear that the British Post Office has just recalled their latest stamps?
**A:** Well, they had photos of Sunderland players on them and folk couldn't figure out which side to spit on.

**Q:** What does a Spurs fan do when his team has won the Champions League?
**A:** He turns off the PlayStation.

### A FRIEND LIKE YOU!

Two men are hiking in the mountains. One suddenly stops, removes his hiking boots, and starts putting on sneakers. The other asks why he is doing that.

The first man answers, 'I thought I heard a bear.'

The second argues, 'You can't outrun a bear, not even with sneakers.'

The first responds, 'I just need to outrun YOU!'

**Q:** What do you say to a Burnley supporter with a good-looking bird on his arm?
**A:** Nice tattoo.